LOYALNOMICS™

The

Power

of

Branding

KIM D. ROZDEBA

LOYALNOMICS™: The Power of Branding by Kim D. Rozdeba

Published by Rozdeba Brand & Co.

Calgary, Alberta, Canada

Rozdeba.com

Cover by David Drummond www.salamanderhill.com

Editing by Jess Shulman JessShulmanEditorial.com

Proofing by Kelly Laycock kjleditorial.wordpress.com

Interior Design by Jennifer Stimson www.bookdesignmaven.com

ISBN: 978-1-7780090-5-1   (Hardcover)

           978-1-7780090-7-5   (Audiobook)

LOYALNOMICS™ is a trademark of Rozdeba Brand & Co.

First Edition: November 2024

RB&C
ROZDEBA BRAND & CO.

To all the brand builders

Contents

PREFACE

"Products are made in the factory,
but brands are created in the mind."
—WALTER LANDOR, BRANDING PIONEER AND FOUNDER OF LANDOR

What Is a Brand?

A brand isn't about what it says or does but how it makes its customers feel. Ultimately, it's the customer who owns the brand relationship. So, if they own it, why should you care? Like many earthly wonders, branding is part science and part art. A company can shape, influence, and direct a brand. It can define the brand's business model, ultimate promise, intrinsic and physical attributes, customer benefits, messaging, governance, and values. What the company can't do is translate the myriad of brand touchpoints into a meaningful emotional connection with the customer. That magical connection is based on expectations, memories, stories, and experiences. The purpose of this book is to define how a business can create a brand whose existence a customer will willingly embrace by allowing it precious space in their busy, complicated life.

I still cherish the first brand relationship in my life (that I can recall). Unfortunately, I don't remember the actual first time I engaged with it, as I was a kid. Still, I do remember the anticipation of Sunday evening, when the whole family would gather around the tiny black and white television. Every time Tinkerbelle, the fairy queen, opened the Wonderful World of Disney show with her wand and a trail of fairy dust, it was a magical moment. I remember Mr. Walt Disney introducing the evening show from his office with pictures of Micky Mouse on the walls. He looked like a wise grandfather who understood entertainment's secret, even in black and white. In the mid-1960s, my parents finally bought a color television, and the Wonderful World of Disney was elevated to Technicolor.

I was a young, impressionable child, and product brands were everywhere—creating new memories and relationships with me. Some toys helped build character, agility, and fine motor skills, such as Hot Wheels, Matchbox cars, Tonka trucks, Mr. Potato Head, Nerf balls, Etch a Sketch, Slinky, and Spirograph. Then there were board games to stimulate competition, social skills, and cooperation like Clue, Operation, Yahtzee, and Monopoly.

I associate comfort and love with brands like Campbell's Tomato Soup, grilled cheese sandwiches made with Velveeta cheese slices, and a Bick's Baby Dills pickle on the side. There were times when I was sick at home when only Campbell's Chicken Noodle Soup could make me feel better. If I close my eyes, I can still see the steam drifting from the cup of soup. It was "M'm! M'm! Good!" That was over fifty years ago, but I still look forward to a mug of Campbell's soup when I'm under the weather. It's a simple pleasure, but it always makes me feel better. I think it's because Campbell's soup is more than just a meal. It's a reminder of a time when I was safe and loved. It's a taste of home.

Then there's ketchup. Who doesn't love a great french fry? But sometimes I think I only love fries because of Heinz Tomato Ketchup. Without Heinz, fries just aren't great. Have you ever watched people eat their fries with ketchup? Some pour it all over them. Others pour it on the side and carefully dip each fry into it, maybe once or several times. That's me.

All of these brands are loaded with happy memories. Sure, there were also the times I accidentally fell stepping onto a Matchbox car or lost my Nerf ball when the neighbor's dog ran away with it, and I certainly failed at board games many times, especially Yahtzee, but that's not what sticks in my mind. I remember being upset at my grandma's house when I had to eat my eggs with some no-name brand of ketchup—but mainly because I have such fond memories of Heinz itself. For some reason, we mainly remember the good times—a rosy retrospection of life.

Our positive feelings make a brand's good memories persist in our minds. It's simple: brands that make us feel good are the brands we have an affinity with. The constant reliability of the taste of Campbell's soup keeps me stocking it in my cupboard. I still love the tanginess and crunch of a Bick's pickle straight from the jar, and I'm still a die-hard fan of Heinz's ketchup. A brand isn't a physical thing but a feeling that comes from the experience of interacting with it.

Do you remember your first wallet? Probably not—unless it was a Gucci, Fendi, or Louis Vuitton. Maybe a graduation present? But what is likely more memorable is the first bank card and credit card you carried in your wallet. Chances are you're still dealing with the same bank or using the same credit card (as long as the relationship didn't sour for some reason). In Canada, we have five large banks: Toronto-Dominion (TD) Bank, Royal Bank of Canada (RBC), Bank of Montreal (BMO), Canadian Imperial Bank of Commerce (CIBC), and Bank of Nova Scotia (Scotiabank). I started my first relationship with RBC. That was where my parents banked. But my longest and dearest relationship is with Scotiabank. They were the first to accept my Visa credit card application. I was seventeen and needed one to travel the world. RBC had refused me. So that's where my business went.

I've been with Scotiabank for almost fifty years and have multiple accounts. Last year, I opened a business account for my book publishing when I released my first book, *Branding Queens*. The bank manager asked me if I was having a book-signing event and said she would love to attend. I said no; I didn't want all the fuss. A week later, I got a call from the manager asking me if Scotiabank could organize a launch party for me. They would invite the members of their Women Initiative. The Scotiabank Women Initiative is a program to support women entrepreneurs as they grow, scale, and operate their small businesses. They thought my book was a perfect fit. Brand occasions like these are almost impossible to buy, but they are real. Significant events in our lives can be critical moments for triggering less frequent and more expensive brand purchases or changing our lifestyles indefinitely, like going to college, starting dating, moving to a new city, starting a new job, buying a condo, getting married, having a baby, getting divorced, remarrying, having a second baby, losing a parent, helping your kids go to college, getting a promotion, downsizing, and retiring. All these events have a ripple effect on how we live, and they change our consumption patterns. Sometimes we lean into our go-to brands, and other times we shift abruptly. External facts and perceptions also have a profound effect on our brand choices. Think about how the pandemic affected your brand choices and buying patterns. Changing interest rates will also change our decision-making processes and brands.

When our first daughter was born, I walked into a children's store for the first time in a mall I had been shopping at for years. I asked the salesperson when they'd opened, as I had never seen the store before. She smiled and said I must be a new dad. They'd been open since the mall opened, more than ten years before. Before that day, I had never known the store existed. Having a child provided the opportunity for this new brand relationship to form.

This book aims to peel away the multiple layers and complex dimensions of what makes a product a brand and why we care about it. I have had over thirty years as a boomer, a student of life, and a marketing and communications expert, watching brands thrive and die. I have witnessed brands endure multiple generations while others meet a sudden demise. Every day, a new one desperately tries to find a place in my heart. Some are succeeding, some aren't really trying, and some are failing. I have worked for and with many iconic global brands, helping them evolve to remain relevant as the world changes. I have also tried to revive dying brands; some of these attempts have been successful, and others have not.

I created this book based on my experiences, observations, and endless search for knowledge. I love brands. I love what many of them stand for. They're more faithful than a dog, eager to please us. They have raised people out of poverty and connected the world into a global community. Are they perfect? No. But they will outlive us all if they are sustainable, adaptable, and relevant.

In this book, I aim to show you how to build and nurture a brand into an iconic one that customers love. You'll learn how to start a customer relationship from a place that matters—from their perspective. We'll talk about how to genuinely support the customer, helping them manage their daily complexities, simplify their burden of choices, and reduce their cognitive load. My goal is to provide a road map for making your brand stand *for something* and stand *out* enough that customers reward you with profits and loyalty.

INTRODUCTION

> "With great power comes great responsibility."
> —VOLTAIRE (AND LATER UNCLE BEN, GIVING ADVICE
> TO PETER PARKER, AKA SPIDER-MAN)

Economics of Brands

Brands play an intrinsic role in our lives. Over the years, some brands have mimicked culture, while others have created and driven it. Brands have provided economic growth and human development. In 2022, the world's 500 largest companies employed over 70 million people while producing $41 trillion in revenue and $2.9 trillion in profit.[1]

Brands have brought the world to our doorsteps. They have taught us about global values and uplifted our spirits. They have poured billions of dollars into our communities. Brands make the world go 'round. And, as the saying goes, with great power comes great responsibility.

Can you imagine a world without brands? It would be a world of lifeless commodities and generic products, void of personality, aesthetics, emotion, or aspiration. Brands have brought us together in joy, happiness, and pleasure (and yes, also in anger, hatred, and desperation). Brands have been the catalyst for change and innovation. They have inspired art, technology, government, and social causes. They are friends who remain loyal, delivering on their promises worldwide. Brands have also made a lot of money, having a positive impact on society as the wealth of nations increases. Good brands understand and respond to their consumer's needs, delivering value to both them and shareholders. Everyone wins.

Critics argue that greedy global brands, with their vast appetite for natural resources, are destroying forests, ruining oceans, and polluting our environment. Human resources are also taken advantage of, with low pay and poor working conditions. Brands are seen as the source of the plastic pollution pandemic and linked to the destruction of rainforests and the extinction of wildlife. Brands are the motivation behind society's endless consumption. Brands have created a disposable society with a one-use, throw-it-away mentality.

There is no question that some brands' ethics and motives aren't acceptable. It often takes a disaster or a WikiLeaks-style exposure to inform the public of atrocities, but then unacceptable conduct is usually addressed quickly via financial pain through boycotts and brand-damaging messaging.

Billion-dollar tech brands like Amazon, Apple, Google, and Facebook have captured unprecedented market share in the new digital world. These brands and others like them collect large amounts of personal data, and they sometimes misuse it. According to StockApps research, the company that collects the most personal data is Google, followed by X (formerly Twitter), Amazon, Facebook, and Apple.[2] Using your data, these brands can map your behavior, becoming so accurate and detailed that they know your next move before you do. If (and when) they share this information with a third party, you have a political mess. Unethical brands' misuse of information will continue to be a threat.

Think about it: Uber, the world's largest taxi company, owns no vehicles and only collects logistical data. Facebook, the world's largest advertiser, creates no content but has eyes on every like, share, and comment. Alibaba, the world's largest e-commerce retailer, has no inventory but has billions of transaction data points. Airbnb, the world's largest accommodation provider, owns no real estate but knows where you sleep.

Good brands are seen as nurturing the planet and promoting human well-being, while bad brands are seen as exploiting the Earth and its people. At the end of the day, consumers will decide which brands win. We vote every day with our purchase decisions.

In 1949, Harry Truman said that "more than half the people in the world are living in conditions approaching misery." That same year, Minute Maid Orange Juice, Sony, H&M, 20th Century Fox Television, Burger King, Adidas, McDonald's, and Visa made their brand debuts. Shortly thereafter, Walmart, Nike, Mastercard,

Intel, and The Gap made their presence felt around the world. World War II was finally over, and the Bretton Woods Agreement (which created a system of global exchange rates promoting international economic cooperation) had been signed, opening the world to a new free-trade system.

Poverty rates started to collapse as the world shifted to free markets in the 1950s. The world's population was around 2.52 billion, and more than 70 percent (1.81 billion) lived in extreme poverty, making less than $1.90 per day. Experts attribute two-thirds of poverty reduction to economic growth and the third to greater equality. By 2015, the world's population had nearly tripled (thanks partly to the baby boomers) to 7.35 billion. Over the same period, extreme poverty dropped to less than 10 percent of the world's total population.[3] Over these sixty years of incredible economic growth, we saw the globalization of brands worldwide. Even with the explosive population growth, illiteracy rates dropped and life expectancy increased. This progress was thanks in large part to brands investing in countries, communities, and people. Everyone profited.

World War II was also a turning point for women, especially in North America, where they played a significant role in the workforce and broke down psychological barriers. Julia Blackwelder, in her book *Now Hiring: The Feminization of Work in the United States*, said, "The war so profoundly altered labor demands and women's expectations that women entered the workforce in even greater numbers after the war."[4] In 1950, 34 percent of women were part of the labor force; by 2016, they grew to almost 57 percent.

Brands clearly understood the major shift in the consumer landscape. In the 1960s, brands came under scrutiny from feminist groups for how women were being portrayed in advertising. Over time, a greater emphasis was placed on independent women who were just as likely as men to own a car, have a career, and participate in significant purchase decisions. Today, there is still plenty of room for improvement in the areas of pay equity, discrimination, and sexual harassment. But advertising images of women doing "men's work" helped make women the target audience of many new brands.

Generics are copycat brands that are generally cheaper and come with no-frills packaging. In some cases, generic brands offer products of similar quality, while in others, the difference is much more noticeable. Generic ketchup isn't Heinz, no-name cola doesn't taste the same as the "real thing." The generics are about price with no branding, innovation investments, or product support.

As with most things, you get what you pay for. The branded version is about loyalty and building relationships based on quality, craftsmanship, and support services. Good brands are always anticipating future customers' needs. They might be more expensive, but brands that make more profits can do more research and development. Brands care about innovations and continuous improvements to keep them relevant. Generics only care about selling you as much of their product as possible. Generics don't invest in communities or new technology; they aim to make as much money as they can, without spending anything more than the absolute minimum.

Brands evolve. Generics come and go while brands create new technologies, industries, business models, goods, and services. A new version of the iPhone is anticipated and expected as an annual event. But new technologies can make older ones obsolete, shutting down outdated production systems while displacing workers. These rapid changes can also destroy traditional work and social relationships that once played an essential cultural and economic role in the lives of a community or country. The Apple iPod and Amazon Kindle reader had a profound effect on the music industry and the book industry, respectively. Airbnb and Uber are creating havoc in the traditional hotel and taxi industries. These changes come with serious trade-offs that don't necessarily make it clear whether the future will be a better place.

Karl Marx predicted in *The Communist Manifesto* that large multinational brands would wipe out local businesses, and that local culture would be lost forever. This prediction has largely come true. Go almost anywhere in the world, and you can find a Starbucks, McDonald's, KFC, or Pizza Hut. And thanks to e-commerce, you can access almost any brand, with delivery right to your door, even within twenty-four hours if you subscribe to Amazon Prime.

Multinational brands became mega brands and wiped out local vendors because consumers supported them. Customers will line up for days to get the newest model of the latest product and spend their entire paycheck to display the brand logo proudly. No local grocer is a match for a large multinational brand like Walmart, with its global resources of outsourcing, data and digital management, and low-margin, high-volume sales model. It doesn't matter how many years the local grocer spent building their business with personalized service, one customer at a time.

We have, however, seen a resurgence in local premium products like craft beers, spirits, soda, natural energy drinks, ice cream, and coffee. Consumers want the best experience at the best price while supporting local businesses and getting elevated-quality products.

People build culture and brands. More than ever, brands are shaping our lives. Microsoft has shaped the way we work, learn (Microsoft Office Suite), communicate (Outlook), and play (Xbox) while Airbnb has disrupted the hotel industry and reshaped the way we travel and experience new destinations. We are addicted to our smartphones and the social networks we live on. Author Thom Braun says,

"Brands and branding are fundamental to the way we experience modern life—and the way we give 'meaning' to it."[5]

We can't live without brands. In some cases, they define who we are. Brands aren't just extended objects in our disposable lives; they give us meaning by intertwining their narratives with our personal stories and experiences. Novelist Paul Auster said, "If we didn't have stories to tell each other, I don't think we'd be able to understand the world at all." In the book *Storytelling: Branding in Practice*, authors Klaus Fog, Christian Budtz, Philip Munch, and Stephen Blanchette say, "It is, therefore, no coincidence that an ancient tradition like storytelling should appear in a new form as a tool for brand building…"[6]

Good brands work to shape culture in order to remain relevant and break through the clutter. The best brands try to champion a societal need and change attitudes or behaviors, aiming to make the world a better place (and sell more products). Nike's support of Colin Kaepernick's racial injustice cause is a case in point. As the ad said, "Believe in something. Even if it means sacrificing everything. Just do it."

Brand Domination

Thanks to digitization and globalization, popular brands are getting bigger by the second.

While in 2023 Amazon remained the dominant online leader with over 37 percent market share according to estimates, with Walmart trailing far behind in second place with only 6 percent, the more extensive play is still in the brick-and-mortar, where Walmart dominates the retail landscape with approximately 240 million customers who visit more than 10,500 locations in over twenty countries, with over 2.1 million employees and annual sales of over $605 billion.[7] With this clout, it can dictate the terms and define the products with a network of 3,000 diverse suppliers. Walmart's global website says, "We want to use our size for good." Let's hope so, because they are massive!

Coca-Cola uses about 289 billion liters of water (a fact listed on its website) to produce its forty different products each year. In perspective, that is about 115,600 Olympic-sized pools, almost one week of water flowing over Niagara Falls, or nearly a year of the city of Toronto's water consumption. The company claims it takes about two liters of water to produce one liter of product. While agriculture accounts for 70 percent of all water consumption globally, Coca-Cola recognizes that a sustainable approach to water is essential to its business.

McDonald's has over 36,000 restaurants worldwide and serves 69 million people daily. According to Bloomberg, McDonald's sells four million kilograms (nine million pounds) of fries daily. A year's worth of its potato supply would fill the entire Madison Square Gardens to the ceiling. McDonald's employs about 1.8 million people in 119 countries and has become so central to global trade that *The Economist* values foreign currencies against the dollar using the price of a Big Mac. One in eight US workers has been employed by McDonald's at some point in their career. McDonald's has helped put a lot of people through college.

Brand Responsibility

In a world inundated with brands, it is clear that they hold immense power and influence over our lives. Brands can evoke emotions, shape culture, and drive prosperity. They can unite people, inspire change, and create a sense of identity. However, with this power comes great responsibility.

While some brands contribute to economic growth, social progress, and empowerment, others are criticized for unethical practices, environmental damage, and exploitation. The dichotomy of good and evil is a reminder that brands must be held accountable for their actions.

As consumers, we have the power to shape the landscape of brands. Our choices and preferences determine which brands thrive and which fade away. Our responsibility is to support brands that align with our values and prioritize sustainability, social justice, and ethical conduct. By embracing brands that nurture the planet and promote human well-being, we can create a future where brands are a force for good.

Successful brands understand this dynamic and strive to build strong consumer relationships. They create experiences, deliver value, and cultivate emotional connections that foster brand loyalty and love. In this sense, the person experiencing and owning the relationship with the brand becomes an integral part of the brand's identity and success.

To truly understand the dynamics of brand-consumer relationships, we must delve into brand loyalty. While a brand's legal ownership may lie with a specific entity, its actual ownership and power lie in the hands of the consumers who form deep connections with it and actively participate in its growth and success.

The world's challenges, like climate change, obesity, population growth, and dwindling natural resources, are so complex that they require collaborative solutions beyond any brand or government. The world's mega brands can help address social concerns beyond their own backyards, and they have the resources and ability to bring about lasting change. They can define and uphold universal values. Every day, they must answer to their customers (and shareholders) because the customers choose to buy their brand and keep it relevant. They must keep their brand promises, nurture the planet, and promote human well-being. The world would be very different without brands that make the global economy go 'round.

Everything is a brand today. (Brand experts even tell us that we must each build our own personal brand.) In a given day, we can be bombarded with 3,000 to 10,000 brand messages, of which only about twelve get any brain attention. The online publication *The Drum* tried to determine how many ads we see daily—is it 3,000, 5,000, or 10,000?[8] They argued that if an average adult is awake for sixteen hours and seeing 10,000 ads in a day, that would make 625 ads an hour or ten a minute. Even at the low end, it's three ads every minute. It's estimated that the world's advertising spend will exceed $1.3 trillion by 2029.[9] The cognitive overload with a sense of mental clutter is real. There is an environmental cost from the visual pollution as well as a psychological effect contributing to materialism and unrealistic expectations. Media expert Ed Papazian says the problem isn't about advertising clutter but avoidance. Over four million new brand names are added to the shopping list annually. Do we need over fifty shampoo brands and hundreds of specialized types essential to having the perfect bouncy, curly, wavy, shiny, or smooth tresses?

Barry Schwartz, Ph.D., a Swarthmore College psychologist and author of *The Paradox of Choice: Why More Is Less*, explains, "There's a point where all of this choice starts to be not only unproductive but counterproductive—a source of pain, regret, worry about missed opportunities and unrealistically high expectations."[10]

Have we reached a state where a brand can no longer differentiate itself from other brands? How many deep brand relationships do we want or can handle in our busy lives? Are we reaching a point of saturation where the proliferation of brands is doing more harm than good?

A Gallup research study found that, on average, Americans say they have about nine close friends, and the older they get, the number maxes out at thirteen close friends.[11] So, can we expect more from consumers regarding a meaningful relationship with brands?

The First Brand

We can credit Japan with starting some of the world's first and oldest brands, such as Kongō Gumi, established in the year 578, and Hōshi Ryokan, founded in 718, according to William O'Hara's book *Centuries of Success*. Kongō Gumi is a construction company that built Buddhist temples, Shinto shrines, and castles. But after surviving fourteen centuries (1,428 years!) as a family business, it closed its doors in 2006. There wasn't a huge demand for building temples anymore, which occupied 80 percent of the company's business focus. Hōshi Ryokan is a Japanese inn in Komatsu that has been operating for over 1,300 years. You can book a room today on Booking.com. In a study, the Bank of Korea discovered more than 5,586 companies that are over 200 years old in Japan, 837 in Germany, 222 in the Netherlands, and 196 in France.[12]

But brand age doesn't guarantee brand success. Jim Collins, a co-author of *Built to Last: Successful Habits of Visionary Companies*, says brands must follow unchanging and sustainable principles of who they are, yet constantly change their actions and how they do it.[13] Today, many brands know who they are but don't dare to change what they do, such as old favorites Kodak, BlackBerry, Blockbuster, Nokia, and Hummer.

On the Fortune 500, 88 percent of those listed in 1955 no longer appear on the 2014 list. Brands continually get destroyed by mergers, acquisitions, bankruptcies, or break-ups. As a result, there is a healthy churn in brands coming and going. Steven Denning reported in *Forbes* that fifty years ago, the life expectancy of a firm in the Fortune 500 was around seventy-five years. Today, it's less than fifteen years and declining constantly.

That said, about 250,000 new brands are launched each year globally, keeping the world's advertising agencies busy. However, Lynn Dornblaser, an analyst at market research firm Mintel who tracks new products, says the typical failure rate of new product launches can be anywhere from 85 to 95 percent. That's a lot of new business cards and advertising wasted. For example, Schneider Associates and research partner Sentient Decision Science did a consumer survey in 2016 that found that 50 percent of participants couldn't name a new product brand.[14] To succeed with a brand launch, you need your prospect to see your brand on three to six channels. Research suggests that it takes an average of three to six touchpoints for a prospect to remember and engage with a brand. By using a combination of channels such as social media, email marketing, advertising, PR, and website content, you can create a cohesive brand presence that resonates with your target audience. This omnichannel approach can help reinforce your brand messaging and increase the likelihood of getting on a buyer's shopping list.

None of this, however, has stopped companies from extending their brands and introducing new products.

Many brands have tried to extend their brands from their original offering to capture new markets and target groups—some successfully, and others with less clarity.

Sir Richard Branson has taken the irreverent and fun Virgin brand and stretched it across 350 products, from life insurance to lingerie with great successes and failures.

Sub-brands have unique attributes, quality, and value levels. For example, Coca-Cola has its classic Coke, as well as Diet Coke, Caffeine-Free Coca-Cola, Diet Coke Caffeine-Free, and more. Increasing the number of choices you offer can cater to different consumer preferences and needs, allowing you to capture a larger market share and increase brand loyalty. On the other hand, sub-brands can dilute your core brand identity and cause consumer confusion, not to mention adding potential quality control challenges and operating complexities.

Everything in life is moving faster and faster, and digital technologies are changing everything. The human brain, however, still only has so much memory power and capacity to retain and process information. Bob Nease, behavioral scientist and author, explains that the brain can process 10 billion bits of data each second, but when it comes to the "decision-making part of the brain, [it] only processes a maximum of 50 bits per second."[15] This is a significant bottleneck in decision-making that won't change any time soon. We literally have a bandwidth issue in our brains. The proliferation of brands and branding messages means there are fewer chances that new brands will find a permanent place in consumers' minds. On his return to Apple in 1997, Steve Jobs said, "Marketing is about values. This is a boisterous world, and we're not going to get a chance to get people to remember much about us. So, we must be clear about what we want them to know about us."[16] Almost thirty years later, Jobs's comment is even more relevant. A simple route to the consumer's head and heart no longer exists.

We can get a new product brand to market faster and more efficiently than ever. We have more channels to get our message out than ever before. However, the resulting complexities have created brand apathy. As we continue along this path, brands have less of a chance to be successful. Aldo Cundari, CEO of the Cundari marketing agency, explains, "The new customer behavior has serious implications for all brands. If organizations don't commit to meeting their customers' expectations today, customers will go elsewhere tomorrow."[17]

What Cundari says isn't revolutionary thinking, but the warning signs are everywhere—consumers are reaching a point of brand overkill. It's like a stadium full of brands screaming to persuade potential customers to go for their product. The noise is deafening.

Havas Media Group's annual global *Meaningful Brands* survey has been consistent in the last ten years in saying, "Most people would not care if 75 percent of brands disappeared."[18]

Who owns a brand? This is a trick question. While owners and shareholders own *companies*, those companies' *brands* are owned by their customers. It's the consumer's experience with the brand that matters—their relationship and perception. As brand steward, the company must protect the brand and ensure its promise is delivered every time, every place, so they don't screw up the relationship between the customer and the brand. They—*you*, assuming you work for a company with one or more brands—must understand the psychological connection between the customers and the brand in order to continue to do what keeps them coming back, and to hopefully attract new customers as well. Your loyal customers are your brand advocates (especially if something goes wrong).

Without a product/service, there is no brand experience. Can you control the experience from the beginning? You can try, but it's loyal and faithful customers that really build the brand. While you can control every physical aspect of the brand—its features, attributes, and even benefits—you can't control how a customer feels about it. The most potent marketing tool is still word-of-mouth, perhaps better phrased as "word-of-social." You can create the brand environment, but, in most cases, you cannot control how customers will interact with your product.

Here's a case in point. Calvin Klein started in the 1970s as a youthful women's wear brand. In the early 1980s Calvin Klein made a strategic move into the men's underwear market, which was then dominated by established brands like Hanes and Fruit of the Loom. Quickly they changed the face of men's underwear, sparked by the semi-nude body of Marky Mark (Wahlberg) modeling the CK briefs. Today, Calvin Klein's men's underwear line remains a prominent and iconic part of the brand's identity, demonstrating the power of strategic marketing and brand evolution in shaping consumer perceptions and driving success in unexpected product categories. Currently, CK men's and women's underwear account for more than a billion dollars annually.

Betty Crocker (not a real person but a brand mascot), the revered expert on cake-making going back to 1921, stumbled when it changed its cake mix recipe in the 1950s. The company introduced a "just add water" product, which its loyal following rejected outright. It seemed the brand managers of Betty Crocker didn't understand the brand experience; by creating the mindless cake mix, the company reduced the baker's role in the process to nothing. The brand insight was that to bake a cake was to show appreciation to one's family. Making it a mindless effort eliminated the appreciation toward the baker.

Another famous marketing blunder was Coca-Cola's attempt to change Coke's recipe in 1985. While the new formulation was intensively researched, no one had asked the customer how they would feel if they lost their original Coke, a recipe that had been around since 1886. The backlash and PR nightmare forced the Coca-Cola Company to reintroduce Coca-Cola Classic, and rename New Coke to Coke II.

Today, customer backlash is almost instantaneous, and the impact on the brand can be drastic and global. Any brand crisis quickly becomes an online reputation crisis thanks to the real-time nature of social media. Suppose a brand faces a problem with its image, product failure, or mistreatment. I don't have to tell you how quickly it will become the latest news across social media platforms and mainstream media outlets. Many brands, like Abercrombie & Fitch, Lululemon, Heinz Tomato Ketchup, Facebook, Instagram, Tim Hortons, Maple Leaf Foods, and even Apple, have felt the wrath of unhappy customers following product changes and issues, policy and production changes, and inappropriate behavior of management and staff.

The digital communications revolution has completely transformed the balance of control. The consumer's voice has become louder and much more public. Consumers can publish their brand experience and compare it with their knowledge of other brands. How a brand responds under pressure can profoundly affect its future and customer relationship.

Never forget that brands are owned by their consumers. They can be the best ambassadors and brand advocates—or the brand's worst enemy. They are the true voice of the brand.

Brand Future

While Meta's new Threads platform reached over 100 million users in five days, ChatGPT's OpenAI chatbot took two months to reach the same milestone.[19] However, ChatGPT's user base is more active, with about 60 million website visits daily, whereas Thread struggles to maintain 23.7 million users monthly.[20] Generative AI is quickly becoming integral to many people's personal and working lives for activities traditionally thought to be exclusive to the human mind, such as generating content and brainstorming. Beyond the written word, it can create images, video, audio, and music. Before the world realized what was happening, a fake song called "Heart on My Sleeve" mysteriously appeared with the life-like voices of Drake and The Weeknd and racked up millions of plays across TikTok, YouTube, and Spotify. Then there was Pope Francis, portrayed wearing a puffy white winter jacket, talking about climate change in a viral deepfake video. Forty-six years ago, the legendary Beatle John Lennon wrote a song called "Now and Then." In 2023, thanks to AI, this final Beatles song was released. AI could take a poor-quality cassette recording of John Lennon singing in his living room in New

York City just before his death, clean it up, and then fuse it with a recent recording of Paul McCartney and Ringo Starr. Without AI, we would never have heard about this gem. The power of AI can be used for good and for evil. The internet is full of fake news, propaganda, deepfakes, and false social media accounts—as well as some pretty great, creative stuff.

Despite the potential downsides, the impact of generative AI will be enormous. Its mass adoption by consumers in an unprecedented time frame indicates the technology's usefulness in many areas. Marketers have been talking for years about personalization, but earlier efforts toward it always relied on significant human intervention and manual content creation; AI will make it possible on a grand scale. Generating customized content for hundreds and thousands of customers just wasn't possible before AI. Predictive modeling on a micro level has never been feasible until now.

At the same time, protective mechanisms will be necessary, in addition to reasonable caution. As consumers continue their journey with generative AI, it will be up to all of us, including organizations and regulators, to ensure that its full potential is used positively.

In this book, my goal is to guide you in creating a cohesive brand identity that weaves like a red thread through everything the brand presents and does, consistently reflecting the brand's essence across all touchpoints, ultimately fostering a strong emotional connection and loyalty from customers. I'll show you how to start a relationship from a place that matters to the customer—how to be where they want your brand to be, solve their problems even before they exist, and eliminate the need for them to make another decision or remember another brand name.

You'll learn about automating to eliminate repeating issues or tasks, making customers feel good (even when your brand isn't about feeling good), and helping them navigate a complex, busy world. Stop yelling and start listening more. Your brand will be rewarded for its simple solutions, not for providing more choices. Remember, less is more, and always be empathetic and relevant. Through all of this, I'll teach you how to embrace what I call the "five C's," which serve as a blueprint for establishing your brand's identity and differentiating it as one that warrants a consumer's loyalty.

1 | ECONOMICS OF LOYALTY

"An ounce of brand loyalty results
in a pound of brand equity."

—ADAPTED FROM A QUOTE FROM ELBERT HUBBARD

Value only exists if it's perceived by the customer. For example, water flows free as a natural resource, but once you bottle it and place a brand label on it, it becomes valuable. Brands must consistently create and deliver a valuable, differentiated, trustworthy experience to fulfill the economic imperative of value creation for customers and the business. Without this focus on value creation, nothing else in business matters.[21]

In 1975, 83 percent of the S&P 500 companies' total assets comprised tangible assets such as buildings, equipment, cash, bonds, inventory, and land. Since then, a complete reversal has occurred. In 2020, intangible assets (i.e., intellectual property and brand equity) account for over 90 percent of total assets among S&P 500 organizations.[22] Intangible assets have come to represent over $21 trillion in the S&P 500—and that number's growing. Globally, 2021 intangible assets were estimated to have been worth over $74 trillion, representing between 71 and 93 percent of the total assets of the top twenty economies.[23] Rita Clifton, the former chair of Interbrand UK, believes brand value is a fundamental asset for any company's enduring success and stability. It is an asset that transcends a business's physical and personnel components and can create demand and customer loyalty. Clifton breaks the role of brand value into two components: its role in creating earnings (for example, in luxury brands, over 70 percent of earnings is attributed to the brand) and its role in determining how secure those earnings are for the future.[24] Brands contribute to a company's financial well-being and play a significant role in national economies.

If a brand is what a customer feels, then it is a psychological entity that manifests economic value. We might ask ourselves *when* a customer becomes brand loyal. Of course, it depends on how often they purchase the product or service: daily, weekly, monthly, bi-annually, annually, or at longer intervals. Nevertheless, in a study by Yotpo, shoppers said they consider themselves loyal after three to five purchases.[25] Remember, to build a loyal customer, each purchase experience must be as good if not better than the last. Customer loyalty is the intent to keep the relationship going.

So what makes a customer loyal to a brand? Yotpo's research says it starts with the product or service itself, and is followed by price, customer service, convenience, social responsibility, and coolness.[26] While product quality is paramount, the rest of these factors are more about the customer's persona and personal situation. University students and young families watching their budgets have a greater chance of becoming loyal IKEA customers than higher-income older professionals. A dry cleaner next door to your office has a greater chance of making you a loyal customer than a dry cleaner four blocks away. The customer defines the value of the service. Some customers want interaction and recognition, while others want a fast and straightforward experience like Starbucks's mobile pick-up system. Building loyalty is about understanding what is essential to your customers. The five C's of branding, which we are about to discuss at length, are about building a brand that people love so much that they become loyal fans.

Customer loyalty has a significant impact on brand equity. Brand equity is the value premium a company realizes from having a highly regarded reputation beyond its category and industry. It is created through consumer perceptions, which include awareness of the brand, the associations consumers have with the brand, the perceived quality of the brand's products or services, and the level of brand loyalty. Customers loyal to a brand are more likely to have positive attitudes and perceptions toward it, leading to increased brand equity. Some economists have tried to examine outrageous stock prices that exceed book values by trying to measure *customer capital*—the notion that loyal customers are capital for a brand.

Loyal customers can bring many benefits, like repeat purchases and active recommendations to others, which can result in higher sales and market share. This word-of-mouth or word-of-social promotion from loyal customers helps to build a strong brand reputation and increases sales.

Moreover, customer loyalty can increase Customer Lifetime Value (CLV) or Lifetime Value (LTV). CLV and LTV are the total revenue a customer generates over their lifetime for a brand. Loyal customers tend to spend more and be less price-sensitive, and thus have a higher CLV. Customers loyal to a brand are less likely to switch to competitors, even when presented with price discounts or promotional offers. Loyalty provides a competitive advantage and helps maintain and strengthen brand equity over time.

So, how do we successfully get our brand into a customer's brain? The easiest and most successful way is to tell and live a story they can relate to and align with emotionally. Storytelling creates emotional connections that make memories.

Imagine a local coffee shop, Java Joe, known for its rich, diverse, aromatic brews from around the world. Each cup is a testament to its quality and provides a satisfied start to a customer's day. The shop's interior feels like a comfortable living room with relaxing couches and chairs. Patrons return for the coffee, the environment, and the warm, personalized greetings from baristas who remember their names and orders. This personal touch and homey environment keep customers going back.

One rainy afternoon, a regular customer comes in in a hurry, wet and without her wallet, unable to pay for her coffee. The cashier doesn't turn her away, but instead fulfills the order and tells her she can pay next time. Understanding the customer's highly stressed situation, the cashier includes a pastry to make her feel better. These thoughtful acts turn into a memorable moment, reinforcing the customer's attachment to the Java Joe brand.

Java Joe doesn't just sell coffee; it sells stories. The shop walls are covered with photos of customers and employees traveling worldwide, emphasizing Java Joe's quest to learn from every corner of the globe, as coffee is the medium through which these stories are shared. Java Joe understands that behind every cup is a narrative of community, sustainability, and the shared human experience. The brand sees itself as an educator and a student, learning from each interaction with the global coffee community and imparting this knowledge to its customers. This narrative weaves the customer's daily ritual into a larger tapestry of a worldwide commonality and shared values.

Value is perceived in every interaction. While Java Joe might not be the cheapest shop on the block, customers feel they get their money's worth there, and more. The shop's reputation is the talk of the community, built on countless positive experiences and word-of-mouth praise. And when Java Joe makes an occasional misstep, it listens and adapts, treating feedback as a golden opportunity for growth.

The brand extends beyond its four walls by hosting local travel destination nights called Java Joe Journeys, turning customers into a community of coffee enthusiasts, travelers, and culture lovers. This creates a sense of belonging that turns a simple coffee shop into a hub of travel enthusiasts and world adventurists.

Java Joe doesn't merely retain customers; it cherishes them, creating an ongoing story where every journey is an opportunity to deepen the bond—a narrative that makes the second or third visit as exciting as the first. At the heart of Java Joe lies a profound "why" that transcends the mere selling of coffee. It is a brand with a quest, a mission fueled by a passion for exploration, discovery, and the rich tapestry of global cultures. This is how you turn customers into loyalists, eager to return to where they are known, valued, and delighted.

Brand Economics

Happy customers create profitable brands. McKinsey & Company estimates that the value of one lost customer is equivalent to acquiring three new ones. Happy customers can be measured by share of wallet, repeat purchases, and net revenue retention. A five-year McKinsey analysis showed that brands that are leaders in customer experience achieved more than double the revenue growth of those with poor customer experiences.[27] At the core of brand economics is the concept of value creation. Brands are powerful tools of differentiation, enabling companies to stand out in crowded markets. By cultivating a strong brand identity and strategically positioning themselves, companies can command premium pricing, secure customer loyalty, attract the best talent, and ultimately enhance their revenue and profitability. This differentiation also helps reduce reliance on aggressive pricing and promotion strategies, and it can decrease marketing costs over time due to the established customer trust and recognition.

To understand the value a loyal customer can bring to a brand, we must measure the customer's lifetime value (CLT or LTV). The simplest way to do that is to take the average dollar value or profit of a customer's purchases (average purchase value (APV)) and multiply it by the average annual frequency at which customers buy your brand (average purchase frequency rate (APFR)). The result is your customer value (CV). Once you have your CV, multiply that by your average customer lifespan (ACL).

$$CLV = APV \times APFR \times ACL$$

To illustrate this formula, let's use a dry-cleaning business as an example. Dry cleaners generally have a lot of repeat customers, such as business people who visit them on a weekly or bi-weekly basis to have their dress shirts laundered. Let's say this business owner has just one location with an average loyal customer spending $40 twice a month to launder ten shirts. The profit from each shirt is about a dollar, so the owner makes $10 each visit—that's the APV. If the loyal customer comes in twenty-four times yearly (the APFR) for an average of four years (the ACL), that gives:

$$\$10 \times 24 \text{ times yearly} \times 4 \text{ years} = \$960$$

To be clear, this is a conservative number, as we know a customer is likely to have other items cleaned over time, like suits, pants, jackets, and dresses, which will increase the customer's value. But this baseline number helps you determine what your branding strategy should be.

Creating Value

Market research company Market.US estimated that the global market for bottled water was worth about $329 billion in 2023 and that it will continue this trajectory to over $551 billion by 2033.[28] In North America, more bottled water is sold than milk or beer in volume. The volume of bottled water sold globally is projected to reach 515 billion liters by 2027.[29] The United States remains the fastest-growing bottled-water market outside of Asia, mainly due to more health-conscious consumers shifting away from sugary carbonated soft drinks.

In many emerging markets, the scarcity of clean water makes bottled water a necessary staple rather than a value-added refreshment like juice or soda. In North America, the water in your tap is generally the same stuff you buy in the bottle. The big difference is that tap water is constantly tested to ensure it follows drinking water quality standards. Bottled water doesn't have the same stringent guidelines, except that it does not contain any "poisonous or harmful substances."

Clean, drinkable water is generally available throughout North America, where bottled-water companies position their brands on quality (it's a "healthy choice") and convenience (it's "portable and handy"). This foundation makes the category complex with pricing strategies, water sources, and lifestyle attributes.

In their show *Bullshit*, magician duo Penn & Teller did a spoof on bottled water. In a fine dining restaurant in Southern California, they proved that the public couldn't tell the difference between tap water and $4-a-liter bottled water. You can find it on YouTube.

ABC's *Good Morning America* conducted a blind-tasting experiment in 2001 where they sampled branded bottled water such as Poland Spring, O2, Evian, and the famous New York City tap water. The results might surprise you—Big Apple water beat them all.

If bottled water (spring or no spring) can't be distinguished from tap water, the real difference is branding. Tap water is a commodity with no brand. It comes from any unmarked tap—hot or cold. But if you take the same thing and build a formidable brand image, you can extract a premium.

So how do you do this? This book will take you through five branding principles that all successful brands possess: Commitment (the why), Construct (the what), Community (the who), Content (the where), and Consistency (the how). While the balance and intensity of these components differ from brand to brand, the five C's of branding are what help make a brand unique. Brands are just as complicated as human beings. A formula can't determine what brands or people will succeed or fail. And while technology has changed how we interact with a brand, the fundamentals of how people think and act haven't changed since brands began.

Kantar BrandZ, which puts out a list of the world's top 100 most valuable brands, estimates the total brand value of the 2023 list to be over $6.9 trillion—a 138 percent increase since 2014. The most valuable brands on the list are the same ones at the top of my mind, such as Apple, Google, Microsoft, Amazon, and McDonald's.[30]

The Five Branding Principles

We're about to embark on a journey through the enigmatic world of branding. But first, let's clear the air about what branding *isn't*. It's not a magical elixir that transforms the taste of a product or elevates its performance; if a product is subpar, no amount of branding will sweeten the bitter truth. Branding can't mask a flawed promise or conjure up fond memories where none exist. It is not a marketing or advertising campaign. Your brand's steadfast performance cements the customer relationship, and with higher price tags come loftier expectations. The brands that stand out consistently exceed these expectations, delivering unexpected delights and rekindling the warmth of past pleasures.

In our results-oriented world, brand-building efforts can be quickly derailed by performance marketing focusing on short-term results and measurable ROI through campaigns that generate sales, leads, or clicks. This approach is attractive because it allows for targeted campaigns with precise results, addressing the age-old advertising dilemma of not knowing which part of the spending is practical. Studies have shown that excess performance marketing can undermine long-term brand-building efforts. Brand-building activities include novel packaging, new products, distinctive services, innovative distribution, and creative advertising. Jim Stengel, former global marketing officer of Procter & Gamble, said that performance marketing and brand building should be at odds for budget resources but be guided by a single North Star metric for brand equity that can be linked to both current and long-term performance metrics.[31]

Like people, brands are complex creatures without a clear path to success or failure. Despite the digital revolution that continues to reshape our interactions, the core principles of branding remain timeless. Think of a brand's stumbles as akin to our own occasionally off days—like the time you were dashing in for a quick Big Mac, only to be disappointed as a Filet-O-Fish landed in your hands. Frustrating? Absolutely. But does that one slip-up spell doom for a brand relationship? Hardly.

We expect brands to recover gracefully from their missteps and turn our next experience around. If mishaps become the norm rather than the exception, we'll naturally drift toward new brand horizons. "Slapping lipstick on a pig" is futile. Branding isn't about concealing flaws, it's about genuine connection—and a failed product is ultimately a failed brand.

Now, let's delve into the five C's of branding—a proactive blueprint for nurturing an enduring and positive brand experience at every touchpoint. These principles are not just for the elusive luxury brands we long to touch but also for the everyday names that weave through our lives—the cars we drive, the shoes we wear, the toothpaste we use. Even these familiar faces can falter, but with commitment at the core, there's always a way back to redemption.

This book is your atlas through the landscape of brands—corporate giants, niche players, personal identities, service providers, and every other incarnation you can imagine. Each 'C' will resonate differently depending on many factors, from product category to market size to risk appetite. Branding is a complex dance of variables—some within your grasp and others beyond your control. It creates a never-ending adventure of learning and refinement that makes for an exhilarating pursuit.

As we explore these five branding principles together, let them guide you and ignite your imagination about crafting an iconic brand—whether you're building empires or nurturing start-ups. Welcome to the art and science of branding, where every chapter is an opportunity to sculpt your brand's legacy in the hearts and minds of your audience.

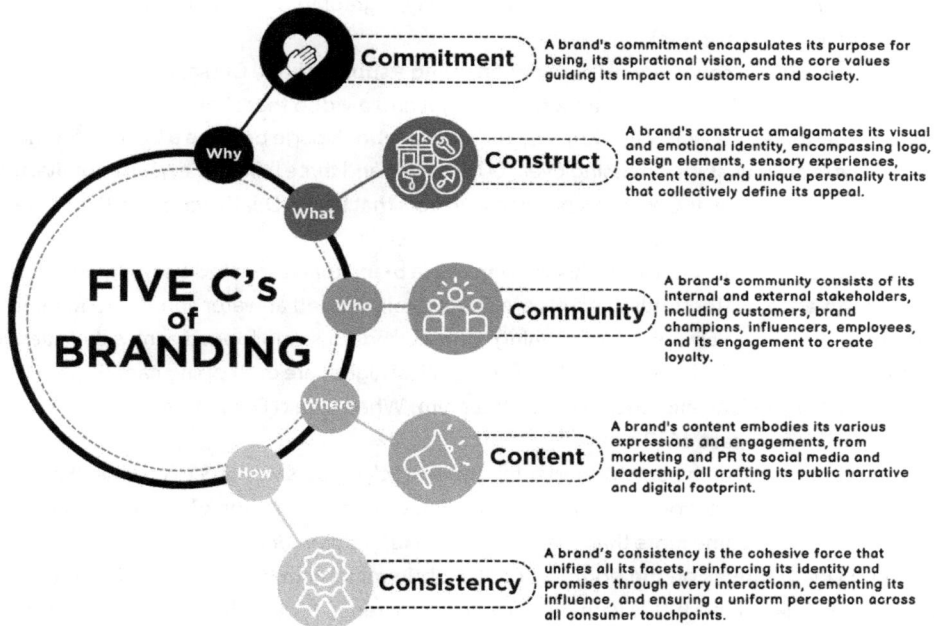

FIVE C's of BRANDING

Why — What — Who — Where — How

Commitment — A brand's commitment encapsulates its purpose for being, its aspirational vision, and the core values guiding its impact on customers and society.

Construct — A brand's construct amalgamates its visual and emotional identity, encompassing logo, design elements, sensory experiences, content tone, and unique personality traits that collectively define its appeal.

Community — A brand's community consists of its internal and external stakeholders, including customers, brand champions, influencers, employees, and its engagement to create loyalty.

Content — A brand's content embodies its various expressions and engagements, from marketing and PR to social media and leadership, all crafting its public narrative and digital footprint.

Consistency — A brand's consistency is the cohesive force that unifies all its facets, reinforcing its identity and promises through every interactionn, cementing its influence, and ensuring a uniform perception across all consumer touchpoints.

BRAND FIRST, PRODUCT SECOND

A visionary emerged with a radical concept in the saturated marketplace of branded bottled water. Mike Cessario, a former creative director with a penchant for the unconventional, looked beyond the liquid to identify the essence of a market disruptor: he wanted to create a brand that could captivate before a single drop was bottled. Thus began the saga of Liquid Death, a brand that dared to quench the world's thirst with audacity.

Liquid Death was not born from the springs of innovation but from the wellspring of imagination. Cessario's epiphany struck when he saw empty Monster energy drink cans being filled with water to serve punk-rock bands' needs. The message was clear: the vessel and its branding were more potent than the beverage. While most companies meticulously refined their product before branding, Cessario flipped the script. He posited a simple yet revolutionary question: What if the allure of a brand could precede the existence of its product? Turn water into a cultural statement that goes against the current.

His answer was a brand that would resonate with an edge—Liquid Death, encased in an eco-friendly aluminum tallboy can, reminiscent of a craft beer, yet filled with only H_2O. The name itself was a declaration, a battle cry, and it came with a slogan that promised no less than to literally "murder your thirst." The skull logo and heavy-metal typography were not mere design choices, but precursors of a brand seeking its clan.

Before securing a source for his water or finalizing a supply chain, Cessario launched Liquid Death into the digital realm. With a modest budget and a video that showcased mock-ups of his vision, he sparked a viral sensation. The brand's Facebook page became a beacon for those drawn to its rebellious spirit, amassing over 100,000 fans and three million views. This digital fortress of brand identity was Cessario's proof to investors that Liquid Death was more than a crazy idea—it was a water movement.

The physical product remained elusive even with a brand that resonated deeply in the virtual world. In America, water bottling plants are strategically placed at water sources to minimize costs—and none were equipped for canning. Undeterred, Cessario looked across the Atlantic and found his solution in the Austrian Alps. The logistical nightmare of shipping cans 6,000 miles to their thirsty American audience did not deter him. When Liquid Death finally hit Amazon, it sold out at $20 for a case of 12.

By 2019, Liquid Death had stormed retail stores, racking up sales of $2.8 million. Fast forward to 2023, and projections soared to $250 million—a feat Monster took 11 years to achieve.[32] Liquid Death has become more than a brand; it's a cultural statement.

Liquid Death thrives on the edge, its content brimming with horror, absurdity, and dark humor—not unlike in the 1990s with *Pulp Fiction* and *Scream*. It's a niche carved out precisely, catering to those who delight in the outrageous.

Is Liquid Death a fleeting craze or an indication of branding's future? All signs point to the latter. The success of Liquid Death has not only rewritten the playbook for commodity branding but also foreshadowed a seismic shift in how products will come to market in the burgeoning age of the metaverse and virtual reality. In these expansive digital realms, companies can architect and refine their brands in immersive environments, engaging with consumers and building vibrant communities before a physical product even exists.

This digital-first approach is set to revolutionize product launches. It will allow a brand narrative to be fully experienced and embraced in virtual spaces, creating demand and loyalty that transcends the physical world. Brand first, product second.

Part One

BRAND COMMITMENT
THE WHY

"People don't buy what you do;
they buy why you do it."
—SIMON SINEK

The why is the most critical question of all the five C's of branding. It may also be the easiest or the most difficult to answer. Why?

Have you ever wondered why people line up for the latest Apple gadget but not for a Microsoft one? Why do some brands become more emotionally connected to their customers than others? Why does a 149-year-old brand like Heinz ketchup have over 84 percent of the market share in Canada and over 62 percent in the US? Why do people still want to buy the world a Coke? The secret behind the success of these and many other beloved brands lies in one question: "Why should I buy your product?"

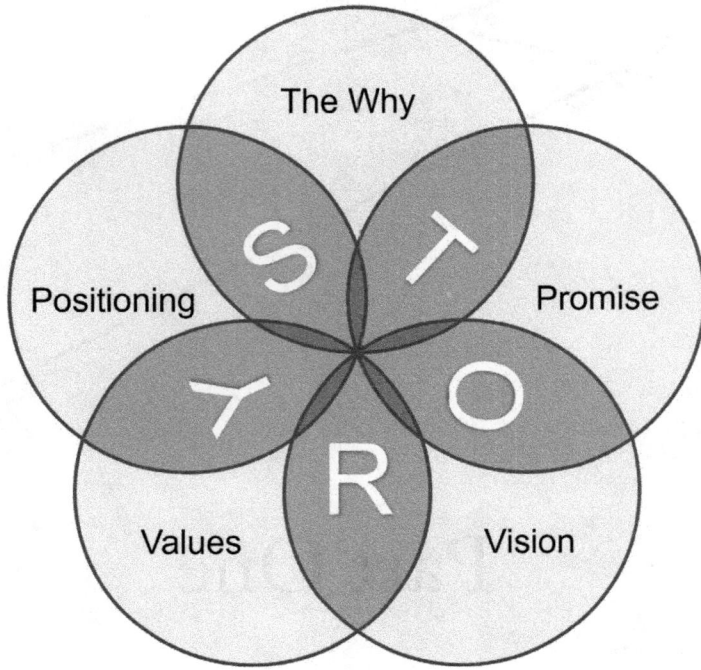

2 | BRAND STORY

The best brand stories aim to get the audience to care by answering their question—"Why should I care?" Many successful brands talk mainly about the "why" and very little about the facts of what they are selling. Author Neil Patel says that when someone is "interested in your brand's story, they feel connected in a powerful way. This feeling of connection then turns them into customers."[33]

Shoe company Toms uses storytelling to convince thousands of people and customers to go a day without shoes in its annual "One Day Without Shoes" campaign, which raises awareness of the millions of children worldwide who have no shoes. During the campaign, if you post your bare feet on Instagram with the hashtag #withoutshoes, they will give a new pair of shoes to a needy child.

In *Winning the Story Wars: Why Those Who Tell (and Live) the Best Stories Will Rule the Future*, author Jonah Sachs says, "It's critical for brands to shift from messaging to storytelling. After all, a brand is nothing more than an ongoing story—a set of meaningful emotional experiences—unfolding between itself and its audiences."[34]

We need to step back to around 30,000 years ago to observe the first documented storytelling on the walls of a cave in the South of France. In ancient Egypt (about 5,000 years ago), hieroglyphs were first used to communicate stories. As humans developed an oral language, stories became word-of-mouth until the transition from oral to written began about 1,250 years ago. But it wasn't until Johannes Gutenberg invented the printing press in 1439 (583 years ago) that the masses started to share stories widely. The first newspaper was published in 1690, followed by the first photograph in 1826, then the first silent movie in 1888, then the first radio broadcast in 1922, followed by the first television broadcast five years after that.

The dawn of storytelling is marked by the ancient poem *The Epic of Gilgamesh*, which was inscribed on twelve clay tablets around 2100 BC. Fast forward to the digital age, and Google's sophisticated algorithms reveal that by 2010 a staggering count of over 129.8 million books had been printed globally. Since then, an additional 26.4 million titles have joined this literary tapestry, according to research by writer Talon Homer, bringing the total to an impressive 156.2 million printed books by 2022.[35]

This history lesson aims to illustrate that storytelling has been around for thousands of years, but that as humanity has developed, so has the number of stories and the ways we communicate. We are inundated with more wisdom and important stories than are possible to consume in one lifetime. So, we've learned to rely on our basic instincts and extract general patterns or relevant meanings.

Stories are foundational to humanity. Storytelling has been a famous branding and marketing tool for years. In an *Adweek* article, creative director Jon Hamm of Momentum Worldwide emphasizes the significance of brand storytelling by noting its role in transmitting collective knowledge, principles, and ethics. Storytelling serves as the mechanism by which we interpret the world and our place within it, he says, offering a narrative framework for our existence. He adds, "Audiences have always known this and asked for stories—they've never asked for content."[36]

It seems that social media has given new life to storytelling. Attracting consumers with captivating, engaging, significant, and meaningful stories is a competitive edge for brands. You wouldn't need advertising if all employees could tell the company's brand story (or brand promise) on social media with passion and emotionally charged, descriptive language using no facts and figures. Susan Gunelius, a marketing veteran, says, "Stories are the perfect catalyst to building brand loyalty and brand value." A good story can emotionally connect a customer with a brand where the "brand's power will grow exponentially."[37]

A case in point is that over 8.5 million people have watched Coco Chanel's story on YouTube—which is about transforming women's fashion and the transformation of the woman who built the Chanel empire.

Successful brands tell the story of who they are—not only of the people behind the brand, but also of how their customers connect to their products in ways that give them the ability to do more with their lives. Such stories inspire passion in life and illustrate the *why* and *how* behind the *what* and *where*.

Marketing guru Seth Godin reminds us, "Great stories agree with our worldview. The best stories don't teach people anything new. Instead, the best stories agree with what the audience already believes and make [them] feel smart and secure when reminded how right they were in the first place."[38]

AN APPLE A DAY

Consumers don't need complicated details about your brand; they want you to improve their lives. It's that simple. Yet brands often want to tell their customers about all the craftsmanship and technology that goes into making their products. They can't help but talk about everything that makes their product superior, faster, and smarter. Brands that do this serve their own best interests instead of their customers' desires.

Rest assured, consumers do care that you have the latest, greatest, best quality technology, but don't bore them with the details. Apple understood this from the beginning. Their products inspire consumers because they're idiot-proof—all you have to do is turn them on.

Steve Jobs didn't talk about how they built the iPod's mercury-free, LED-backlit display, nor did he elaborate on its OS X v10.6.8 system requirements. Instead, he discussed the big "why" of changing the digital world forever. As his commercial said, "The people who are crazy enough to think they can change the world are the ones who do."[39] Steve Jobs was one of the crazy ones because he and Apple changed the music and smartphone worlds forever.

Brands led by a visionary or focused on a specific cause start from a passion for doing something right for their customers and the world. Not only do customers relate to this approach, but they also become emotionally invested in these brands.

FRENCH FRIES' BEST FRIEND

Did you know that over 650 million Heinz ketchup bottles are consumed annually?

The founder of Heinz, Henry J. Heinz, revealed the company's secret to success as "doing a common thing uncommonly well." He was adamant that customers should see what they were getting in every bottle, hence the clear glass (which was more expensive). He insisted on strict quality control, providing farmers with Heinz's own tomato seed—6 billion seeds every year. This guaranteed firmer tomatoes that stayed riper longer to give the ketchup's trademark thick, rich taste. There's even a quality specification on the speed at which the ketchup pours from the bottle, set at a maximum of 0.28 miles per hour. If it pours faster, it doesn't reach the store shelf.

Few people know the lengths Heinz goes to in the quest for the perfect ketchup. Heinz doesn't inundate you with these details to try to sell its product; it simply delivers consistent results that drive consumer loyalty.

Esquire restaurant critic John Mariani describes Heinz ketchup as, quite simply, "one of the few things in the world brought to such an honest state of perfection."[40] This is all that people want to know—that the company cares enough to ensure every bottle is perfect.

As a side note, Heinz ketchup will come out quicker if you tap the bottle at the "57" on the neck. Skip hitting the bottom of the bottle—that's for amateurs.

Caring Brands

"Start something that matters" is Blake Mycoskie's motto and the foundation of his booming shoe and accessories company, Toms. His business concept is firmly planted in the "why" and has sparked many companies to adopt the buy-one-give-one business model. His advice is to "stay true to what you believe."

Making a difference in people's lives and explaining the "why" seems to be the starting point for all successful brands. The ultimate key to success is to elevate the purpose beyond a consumer's functional wants and needs to a higher good of fulfillment, identity, affiliation, and societal or environmental altruism.

It is this passion for a brand's "why" that gives customers a reason to embrace the product. In the book *Start with Why*, author Simon Sinek explains that successful brands communicate the whys (beliefs, causes, visions) before communicating what they do and how they do it. Martin Luther King Jr. said, "I have a dream," not "I have a plan." It's all about the why.

Allen Adamson, author of *The Edge*, says, "A company that looks at its brand and asks not simply what promise does it make, but what purpose does it serve, to its customers and its shareholders, and brings this purpose to life through every customer experience will be the company most likely to beat its competition. When an employee can answer the question 'Why am I here?' in a positively motivating way, everyone benefits."[41]

A brand purpose must be simple and clearly understood by everyone in the company so they can emulate it daily. It must be single-minded in its focus and speak with one voice. It also helps to have a leader who is passionate about what the brand stands for and keeps everyone focused on what matters.

Start asking "why" your brand should be above the rest, and results are sure to follow.

3 | BRAND VALUES

Brand values are the ethical compass of a company, representing the core principles that guide its behavior, actions, and decision-making processes. They are essential for establishing a company's identity and serve as a benchmark for evaluating its interactions with customers, employees, and other stakeholders. Brand values help to create a strong, relatable, and trustworthy image that resonates with the target audience. They are not just abstract concepts but are meant to be lived and breathed throughout every layer of the organization. When brand values are clear and consistently upheld, they contribute to a cohesive brand culture and identity, enhancing customer loyalty, employee engagement, and overall brand equity.

For example, Patagonia's commitment to environmental sustainability is not just a part of its marketing strategy; it's woven into the fabric of its business operations. From sourcing eco-friendly materials to advocating for environmental causes, its values are evident in everything it does, which has helped Patagonia to build a loyal customer base that shares these values. Another example is the technology giant Apple, which highly values innovation and design. This focus is evident in every product it releases and its retail spaces' clean, minimalist design. By consistently applying their values, these brands create a distinct and enduring presence in the marketplace, fostering a strong connection with consumers who share similar values.

Having consistent brand values is crucial for a company's success. Internally, these values provide a sense of unity and direction for the staff. Externally, they help distinguish the brand from its competitors and foster genuine relationships with customers. In the absence of coherent brand values, companies often find it challenging to preserve their integrity, especially during times of accelerated expansion or adversity.

Therefore, it's no surprise that Patagonia donates 1 percent of sales to environmental nonprofits, sources sustainable materials, and empowers customers to repair rather than replace its products. This alignment between brand values and actions breeds trust and loyalty. In contrast, Volkswagen's emissions scandal revealed a gap between its brand values and unethical engineering practices, leading to reputational damage. Embedding brand values through policies, procedures, and behaviors provides consistency and meaning that sticks with stakeholders. Brand values are a strategic platform for making choices that continually reinforce what the brand stands for. The values are the measuring stick to evaluate all brand and corporate actions.

HAPPINESS IN A BOTTLE

Coca-Cola understands the magic in the bottle. The company's advertising stays away from product attributes, focusing instead on how its product makes you feel. Coke has successfully appealed to the consumer's heart and not their stomach.

Jim Stengel, in his book *Grow*, says, "Everything they do is inspired by this idea of, how do we promote, develop and create happiness?"[42] The company has never lost focus on why it exists, even when it introduced the failed New Coke. Stengel explains that "they never forget why they started and where they came from, which means a lot to consumers."

Richard Laermer, co-author of *Punk Marketing*, says the secret to Coca-Cola's brand is its ability to transfer adults back to their childhood, "a time people relate to being happy and worry-free."[43] Every cola can give you a sugar high, but Coca-Cola can also provide warmth and nostalgia. The company has successfully tied the brand to sentimental thoughts and stayed clear of being informative.

ALWAYS ON THE EDGE

Gillette has dominated the razor and blades market since 1901, with nearly 65 percent of the global market share in 2017. The brand started with the single safety razor and, over time, moved toward multiple-bladed versions. Gillette has been relentless in developing product innovations that are heavily patent-protected, while pouring funds into sports marketing and advertising to justify their hefty price tag. From the beginning, Mr. Gillette understood the brand's purpose was to transform men from prehistorical brutes to civilized males. As a 1910 advertisement eloquently stated, "The country's future is written in the faces of young men."

It wasn't until the late 1980s that the Gillette brand decisively started articulating the brand's why with the slogan "The best a man can get." This purpose was brought to life by emotional images of men as devoted sons, fathers, husbands, and boyfriends, all devoid of facial hair.

This doesn't mean, however, that the company hasn't occasionally fallen into the technology trap of explaining the "what" and "how" of their cutting-edge, stainless steel, micro, anti-friction, Pro-Glide, FlexBall razor that can cut hair one-fortieth of a millimeter shorter than its competition.

Today, the Gillette brand is under attack from lower-priced upstarts like Dollar Shave Club and Harry's, but if it keeps true to its follicle roots of "why," it should continue to protect its competitive edge.

4 | BRAND VISION

A brand vision is the guiding star for any business, embodying a company's aspirations and ultimate purpose beyond just profit-making. It serves as a strategic compass, providing direction and meaning to every aspect of an organization, from decision-making to brand communication. A compelling brand vision aligns the company's values with its long-term goals, ensuring all stakeholders work toward a common objective. It inspires and motivates employees by giving them a sense of belonging and purpose and helps build a consistent customer experience. When customers identify with a brand's vision, they develop a deeper emotional connection, which can lead to increased loyalty and advocacy.

For instance, Tesla's vision "to accelerate the world's transition to sustainable energy" is not just about selling electric cars; it's about leading a movement toward a more sustainable future. This vision helped Tesla carve out a unique position in the automobile industry and garner a passionate customer base. Similarly, Google's vision "to organize the world's information and make it universally accessible and useful" goes beyond the scope of a traditional search engine. It speaks to the transformative impact Google aims to have on global information consumption and accessibility. These examples demonstrate how a well-articulated brand vision can guide a company's trajectory and foster an emotional connection with its audience.

A clear and compelling brand vision is vital for companies looking to establish meaningful connections with their customers and differentiate themselves in a competitive market. A brand vision is a forward-thinking, aspirational statement that describes the ideal customer experience a brand aims to deliver. In essence, it articulates what a company hopes to achieve for its customers through its brand identity and offerings. An impactful vision aligns a company's leadership, inspires its employees, and gives its customers a reason to choose it over competitors.

For example, Disney's brand vision is "to make people happy by providing the finest in entertainment for people of all ages, everywhere."[44] This simple but bold vision guides Disney's business decisions and helps create a consistently magical customer experience. Apple's brand vision of "think different" empowered it to disrupt industries with innovative, customer-centric products and marketing. In contrast, companies without an apparent brand vision often struggle to connect their work to strategic goals that resonate with stakeholders. Research shows that brands with well-defined identity and vision statements outperform the competition on revenue growth and customer acquisition.[45]

5 | BRAND PROMISE

A brand promise is a personal commitment or covenant between a brand and its customer. A compelling brand promise expresses the unique value a customer can expect from a brand. It's an assurance to consumers about the benefits they will receive from the brand or how it will make them feel—like McDonald's "I'm lovin' it" slogan. As branding expert Scott Davis explains, a compelling brand promise captures "the company's pact with the customer—a pact that conveys the fundamental nature of the company or brand."[46] It gives customers a reason or rationale to choose one brand over another.

A brand promise is the declaration of the experience a brand commits to delivering to its customers. For example, the hospitality chain Ritz-Carlton promises, "Ladies and gentlemen serving ladies and gentlemen." This brand promise speaks to the respectful, dignified service one can expect at their hotels. It shapes Ritz-Carlton's staff training and customer interactions to meet this standard. It's crucial because it defines the customer's anticipation and drives the organization's internal strategy and culture, ensuring that every facet of the company is aligned with delivering on this pledge. When a brand consistently fulfills its promise, it can build a loyal customer base and differentiate itself from the competition.

Similarly, De Beers's decades-old brand promise that "A Diamond Is Forever" suggests diamonds are enduring symbols of commitment and love. A compelling brand promise that a company delivers consistently in all brand touchpoints leads to meaningful differentiation and emotional connection with the customer. Another iconic brand promise is BMW's "Sheer Driving Pleasure," which the company has used as a tagline globally (except in North America) since the 1930s. The essence of the BMW brand is a person's pleasure from driving one. As Joachim Blickhäuser, head of brand identity at BMW, said, "Joy is universal. It is a human emotion that binds us all together. So, I think [our tagline] will remain just as relevant in the future as it is now."[47]

Because a brand promise is ultimately a declaration, it's not unusual to see it as a tagline, rally cry, slogan, or motto. We'll talk more about these in Part Two: Brand Construct.

FLOATS ABOVE THE REST

Since its launch in 1964, Unilever's Dove soap brand had always used its unique selling proposition of its one-quarter moisturizing cream formulation. By the late 1990s the market leader's Dove sales were surpassed by Procter & Gamble's Olay brand in the United States.[48] The brand's "what" wasn't keeping it ahead of the competition. In 2004, Dove finally understood the importance of a higher purpose, and it launched the "Real Truth about Beauty" campaign that targeted women. To reach this point, they had probed deeper into emotional insights with their customers, moving past the functional benefit of one-quarter moisturizing cream to a more inspiring discussion of what defines beauty. In the end, they started a movement about self-esteem. *Advertising Age* reported that Dove's sales increased to $4 billion in 2014, compared with $2.5 billion just a decade earlier.[49] Moving from "what" (one-quarter moisturizing cream) to "why" (true, honest beauty) is a beautiful investment.

6 | BRAND POSITIONING

Understanding how the human brain works and how we communicate is essential to building a lasting brand relationship.

The human brain is an incredible machine. In the book *Kluge: The Haphazard Construction of the Human Mind*, author and psychologist Gary Marcus tackles the idea that we have two thinking systems inside our skulls. He argues that human evolution has created two distinct ways of thinking—an ancestral system that is instinctual and reflexive, and a more modern, deliberative one that involves reasoning. He explains that humans developed "contextual memory," which means we pull things from our memory by using context or clues that hint at what we are looking for; therefore, we are better at quickly retrieving general information than specific details. Examples of this are seen in branding daily, where we categorize complex products into a simple "first" attribute or benefit, like safety = Volvo, fights cavities = Crest, tastes awful = Buckley's (a cough medicine sold in Canada), magical = Disney. You get the picture.

Marcus says most pleasures are attributed to the ancestral, reflexive system. This would explain why we are constantly distracted and attracted to anecdotal and emotional hearsay that affects how we see the world, filter information, and make irrational decisions.

While we portray ourselves as highly evolved, logical, reasonable bioforms, we are explicitly tied to our basic instincts. Tapping into this insight, brands must have a connection to the non-rational side of the brain. This explains why many successful products have built their brands on emotion and why the best technically superior products don't necessarily win. A perfect example is the failed Blu-ray disk player.

To etch a brand into the long-term memory of a consumer, first we must understand the mechanics of memory formation. The hippocampus is the brain's memory architect, constructing new recollections by weaving a web of neurons and synapses. It organizes memories, clustering similar ones—like language-based memories near the language centers and visual ones near the visual cortex. When memory is revisited, its neural connections are reinforced, embedding it deeper into the brain's cortex.

For a brand to become memorable, it must captivate the consumer's senses, creating a multisensory brand experience. But mere attention isn't enough. The brand experience must be enjoyable, unique, significant, and delivered consistently to lay the foundations of a new memory. Repetition is crucial; it cements the experience, transforming it into a long-term memory.

The most effective strategy for securing a brand's place in a customer's mind is storytelling. A compelling narrative that consumers can identify with and emotionally connect to is not just heard; it's felt. These emotional connections are the building blocks of lasting memories.

Thanks to technology, we have more ways to tell stories than ever before, through instant photography, motion pictures, smartphones (voice and image), radio, TV, books, magazines, digital media, mobile media, and social media. The problem is that consumers can only hold so much information and memories in their brains. While our brain's volume has grown from that of *Homo erectus* (1,250 cm^3) to that of *Homo sapiens* (1,500 cm^3) in the last million years, our brain capacity is still finite.[50] The average brain storage capacity is 1.25 x 1012 bytes or 1.25 terabytes.[51] Let's put this into relatable terms. For example, one terabyte equals 2 million images (500KB/image), 17.55 million PowerPoint slides, or 472 hours of broadcast-quality video.[52] You have likely encountered your fair share of the ubiquitous PowerPoint slides, maybe even in the millions, yet my guess is that none remain memorable except, perhaps, the customary "Thank You" slide at the end. Embedding a brand's story into the consciousness of consumers is no small feat, but it is advantageous when it's achieved. Those who pioneer with a fresh narrative or an innovative idea stand a greater chance of making a lasting impression—because the first impression is paramount.

First Brands

Al Ries and Jack Trout pioneered the field of branding with their seminal works in the 1990s, penning influential branding books such as *The 22 Immutable Laws of Marketing* and *Positioning: The Battle for Your Mind*. Their central thesis is strikingly straightforward yet powerful: you want to be the first in the customer's mind. This means leading in market positioning within a given category. And the reason? It's simple: people rarely remember who came second—numerous examples back this concept. Consider your personal "firsts"—the first movie you saw in a theater, the first concert you attended, the initial flutter of a first date, or even the name of your first pet. Most people can readily recall these experiences because they mark new beginnings and are often emotionally significant, making them more likely to be etched into memory.

Try recalling the second or third movie or concert you attended—it's not as easy. Unless it's a specific "first" within a category—like your first country music concert or the first horror film you watched. Delving into second or third experiences, especially dates, can get complicated and are often less memorable. To win in the branding war, be the first to offer a new brand promise that is simple and easy for the consumer to consume. If you can synthesize it into a single thought, image, or word, you have a greater chance of locking up a place in the consumer's mind. Here are some examples: iPod with its iconic white earphones; X (formerly Twitter) making the news 140 characters at a time; Netflix streaming movies and shows 24/7 into your home; PlayStation finding something else for boys to do with their hands while barricaded in their bedrooms.

Successful car brands found their place in loyal customers' minds, securing their place as the first in quality, safety, value, adventure, speed, comfort, and/or durability. Then Tesla came along and took the most critical new position of a sustainable energy vehicle, the electric car. Coca-Cola and Pepsi have been wildly successful with two distinctly different brand positions: Coca-Cola is the "real thing" (first in the minds of consumers), but Pepsi successfully positioned itself as the youthful cola, the "new generation" to carve a new category.

We are attracted to brands. They become a reflection of who we are and what we represent. They define culture, values, and status. It's easy to understand why someone might want to wear a Rolex, and why someone else might want to use the same amount of money to buy an economical and environmentally friendly car plus an Apple watch. We live by our brands. And in some cases, for our brands.

BRAND COMMITMENT SUMMARY

In the final analysis of the "why," we can see that a brand's essence is rooted in its purpose—the fundamental reason for its existence. Though deceptively simple, this central question of why is often the most challenging to articulate—yet it is paramount in forging an authentic emotional bond with consumers. We can look to the powerful examples set by Apple, Heinz, and Coca-Cola, brands that have become integral to their customers' lives by effectively communicating their "why." Their success is not just in their products but in the emotional appeal of their brand narratives, which are deeply intertwined with the five C's of branding.

A brand's identity is anchored in its core values, which guide every action and decision. Positioning sets a brand apart in the competitive landscape, underscoring the unique attributes and value it offers to customers—it's a brand's pledge to deliver a reliable and trustworthy experience. Vision propels the brand forward, charting a course for future aspirations and growth. These elements are seamlessly woven into the fabric of a brand's "why."

Storytelling is a pivotal tool in making these abstract concepts tangible, inviting the audience to form a personal connection with the brand. Going beyond the functional aspects of a product, stories capture hearts, as demonstrated by brands like Toms shoes, which meld product promotion with social advocacy. This narrative strategy is as ancient as humanity, yet it continues to be a cornerstone of brand-consumer relationships in the modern era.

The "why" is the bedrock of an enduring brand's commitment to its foundational purpose. Such commitment transcends product functionality and creates a resonance that can weather market fluctuations and changing trends. Brands can nurture lasting loyalty through a commitment to core values, clear positioning, consistent promises, and a forward-looking vision. This chapter's deep dive into brand commitment, underscored by storytelling and consumer engagement, highlights the imperative for brands to engage with their "why" continually. Unwavering dedication to their raison d'être allows brands to imprint themselves indelibly on the hearts and minds of their devoted customers.

When a brand's "why" seems elusive, turning to the most loyal customers can unveil profound insights. These customers often hold the key to making the brand resonate with them. By tapping into this rich source of understanding, a brand can more effectively communicate its essence, strengthen customer loyalty, and secure its unique position in the marketplace.

To discover a brand's commitment through its "why," consider the following questions:

- What is the core purpose or mission that drives the brand?
- How does the brand's story connect with its audience emotionally?
- What values and beliefs are central to the brand's identity?
- How does the brand communicate its "why" to its customers?
- Can customers quickly articulate the brand's "why" and its significance?
- How does the brand's commitment to its "why" influence its product development and customer experience?
- What actions has the brand taken to demonstrate its commitment to its core purpose beyond marketing?
- How does the brand's "why" differentiate it from competitors?
- How does the brand engage with its community and stakeholders to reinforce its "why"?
- Has the brand remained true to its "why" over time, even when faced with challenges or market changes?
- What fundamental beliefs and principles guide the brand's decision-making and actions?
- How does the brand define its unique place in the market compared to its competitors?
- What consistent experience or outcome does the brand commit to delivering to every customer?
- Where does the brand see itself in the future, and what is its aspiration for long-term impact?
- How do the brand's values reflect in its products, services, and customer interactions?
- In what ways does the brand's current image align with its desired market positioning?
- How does the brand measure whether it is living up to its promise and maintaining its values?
- Can customers and employees clearly articulate the brand's values and vision?
- What strategies does the brand employ to reinforce its positioning within its industry?
- How does the brand plan to evolve its promise and values to stay relevant in the future?
- What is the brand's legacy or mark it aims to leave on its community or industry?

- How does the brand's vision inspire innovation and excellence within the company?
- What stories or narratives does the brand share to illustrate its values and vision?
- How does the brand communicate its commitment to its values and vision through marketing and branding efforts?

To better understand a brand's "why," try writing an obituary for the brand. Get the company's most senior leaders to write a final tribute in the past tense. Compare their results to see where the similarities and differences are. You can even extend this exercise to the most loyal customers and compare their language, sentiments, and insights with the leader tributes.

Part Two

BRAND CONSTRUCT
THE WHAT

"A logo is the period at the end of a
sentence, not the sentence itself."
—Sagi Haviv

The "what" is about building a brand image using physical and emotional signals. Use as many of the five senses (sight, sound, smell, taste, and touch) as possible. Each sense uses a different sensory system to transmit information to other brain parts. For example, the ears and eyes react to sound or light waves. Taste and smell are reactions of chemical contact with taste buds or olfactory centers. Each sense has its unique way of picking up information that the brain processes in different parts of the brain. Yet most brands think only about visual parts of their construct, such as logo and product design, colors, fonts, images, and style. Using as many senses as possible gives a richer brand experience and a better chance of being more memorable and impactful.

But don't forget about the less obvious branding elements like tonality, feelings, and personality traits. These are just as important as how you stimulate the senses. Together, the ultimate goal is to construct a brand image with a high coolness factor. Let's start by breaking down the composition of a brand image.

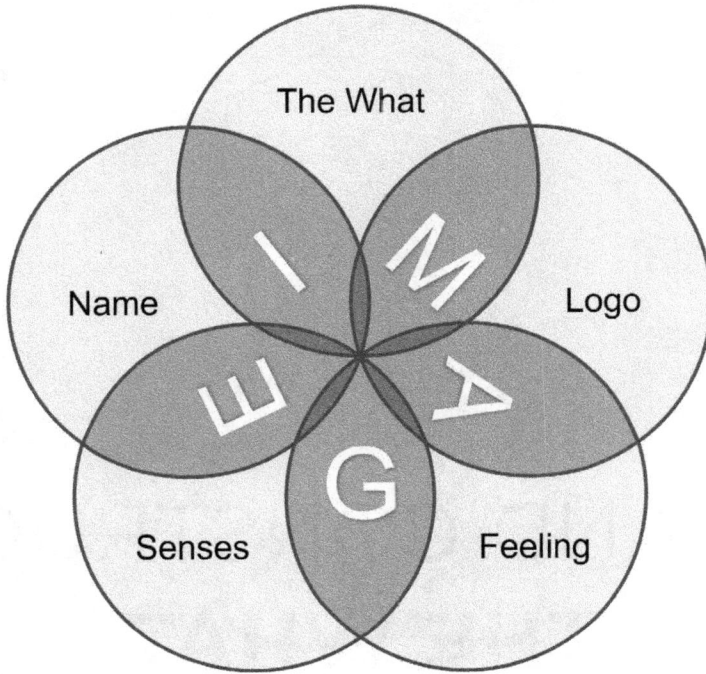

7 | BRAND NAME

No one and no brand can live without a name.

Prince's symbol

The late musician Prince (born Prince Rogers Nelson) tried to live without a name for five years but failed. The pop star dropped his name and requested to be referred to by an unpronounceable symbol he devised. What was wrong with "Prince"? The media was left with an unpronounceable name, so they called him "The Artist Formerly Known as Prince," which was eventually shortened to the acronym "TAFKAP." In the end, TAFKAP went back to his original name, Prince.

A brand's most important visual elements are its name and logo design (if there is one). It's important to have your word mark (name) and design mark (logo design) trademarked and legally protected, both locally and internationally. This is the first priority. If you can't protect it, move on and find something you can. It doesn't make sense to invest millions of dollars in a brand if someone else can use its trade name or mark.

Companies invest millions of dollars in building and protecting brand names. If it had to change its name, a brand could lose all the credibility and loyalty it worked so hard for.

Take a company like Florida-based Wholesale Landscape Supply. There's not much to remember there, right? They changed their brand name to Big Earth, and the following year, they increased sales by 200 percent.

Just like partners struggling to find the perfect name for their newborn, companies spend a lot of time and money finding their ideal brand name. Company owners build a potential list of names and, if they have the resources, conduct customer testing to determine how each name lands. Yet often, research and science factor very little in brand decision-making, with companies spending most of their energy and resources on their product or service instead. In some cases, the brand name becomes an afterthought. "If that's true, those businesses are run by idiots," says Mike Mann, author of the book and blog MakeMillions.com. He says that the brand name is foundational for everything else. Taking shortcuts and relying on your emotional instincts could sabotage your brand's long-term success.

Spend the time upfront to choose your perfect name. Come up with some naming strategies and use data-driven research to help you get to the one unique and memorable brand name. But before you can do that, you must have a clear brand strategy that identifies your brand position, promise, and reason for being. Your eventual brand name should encompass and embody your brand strategy.

Here are five possible approaches to finding your perfect brand name.

People Names

Consulting firms like lawyers, accountants, trainers, and agencies tend to use founder, owner, and inventor names as their brand since their consumers buy expertise directly from people. Logically, their brand names are the actual people behind the brand.

Additionally, many companies have successfully built empires on family names—think Disney, Johnson & Johnson, Johnnie Walker, Maytag, McDonald's, Hugo Boss, Porsche, Procter & Gamble, Walmart, and Toyota, to name a few. Check out Wikipedia's "Companies Named After People" page for a list of almost a thousand family brand names.

Before deciding to use your name as a brand, it's crucial to consider potential issues that could impact your success. First and foremost, privacy concerns should be considered; evaluate how much personal information you're comfortable sharing and whether using your full name aligns with your desired level of privacy. Additionally, be cautious of any negative associations that might be linked to your name, especially if there are individuals with similar names who have controversial reputations. Longevity is another consideration—consider whether using your name allows flexibility as your career or interests evolve. Check the availability of your name as a domain and ensure there are no trademark issues to avoid legal complications. Lastly, conduct thorough market research to avoid confusion with other individuals or brands that share a similar name. In considering these issues, you can assess whether using your name aligns with your personal and branding goals.

Descriptive Names

This is where the left-brain entrepreneurs live. The descriptive brand name communicates, in a straightforward manner, what service or product the company sells. Whether it's tires, donuts, airlines, hotels, banks, restaurants, or pizzas, there are no surprises about what to expect from these brands.

A problem arises, of course, when they want to expand beyond their core product. Dunkin' Donuts, for example, in 2024 changed the brand name to "Dunkin'," so they could extend beyond the donut and compete directly against Starbucks. Tim Hortons had the same problem when it started as Tim Horton Donuts. Today, it offers much more than donuts and is known as simply Tim Hortons (affectionately "Tim's"). Midas Mufflers began as a specialty shop servicing vehicle mufflers, but as time evolved, it added brakes, shocks, tires, and more. Simple solution—it dropped "Mufflers" from its name.

As long as a company sticks to its description, it is golden, but once it wants to branch out, the name can become a detriment. If you're considering getting that granular with your brand name, consider the future and stick to a name that's broad enough to encompass future plans.

Image and Experience Names

We shift now to right-brain thinking. This is where we can use analogical reasoning, draw on metaphors, tap into broader concepts like mythology, literature, art, music, and nature, and consider non-English words. These types of names evoke multidimensional imagery, and they can evolve to create a strong brand story. Sometimes, a brand is much bigger than its product or service and the brand name becomes the underlying theme or promise. Nike, Patagonia, Verizon, Amazon, Expedia, and Virgin are all great examples of names that have a brand story that's more significant than any product.

The $100-billion Nike brand started out as a running shoe built by Phil Knight, a college athlete with a business major from Stanford and his college track coach Bill Bowerman. They first started Blue Ribbon Sports in 1964, as a US distributor for running shoes made by Japanese company Onitsuka Tiger (now known as Asics). But in 1971 they created and manufactured their own running shoes that needed a brand name. They had a graphic design but no name. You've likely heard the story of the graphic design student, Carolyn Davidson, who designed the Nike swoosh for just $35. They came up with two possible brand names, Peregrine (a type of falcon) and Dimension Six, but no one liked either of them. Jeff Johnson, Blue Ribbon's first employee, came up with the name Nike—it came to him in a dream. Nike is the Greek goddess of victory. At the last minute they combined the Nike name with the $35 swoosh and the rest is history. There was no research or focus group testing—they just did it!

Word Names

Wouldn't you love to have been in the room when the agency pitched the brand name "The Gap"? You can hear the creative director reading the Oxford Dictionary definition: "Gap—a break or hole in an object or between two objects." In the end, though, it was brilliant. Take a random word and load it with a new meaning. If you can tie the word to the brand story or promise, you'll create a stronger connection to the brand name. Fruit seems to be a popularly repurposed muse with such brand names as Apple, BlackBerry, Tangerine (a Canadian direct bank), Orange (a French telecommunications), and Peach (a Japanese airline). Lemon and Gooseberry are still available!

Acronym Names

Acronyms and seemingly meaningless letters surround us. Every business and industry has its acronyms and initials. We practically need a decoder ring to make sense of them all. There's even a website, Acronym Finder, dedicated to decoding acronyms and abbreviations, and it contains more than 5 million definitions. We unconsciously use initials and acronyms daily to communicate, such as 24/7, WWW, LOL, TBD, ASAP, FYI, ROI, FAQ, SAP, SOL, KPI, ETA, SEO, SWOT, and OMG, to name a few. Will all brands eventually become acronyms or mindless initials?

Over the years, many companies have shifted to using acronyms and initials instead of their full names. Here are just a few brands that have reinvented themselves:

- Bayerische Motoren Werke to BMW
- The Royal Bank of Canada to RBC
- Kentucky Fried Chicken to KFC
- British Petroleum to BP
- Lucky Goldstar to LG
- YMCA to The Y—a shortening of an existing acronym!
- The Bank of Montreal to BMO

Wisconsin Tourism Federation changed its name to the Tourism Federation of Wisconsin, retiring its unfortunate WTF logo in favor of the innocent TFW. While the TFW name change was about avoiding humiliation, many other brands are doing it for other reasons, such as expanding into new non-English markets or removing words that made the company sound too regional or outdated.

There are also brands that have had a long life as initials, such as GE, IBM, HP, UPS, SAP, AT&T, H&M, MSN, and VW. Most people today couldn't tell you the words that these initials represent.

Developing a unique acronym, then, is another naming solution, as it gets more challenging to establish unique brand names that can be trademarked. IKEA is an acronym with many meanings in so few letters, starting with the founder's initials, "I.K." (Ingvar Kamprad). The "E" comes from the farm where he grew up (Elmtaryd), and the "A" from his home county (Agunnaryd in Sweden).

The charm of initials and acronyms is their simplicity. There is no need to memorize several words, especially if they are long and difficult to pronounce (like the German company Systeme, Anwendungen und Produkte in der Datenverarbeitung, SAP). Globalization has accelerated the use of acronyms and initials because they can transcend languages, cultures, and countries. Graphically, they can be turned into a strong design mark that can also convey emotional dynamics and, more importantly, can be legally protected.

The main problem with acronyms is that many of them mean nothing upfront. Remember your first day in a new company—all those nonsensical abbreviations, just a scramble of letters. Over time, you build a mental library of what each letter represents, even if you can't remember the literal words. Acronyms and initials are inherently not descriptive of the business and possess no imagery or benefit-oriented language in and of themselves. Ideally, you want a brand name to communicate something about the category, a benefit, or both.

Name Equals Benefit

The Government Employees Insurance Company, or GEICO, competes with companies like Nationwide, SafeAuto (acquired by Direct), and Esurance in the car insurance industry. Right away, each of these three competitors' names all tell you something about who they are:

- Nationwide: an extensive network of service and coverage
- SafeAuto: keeps you and your car safe
- Esurance: provides access to insurance online

What does GEICO tell you? The first thing that comes to mind is the memorable little green gecko. GEICO built its brand recognition through extensive advertising.

In 2013, GEICO spent $935 million on advertising, almost three times the average paid by the rest of the ten most significant insurance companies. It's no surprise, then, that their brand is well recognized as an insurance company.

Small and medium-sized companies can't afford the time and money to build a brand from initials unless the letters are exclusive and memorable.

However, there is a way to cheat by using the initials/acronyms as a design mark with total words representing the initials. Consulting firms in fields like law, advertising, and architecture, where people are the differentiating factor, tend to use their founders' or partners' names. The naming origins of one of the world's largest law firms, DLA (Dibb Lupton Alsop) Piper, can be traced to four law firms: Dibb Lupton Broomhead, Alsop Stevens, Piper & Marbury, and Rudnick & Wolfe. After several acquisitions and mergers, the company was called DLA Piper Rudnick Gray Cary, which was then further simplified to the more customer-friendly brand name of DLA Piper. If you go this route, just make sure the final acronym doesn't spell something you couldn't say in front of your mother. (Some companies still push the limit to be memorable, like the trendy clothing store FCUK, which stands for "French Connection UK").

The internet, texting, tweeting, and social media have forced everyone into a new abbreviated shorthand that fits in a limited space, saves time, and is easy to type on a mini keyboard. Many companies have also abbreviated their company names to make more memorable URLs, like Yelpington to Yelp, Flicker to Flickr and Tumblelog to Tumblr. Today, many brands start the name search by securing a URL name first before determining the brand name.

Acronyms and initials are here to stay, and they'll continue to proliferate as more brands become global and digital. Other trends could influence the evolution of brand names into acronyms, such as smart voice devices (Amazon Echo, Apple HomePod, Google Home) and virtual assistants like Amazon's Alexa, Apple's Siri, and Google Assistant. Machine learning and generative artificial intelligence (GenAI), digital assistants, and social algorithms are changing daily communication. How this will affect abbreviating brand names has yet to be seen. The essential brand goal is to ensure customers remember the name—acronym, initials, or not.

Eventually, ABWBA (all brands will become acronyms), but DQMOT (don't quote me on this)!

The real estate you need to secure is your brand name's domain or social handles, but don't sweat it. Joel Gascoigne, co-founder of social media marketing company Buffer, says, "The name [of the brand] itself matters much more than having the same domain name. Pick a great name, go with a tweaked domain name." You might also want to buy misspelled variations of your name before others do. Google owns gooogle.com, gogle.com, gogole.com, goolge.com and googel.com. Most of us have typed all of these variations at some point.

Also, remember that people must be able to easily pronounce your brand name and have it recognized by audio assistants like Alexa, Siri, and Google. If your brand will go beyond the world of English, make sure you understand any linguistic challenges with translations, idioms, slang, cultural associations, and connotations.

Many famous brands didn't get their name right the first time, and many continue to tweak their names to broaden their markets beyond borders and product lines today. For example, Skype evolved from "Sky peer-to-peer," and the Puma brand was changed from "Ruda," which had been based on the founder's first and last names—**Ru**dolf **Da**ssler. If you start with a name that doesn't fit, don't be afraid to return to the drawing board.

Lexicon Branding, one of the leading brand-name agencies in the world, says a great name can make a significant financial difference. And they should know—they have created $15 billion in brand names, including BlackBerry, Dasani, Febreze, OnStar and Pentium. The most iconic brands today don't have mind-blowing works of art for their wordmarks, either. They are simple words that have evolved into powerful brands: Nike, Google, Facebook, Walmart, Apple, and Amazon. A simple name with a powerful branding strategy can (and will) make all the difference.

Trademarks

One of the biggest problems in naming a new company is that the world is running out of pronounceable brand names to trademark. A study found that over 81 percent of the 1,000 most frequently used English words are registered as single-word trademarks; that number jumps to 99.7 percent when considering trademarks that use more than one word.[53] We are making it almost impossible for consumers to keep up. The World Intellectual Property Organization (WIPO)'s annual *Indicators* report shows that trademark demand has exploded from just under 1 million applications per year in 1985 to 11.8 million trademark applications by 2022. Asia, led by China, constituted 67.8 percent of the total global trademark filings in 2022. Since 2017, active trademarks worldwide have skyrocketed by over 90 percent to 82.5 million in 2022.[54]

Securing viable trademarks is becoming increasingly complex, but it's not impossible. As a general guideline, descriptive words are generally too common to protect.

For example, Hotel.com can't be protected, so owning the web domain name is as good as you will get.

Brand names are not only an investment but a liability. With so much money and reputation at stake, many trademark disputes have been about protecting brands. Toy maker Mattel Inc. is always going to court to defend its clean-cut Barbie doll brand against misuse, especially against pornographic misrepresentations. Apple Inc. was involved in litigation for years with the Beatles' record company, Apple Corps. Ben & Jerry's ice cream company sued an adult entertainment company for using parodied names in movie titles such as "Boston Cream Thighs," "Peanut Butter D-Cups," and "Chocolate Fudge Babes."

We classify information in our brains by words (i.e., trademark names) and associate them strongly with images (i.e., design marks). Sometimes, the design mark visually interprets the brand name, such as the pecten in Shell Oil's logo, the "golden arches" representing the M in McDonald's, or the apple logo for Apple. Over time, a brand name becomes loaded with the brand experience, and the design mark (a simple visual element) can be interchangeable with the trademark name. The logo design is not the brand. Nevertheless, it's the anchor of the company's visual identity and a critical component of a brand's success.

The Nike swoosh is a beautiful example of translating the Nike brand experience into an elegant design mark. You might remember the 2005 PGA Masters game when Tiger Woods was at the 16th hole with a chip onto the green. The ball reached the cup as if in slow motion, and then it sat on the lip of the hole for what seemed an endless time. The Nike logo was fully visible on the ball as it finally dropped into the cup. The crowd went wild. For Nike, that little golf ball was worth millions of dollars in building the Nike brand.

Here are some tips to start your quest for the perfect brand name:

Clear and Memorable: Ensure that your brand name is easy to remember and pronounce, allowing customers to recall it easily.

Reflects Brand Identity: The name should align with your brand's values, mission, and personality, effectively communicating what your brand represents.

Differentiation: Your brand name should stand out from competitors and highlight what makes your brand unique.

Relevant: Choose a name that's relevant to your industry, products, or services to help customers understand your offer.

Simple and Concise: Keep the name short and straightforward, avoiding complicated or confusing terms that may hinder recognition and recall.

Avoid Industry Jargon: While being relevant, avoid using jargon that might alienate potential customers unfamiliar with the terminology.

Scalable: Consider the future growth and expansion plans for your brand. Choose a name that can accommodate new products or services without feeling limited.

Global Appeal: If you plan to operate internationally, ensure the name is culturally appropriate and doesn't have negative connotations in different languages or cultures.

Trademark Availability: Conduct a thorough trademark search to ensure that another company hasn't already registered the name you choose. It's crucial to avoid legal issues down the line.

SEO-friendly: In today's digital world, consider incorporating keywords or phrases relevant to your industry, which can help improve search engine visibility.

Positive Association: Create a name that evokes positive emotions and associations, leaving a lasting impression on customers.

Easy to Spell and Pronounce: Avoid complex or ambiguous names that might confuse customers or make it difficult for them to find you online.

Versatile: Your brand name should be adaptable to various marketing channels and platforms, including social media handles, domain names, and packaging.

Timeless: Aim for a name that can withstand the test of time and remain relevant even as trends change. Avoid using trendy words or slang that may quickly become outdated.

Test and Feedback: Before finalizing your brand name, gather feedback from your target audience, stakeholders, and other professionals to ensure that it resonates with your intended market and receives a positive response.

8 | BATTLE CRY, TAGLINE, AND SLOGAN

Fighting for your brand to survive in an ever-changing world isn't for the faint of heart. Getting customers and employees to rally around the brand's purpose, promise, or vision is paramount to winning the war. In today's noisy and cluttered world, having a battle cry of what your brand stands for can be a critical part of your tactical plan. A battle cry invokes patriotic sentiment, arousing an esprit de corps to elevate the brand above the competition. It can give employees a reason to come to work every day and care—and it can reinforce "why" customers believe in your brand in the first place.

Throughout history, the battlefield cry has been used to intimidate the competition in many contexts. It had to be loud, simple, and effective. Mottos and slogans came from the battle cry concept. As marketing and branding have evolved, the words slogan, tagline, motto, and anthem have become blurred and nearly synonymous. New to the arsenal is the #hashtag.

My goal here isn't to try to define each term, as they are used fairly interchangeably. Instead, my goal is to demonstrate how to effectively use a battle cry for different purposes to help a brand become triumphant.

These pithy lines have long been used to sign off print ads, or TV or radio commercials as the final brand message. In some cases, they are incorporated into a brand's sonic/audio signature. However, as brands move away from traditional advertising-centric marketing toward an interactive digital environment, the question must be asked: is a motto or tagline necessary? Today, what's essential to the customer is that the brands be there when they want it, on their terms. It's less about what the brand says and more about what it does.

However, rallying customers and employees around a single idea, action, or thought is still relevant. Especially when consumers are starved for time, a catchy cry can be compelling even in a digital world where we are continually distracted. The line must generally be directly relevant and memorable to gain traction, just like a hashtag that goes viral. In this fast and always-on society with our explosion of acronyms, we have moved away from long-winded blather of vintage advertisements toward concise, powerful phrases loaded with meaning, like MeToo, BLM, Brexit, and IceBucketChallenge. Hashtags have become an extension of the brand battle cry. In some instances they *are* the battle cry.

Some brands, such as Starbucks, Whole Foods, Lululemon, and Nordstrom, have survived on the battlefield without ever shouting a battle cry. On the other hand, more and more brands are turning to hashtags as taglines, such as Audi's #DriveProgress, Kit Kat's #haveabreak, or the epic #LikeAGirl campaign by Always feminine products promoting confidence among teen girls. Here are six ways to use a battle cry to help your brand win the war.

Brand Pitch

Slogans that function as sales pitches are an excellent way to create action from the customer. In many cases, these pitches are short-term campaign initiatives (at least that's the intent). They are focused on a potential customer, and generally tied to a unique product characteristic or benefit, with some urgency. Some of these messages naturally fit as a hashtag or become a musical jingle that can get stuck in customers' heads. Examples include Tide's Power Pods slogan, "Now Stains Can Wait," and Walmart's "Save money. Live better."

Brand Promise

If a brand pitch successfully captures the consumer's psyche, it could become a long-term brand promise. A brand promise is a sales pitch that endures by consistently delivering on the promise. Successful brands have employees who strive to accomplish the brand promise daily for their customers. In essence, it becomes their battle cry. Some brand promises that have survived the test of time (in some cases for many decades):

- Kellogg's Frosted Flakes: They're grrreat!
- Maxwell House: Good to the last drop
- Kentucky Fried Chicken (KFC): It's finger lickin' good

Brand Vision

A brand vision cry is more profound and aspirational than a brand pitch or promise. Sometimes, it reminds the employees that the brand isn't static as the performance bar is constantly raised. Vision statements are created closer to the C-suite, where the company's vision is developed. While these are more ambitious and forward-thinking, they are still relevant for customers today with the future in scope. Here are some examples of a brand vision that rarely changes:

- Disneyland: The Happiest Place on Earth
- United: Fly the Friendly Skies
- Subway: Eat Fresh
- Coca-Cola: Open Happiness

Brand Credentials

Sometimes, brands need to spell out who they are and what they stand for, especially new brands with non-descriptive names and no awareness. Brand names that use a person's name are an excellent example of those requiring a descriptor until they become legends. In such cases, the tagline becomes a subhead to explain what the brand is or does. Generally, the industry or specialty, including law, accounting, insurance, and real estate, is mentioned, followed by a unique benefit. You can also use pure descriptors like lawyers, advisors, consultants, accountants, agents, etc. Here are some great examples of taglines that build the brand's personality while also communicating who the brand is:

- Morse Barnes-Brown Pendleton: The law firm built for business.
- Harris Beach Attorneys at Law: Lawyers you'll swear by. Not at.
- Clark Schaefer Hackett: Strength in numbers.

Brand Cult

The ultimate is when a brand grows a defined cult-like following related to an esoteric anthem that acts as a password. In these cases, the line is less about a call to action and more about how the brand will make loyal customers feel. It almost affirms what makes the brand similar to its loyal followers—reaffirming the feelings and attitudes its followers attribute to their brand experience. These battle cries feel suitable for any customer to yell from a mountaintop, such as:

- American Express: Don't live life without it.
- Harley-Davison: All for freedom. Freedom for all.
- Apple: Think different.
- L'Oréal: Because you're worth it.

Brand Tags

In a mobile world of always-on, many brands use hashtags to entice consumers' online engagement via promotional incentives. About thirty years ago, the first hash symbol appeared online to help label groups and topics. However, it wasn't until 2007 that Stowe Boyd used the first hashtag in a blog post. Then, in 2009, X (formerly Twitter) adopted the hashtag to help users search for specific organic topics, subjects, and groups.

Since then, hashtags have defined trends, movements, events, activities, people, or whatever you want to express as a handle. Hashtags can also be fun, humorous, and just plain silly. Every social media channel has now embraced the hashtag. Brands, politicians, influencers, reporters, like-minded people, celebrities, activists, and more have used the hashtag as their battle cry to create a platform, build a community, or find infamy. Not surprisingly, many brands' battle cries have turned into hashtags or vice versa, creating physical and measurable communities, such as:

- Calvin Klein: #MyCalvins
- Charmin: #EnjoytheGo
- Domino's: #LetsDoLunch

Battle Cry

Our branding consumption has turned into a world of appetizers. We can only stomach bite-size pieces as we face over 5,000 branding messages daily. We gravitate to the sample pack in order to survive the buffet of headlines, videos, commercials, social content, and hashtags we're bombarded with. Brand battle cries have become a staple in this new world of overindulgence. Can a tagline, hashtag, slogan, motto, anthem, or battle cry make your brand famous? Maybe. It depends on why and how you use it. If it's relevant and speaks to the end-user, it has the potential to build a unique bond forever.

Before you send your brand out on the battlefield, make sure it has all the latest weaponry to survive and thrive. A battle cry can be part of the arsenal to make an emotional connection or create an action of urgency. As brand communications evolve using images, pictures, videos, sound, animations, emojis, and memes, the battle cry becomes more relevant in finding a place in the consumer's busy mind. Words are powerful. Victorious battle cries must be simple, unique, memorable, likable, passionate, short, and sweet.

While the power of words continues to create lasting change, new communities, and unique bonds, visual communications continue to grow in strength. Images, pictures, videos, infographics, GIFs, and animatics continue to increase in popularity thanks to social platforms like Instagram, Pinterest, and TikTok. Long-winded verbiage is dying, and the brief battle cry is paramount to help win the war.

9 | BRAND SIGHT

We are quickly turning into a visual society. Based on several annual research studies the number of Americans reading books continues to decline year over year and over the last decade.[55] In 2022 over 50 percent of Americans hadn't touched a book in over a year.[56] Robert Passikoff, president of Brand Keys, says that nearly 75 percent of all communications today are visually based. He predicts that number will increase to 90 percent in the coming years.[57]

People are shifting from traditional television to Netflix, YouTube, and TikTok. The world's second-most used site as a search engine is YouTube, with more than 1.7 billion unique visitors per month.[58] Over 5 billion videos are streamed on YouTube per day, and about 3.7 million new videos are uploaded every day.[59] TikTok is the newer kid on the block, launching and surpassing over one billion monthly users after six years. It took Facebook almost three years longer to reach the same milestone. In 2022, TikTok was the most downloaded app on the Apple App Store.[60] Netflix continues to capture eyeballs with over 269.6 million streaming subscribers as of Q1 2024.[61] Today's challenge is developing consumable content that is worth watching.

According to Nielsen Media Research, in July 2022 streaming video-on-demand services surpassed cable to claim the largest share of television viewing, at over 34 percent.[62] How do brands get in on the action? The traditional fifteen-, thirty-, or sixty-second commercial doesn't fit the new entertainment models. To get your brand message noticed, you must produce your own content for these platforms. Red Bull is a content-creating monster, blending its advertising with entertainment programming such as documentaries, music, and sports events. The company's secret is capturing fantastic moments with breathtaking background scenery like mountains, oceans, and outer space. The message is that anything is possible with a Red Bull.

Brand Color

Do you remember the famous online debate about the color of "the dress"? People argued whether it was blue and black, or white and gold. Color is an emotional trigger that activates memory. Research suggests that cells in the secondary visual cortex (V2) are mainly responsible for how we see color consistency, and begins to explain why a red apple still looks red if we look at it outside, under a lamp, or in different lighting conditions—unless you are looking at a blue or white dress.

A Xerox report on color knowledge points to the connection between color and memory: seeing a logo in color makes it 39 percent more memorable than seeing the same logo in black and white.[63] On a website, color statistics company Colorlib found that color can boost brand recognition by up to 80 percent.[64] Color also drives engagement: adding color to blog posts, product guides, print advertising, and other brand collateral increases readership by 80 percent.[65]

If color increases brand recognition, you must also differentiate your brand from the competition, where there is a kaleidoscope of colors. If you're starting up a new bank, you might want to use a different color than blue, which is used by Chase, JP Morgan, Deutsche Bank, RBS, RBC, Prudential, Barclays, Citibank, Capital One, Union Bank, and Bank of Montreal. For a while it seemed like the color orange was to be the new blue, used by newer banks like ING Bank and Tangerine.

Unsurprisingly, numerous financial institutions and many other brands use the color "true blue," hoping it will evoke a sense of trust and dependability. According to a study published in the Journal of Business Research, customers are 15 percent more likely to return to stores with blue color schemes than those with orange color schemes. But try telling ING Bank that the orange isn't working for them as they turned a profit of over 7 billion Euros in 2023.

A great deal of work has been done in the area of the psychology of color in branding. It's like buying a house: You make the initial decision based on emotion, then rationalize it after the fact to legitimize your purchase. The birth of a brand identity starts with the logo design, which a graphic designer generally does. Depending on your budget, you can employ a single individual or a massive agency team, who will sell you on the perfect color.

For most start-up companies, the brand logo design and color aren't the biggest concerns of the day. It isn't where they invest or spend most of their time, because their biggest issue is getting their product or service to market.

But to believe they have the brand all figured out would be a stretch. You might know where you want to go, but how you get there is not always in your control. College dropouts Steve Jobs and Steve Wozniak, who started Apple Computers in Jobs's garage, didn't have a clear vision of where the Apple brand was going. Their first logo, void of color, could have easily been a cover on a book by Tolkien (author of the famous *The Lord of the Rings* series) rather than a company logo. It depicted Isaac Newton sitting under a tree with an apple dangling over his head. (You know the rest of the gravity story.)

That logo lasted only a year, when the company finally had the funds to commission a real graphic designer, Rob Janoff. He designed the rainbow-colored apple with a bite taken out of it. This logo lasted twenty-two years, until 1997 when the colors were replaced with a more modern, monochromatic look. Such redesigns and modernizations all come with million-plus-dollar price tags from mega graphic design firms, of course.

Starbucks started out with a brown or mocha-colored logo of a siren (or mermaid) from Greek mythology, which made sense since they were selling rich, dark-roast coffee in Seattle, on the West Coast. But, fifteen years later, the logo was refined, and the color changed to green. Why? It is believed the three founders wanted to honor their alma mater, the University of San Francisco, which happens to use a similar green. So much for color research.

Much research has been done to understand the effects of color on consumer's responses. However, as marketing strategist Gregory Ciotti points out, "The truth is that color is too dependent on personal experiences to be universally translated to specific feelings."[66] He explains that gender, background, personal experiences, and culture influence how color perceptions influence consumers.

Nevertheless, we still make all *stop* and *sale* signs red—why is that? In a study published in the journal *Emotion*, Professor Andrew Elliot found that people react faster and more forcefully when they see red.[67] The primary reason behind the phenomenon is that red enhances physical reactions, as it is programmed into our psyche as a cue for danger.

A brand that has used the power of red successfully for over 128 years is Coca-Cola, which sells about 19,400 beverages every second around the world. Coca-Cola started advertising its brand by painting big red signs on buildings and coolers. It continued in the early 1900s with outdoor billboards and traditional advertising. In 1931, the company successfully tied its brand to the man in red—Old St. Nicholas. As the years passed, red has become synonymous with Coca-Cola. This took years and years of persistence and hard-nosed application of the brand principles. As the brand developed over time, the company worked to define and codify the brand's values and its essence. Through this process, the brand color(s) were also encoded into the brand's DNA.

In 2011, Coca-Cola slipped up by changing its sacred red Coke can to white during the December holiday season to celebrate its highly successful polar bear advertising campaign. Within weeks, the white "polar bear" cans were pulled off the shelves because of a tremendous backlash from retailers and consumers, who were confused by the change from the traditional red. Some even complained that the taste of the soda was different—all because of the color of the can!

Getting the brand DNA right takes time, and it's built on what works for the brand's customers. But once the brand color(s) are locked in, you must be ruthless in protecting this relationship to a color and what the brand represents. Can you see a John Deere customer selecting the color they want for their tractor? It comes in green or green or green.

When you think of Heinz ketchup, you automatically think of the red bottle. Yet Heinz had the opposite results when it changed its red bottle to green. The Heinz EZ Squirt Blastin' Green ketchup was a phenomenal success. But to be fair, the red bottle was still available for those customers who didn't want to change. Over 10 million green bottles were sold in the first seven months following their introduction. All because of a simple color change. For some color matters and for other's a change is refreshing. Understand your target audience before you make a radical color change.

Color is a powerful signifier of a brand. When customers visually scan store shelves, they look first at color clues, then at shapes, and finally at the label or name of the brand. Research conducted by the Seoul International Color Expo 2004 found that 92.6 percent of customers consider visual factors the most important when purchasing products, and that color accounts for almost 50 percent of the critical factors. The researcher Satyendra Singh found that people subconsciously judge an environment or product within 90 seconds of initial viewing. Between 62 and 90 percent of that assessment is based on color alone.[68]

The color a company uses to brand itself conveys how trustworthy they are, the quality of their products, how fun they are, and much more. So, you need to have the right color to succeed.

Emeritus professor Paul Bottomley authored a study called "The interactive effects of colors and products on perceptions of brand logo appropriateness." The study demonstrated that the relationship between brands and color is based on the perceived appropriateness of the color used and the particular brand personality you are trying to portray.[69]

Does the color fit what the brand represents? An obvious misfit would be the color pink with a serious law firm brand or a funeral home. While the color pink might differentiate the brand, it might not build a solid brand message. Because there are so many brands today, it is getting harder and harder for new ones to build their own unique brand color positioning, so they are pushing the limits of what is appropriate. Every business category has an outlier that isn't following the color code, like Orange's orange, T-Mobile's neon pink, Veuve Clicquot's bright orangish-yellow, Yahoo's purple, and BP's lime green.

If you want your brand to be synonymous with a color, you need to use your color everywhere, including in the store environment or anywhere else it makes sense. That could mean a fleet of planes painted orange with airline attendants wearing orange uniforms (EasyJet), a fleet of brown delivery vans with drivers wearing brown uniforms (UPS), a tasteful box in robin's egg blue surrounding gold, silver, and diamonds (Tiffany & Co.), or flooding the exterior and interior of the store and staff in yellow and red (Shell and McDonald's). You want to make the color an integral part of the brand experience.

How many brand colors were the result of the whims of a graphic designer exploring the next trend or the personal taste of the CEO's spouse? In the case of Facebook, founder Mark Zuckerberg is blind to red-green colors, so blue was his choice.

Well-thought-out colors can help define a brand's value, strength, and positioning, boosting awareness and customer recall and differentiating the brand from the competition. If chosen effectively, they can even set the emotional stage for the overall brand experience.

Brand Design

Humans have a deep-rooted attraction to beauty and unique designs. Our minds are wired to appreciate the aesthetics of nature, art, and crafted objects that captivate our senses through symmetry, colors, textures, and graceful forms. They elicit positive emotions from appreciation to joy, sparking our imagination and creating a feeling of connection with the world around us.

Insight into this draw toward beauty shapes exceptional brand design across logos, retail environments, and products—especially for high-end brands pursuing timeless elegance. The curve of a letter, the warmth of a palette, and the balance of shapes combine to make customers feel a certain way about a company. Successful brands tap into visceral emotions through conscious design choices.

The iconic Apple logo with its minimalist design and graceful curves, the Chanel logo with its timelessly elegant interlocking Cs, and the solid, structured CBS Eye all deliver the psychological effect of trust, beauty, and craft that draws loyal audiences for generations. Behind many iconic brand logos is a story, and artists who understand that logos should not merely identify a company; they should invite an emotional connection, turning the brands they represent into beacons of trust, desire, and sophistication.

Perfection takes time. Brand names and logo designs are an evolution. Initially, nobody knows your brand, what it stands for, or what it is trying to sell. Any signals you can relay via your brand name and logo are helpful, but as your brand authority and awareness increase, you can drop the descriptors and simplify the logo design to its basics.

A case in point is the Starbucks logo. The initial version contained all kinds of information in the brown design. Sixteen years later, the company began to find its purpose and focus on coffee. Fast forward twenty-four years, and Starbucks has become more than just coffee. Today, it is a universal brand, needing no language at all. Once a brand finds its mojo—becoming more prominent than a product—it can rely on projecting what the customer feels. The mythical twin-tailed siren was said to have the power to lure sailors toward rocky shores to meet their demise. But thanks to Starbucks, the mermaid's allure has transformed over time into the more friendly temptation of a morning cup of caffeine.

Uber is another example of evolving, but not always for the better. Like Starbucks, the company's first logo contained a descriptor to communicate that it was a pseudo-cab business. But depending on your smartphone's operating system (iOS or Android) and who built the logo, you saw a different logo. As the concept shifted from catering to the business elite to a step up from the average taxi to a step below a limo, the brand started focusing on the U, downplaying the name Uber. Unfortunately, the new U was in risk of trademark infringement due to closely resembling the supermarket chain Super U in France. So, in 2011 they had to pivot again.

In 2016, Uber's then-CEO Travis Kalanick decided to rebrand the company—using an internal employee committee rather than engaging external branding experts. This is a cautionary tale about the pitfalls of a top-down approach to rebranding. While the committee's intention was to symbolize the company's evolution from a luxury service to a more inclusive platform across the globe, its execution overlooked a critical aspect. The rebranding effort, driven by an internal perspective, missed incorporating any customer insight or input. It focused on a concept involving bits and atoms, where the box in the center of the logo was the *bit*, symbolizing Uber's technology, the circle-like shape around it depicted the *atom* (humanity) , and the surrounding pattern expressed the world. The idea was that each Uber market would have a different pattern and colors to represent its unique culture. This concept made sense to a tech-focused CEO, but it completely failed to resonate with consumers. The idea that Uber, essentially a taxi company, was bringing together all the bits and atoms in the world to solve all of its problems, seemed grandiose and disconnected from any kind of brand promise, or customer focus. This misalignment highlighted the disconnect between the company's self-perception and public perception.

The fallout from this top-down rebranding was significant: starting from consumers not comprehending the new logo and the complexity of executing a different logo for each city. The effort wasted time and resources, and involved a substantial financial investment that could not recoup its value. The importance of using professional branding experts cannot be overstated. These experts bring a wealth of experience in building cohesive brand identities, and they have the tools and methodologies to effectively gather and interpret customer input. Their external perspective can be invaluable in avoiding the echo-chamber effect that sometimes plagues internal teams, ensuring that the brand's evolution reflects not only the company's self-view but also the marketplace's needs and perceptions.

The expertise of branding professionals in conducting market research, customer interviews, and brand perception analysis is crucial. They can help navigate the complex landscape of customer expectations and competitive positioning. By engaging with branding experts, companies like Uber can benefit from a structured process that integrates customer feedback into the core of the rebranding strategy. This customer-oriented approach helps to mitigate the risk of a rebrand that fails to resonate with its intended audience and ensures that the new brand identity aligns not only with the company's vision but also with the values and desires of its customers.

10 | BRAND TOUCH

The sensation of touch isn't often considered when building a brand, but for some this can be a missed opportunity.

One of the obvious times we use touch is when shopping for clothes. Our first instinct is to touch the fabric to feel it against our fingers. This quick touch tells us many things about a garment—its softness, wearability, durability, and quality. Or think of the last time you visited a car dealership and inspected a vehicle. Your first impression was likely related to how the door handle felt, and how it opened and closed in your hand. If the interior was leather, you assessed the quality by touching the seat or sitting in the driver's seat. At some point, you probably grabbed the steering wheel. With every literal touchpoint, our brains process the information and analyze the vehicle's durability, craftsmanship, and overall quality.

Touch is the first sensory system we develop in the womb, and the one most developed by birth. If you have raised a child, you know that holding, rocking, and rhythmic stroking are all important ways of calming and connecting with babies.

The somatosensory cortex of your brain, which processes touch information, dedicates many neurons to your fingers, lips, and tongue. That's why these areas are more perceptive and finely attuned, maximizing the richness of your sense of touch.

Greek philosopher Aristotle concluded that man was more intelligent than other animals because of the accuracy of his sense of touch. The sensation of touch influences what we buy, who we love, and how we heal. We use touch to gather information and establish trust and social bonds.

In his book *Touch: The Science of the Hand, Heart, and Mind,* Dr. David Linden says that the "genes, cells, and neural circuits involved in the sense of touch have been crucial to creating our unique human experience."[70]

Let's try a touch test. Imagine that you are in a pitch-dark room with no light, and you're handed an object. Through the power of touch, you must determine what it is.

You feel cold glass in your hand. You sense a distinct curvature of the glass in an elongated shape. You determine that it's a bottle. Moving your fingers along the side, you notice subtle smooth groves like ribs that flow up and down the bottle. The glass sweats moisture droplets onto your hand, so you can sense that its contents are cold and wet. When the cap is removed you hear a pop, then move the bottle's neck toward your lips (hopefully someone has told you that it's safe to drink). You feel cold liquid against your bottom lip and tongue. The effervescence of tiny little bubbles tingle against your lip and mouth. You smile. It's the real thing!

If we conducted this experiment, you would have quickly determined that the glass bottle was the most famously shaped soft drink bottle in the world—the iconic contour fluted lines of the Coca-Cola bottle. In 1915, Coca-Cola challenged several glass companies to design a bottle that could be recognized by feel alone. More than a hundred years later, this unique design still succeeds in that objective.

There are two types of touch. (If your mind went to the gutter, you must check out the sexy topic in chapter 15, The Cool Factor.)

The first type is the sensory pathway that provides facts about touch, such as pressure, location, texture, vibration, and temperature. The Coke bottle test uses precisely this type of touching. Linden explains it as "figuring out the facts... uses sequential stages of processing to gradually build up tactile images and perform the recognition of objects."[71]

The second pathway processes social and emotional information from a human touch, such as a handshake, a hug, a caress of the arm, or a pat on the back. Friendly touching communicates trust and cooperation. The *Journal of Personality and Social Psychology* published a study showing that people base their initial opinions of others on a simple handshake.[72] Linden explains, "In both kids and adults, touch is the glue that makes social bonds."[73] Further echoing this idea is Dr. Dacher Keltner, professor of psychology, who explains that "touch is truly fundamental to human communication, bonding, and health."[74]

What does this have to do with building brands? Both types of touch are fundamental in helping build brand perceptions and trust.

Tactile Branding

Tactile branding is all about what the brand or components of the brand feel like. In a *Live Science* article called "Just a Touch Can Influence Thoughts and Decisions," science journalist Jeremy Hsu says, "Hardness may evoke concepts of stability, rigidity, and strictness. Roughness can lead to thoughts of difficulty and harshness, while heaviness conjures up impressions of importance and seriousness."[75]

Professor of Psychology Joshua Ackerman conducted a study in which he had participants sit in hard and soft chairs as they negotiated the price of a new car.[76] Guess who was less willing to move on to their price? You'd be right if you guessed the poor people in the hard chairs were the most rigid negotiators.

Apple is an excellent example of a brand that has embraced the importance of touch. Its smooth, round-edged metal and glass iPads, iPods, and iPhones convey a sense of ease and simplicity. Apple also ensures its customers can touch and feel the merchandise in its interactive stores.

Suppose your brand isn't an actual product but more based on services. In that case, understand that anything you physically give a customer, like a brochure, contract, or correspondence, is tactile and communicates your brand by touch. Your business card, for example, communicates volumes about your brand. Every aspect of your business card should speak to your brand's identity. From the tactile feel of its material, to its heft and texture, to its dimensions and contours, to distinctive enhancements like foil stamping, spot UV coating, and embossing, to the color palette and typography—all of these combine with the details of your logo and contact information to make a statement about your brand.

Amazon takes pride in its shipping experience, using custom-printed boxes and packing tape in a program called "Frustration-Free Packaging." Packaging can be paramount to a brand experience. Again, Apple shines with its packaging. Its new Apple Watch packaging is a masterpiece, making the product seem more significant and weighty than it already is, to heighten the moment of expectation.

Why is a diamond ring box as crucial as the ring itself? The jewelry box must communicate the feeling of love and commitment while showcasing the ring in all its glittery splendor. The most popular materials for ring boxes are velvet (commonly seen on Valentine's Day), silk, and leather—all soft and sensual to the touch.

In the book *Brand Sense: Sensory Secrets Behind the Stuff We Buy*, author Martin Lindstrom shares an example of a supermarket chain in the UK called Asda, which displayed its store-brand toilet paper in a way that shoppers could touch the tissue and compare textures with other brands. The sales for the store brand T.P. "soared."[77]

Human Touch Branding

Interpersonal touch can be euphoric or at least communicate feelings of warmth, safety, and reassurance. The outcome of these feelings is that consumers are motivated to spend and consume more. No brand has been immune to digital technology's changes to the consumer relationship, but technology will never replace the human touch. Brands exist in a highly competitive and fast-moving environment where creating meaningful customer connections is almost impossible. More and more brands are forgoing the brick-and-mortar world for a digital brand connection. But if your brand has any chance to reach out and touch a customer meaningfully, the human touch is a true differentiator.

Have you ever checked into a Westin hotel? Once you have completed the check-in transaction, the staff member moves out from behind the counter to stand face-to-face in front of you. There is a moment of warmth as they welcome you and hand you your passkey. The touch is minimal, but the effect is powerful. But the best part is tucking into Westin's trademarked Heavenly Bed with its luxurious 100 percent Egyptian cotton sateen sheets. Now, you're truly in heaven.

The simple use of touch can be profound when used correctly and authentically. The sense of vision might dominate many aspects of branding, but the subtlety of touch can increase the brand perception immensely. More and more companies have started using the growing field of cognitive neuroscience to help guide product development and marketing decisions.[78]

Look at everything your brand is doing to build relationships. Where can tactile touch fit in to heighten your brand relationship? Are you maximizing human touchpoints? You need to clearly understand how your customers interact with your brand to ensure the right touchpoints are consistently in place to strengthen the brand experience.

Think about the critical moment when the customer interacts with your brand for the first time. Are they excited to open the box or remove the wrapping? Do they need to read a ten-page instruction manual before they start engaging with your brand? Have you made it idiot-proof for them to turn it on? Is the packaging inviting? Does it feel expensive, or simple and clean? Does it reinforce their purchase decision?

IKEA has an obsession with efficient packaging to lower transport costs and ensure their products are affordable. CEO Peter Agnefjäll says, "We hate air at IKEA."[79] However, the packaging has to strike a balance between efficiency and customer satisfaction. Allan Dickner, manager of packaging development at IKEA, admits that they have destroyed products because they were driven by efficiency and not customer needs.[80]

As people age, their sense of touch declines, as do many other senses (like hearing, seeing, and smelling). Today, a large portion of the population is made up of older people. If older people are your target audience, you might need to reengineer or increase the intensity of your brand's sensory touchpoints to create that emotional connection with your brand.

Whether or not your customers physically interact with your brand today, consider the influential power it can have in reinforcing your brand relationship.

11 | BRAND SCENT

Do you know the scent of a new car? It's a sweet smell of success—a blend of new leather mixed with glues, solvents, and plastic smells. While the chemicals might not be healthy, it's recognizable and memorable. The new car smell is so popular that the fragrance industry sells a "new car scent." Of all our senses, the least respected is olfaction, the ability to smell. Without it, our food would be reduced to sweet, sour, bitter, and salty. A glass of wine couldn't have rich layers of cherry, black pepper, and caramel with hints of vanilla, chocolate, and tobacco. For brands that have face-to-face interactions with their customers, their scent is critical.

We use our five senses (sight, touch, smell, taste, and sound) daily to help make decisions and navigate the world of consumerism. Most brands focus most strongly on only two of these—sight and sound. Strong emotional ties are built between a brand and its customers through imagery, design, texture, color, and sounds. However, the most robust sense for evoking an emotional reaction is smell. Let's take a look at the scent of a successful brand.

"When we think about any experience, whether it's personal or commercial, our sense of smell so profoundly plays into how we perceive and make judgments on the experience," says Ed Burke, former director of sales, training, and communications for ScentAir, a company that develops scents for other companies.[81]

As we have become more sophisticated in many aspects of our lives, people have come to use their noses more acutely. Today, we are all culinary experts, embracing new cuisines and using many exotic spices thanks to our noses. Connoisseurs of wine, beer, and scotch swirl their glasses and stick their noses into the vapors. We are refining our sense of smell in many areas of our lives, and we're ever more aware of what we like and don't like—so a brand's smell does matter.

Fortune Business Insights reports that the home fragrance market was worth almost $24 billion in 2023 and could reach $38 billion by 2032.[82]

Aradhna Krishna, a professor at the University of Michigan's Ross School of Business, groups these scent considerations into a category she calls sensory marketing. In her book, *Customer Sense: How the 5 Senses Influence Buying Behavior*, she defines sensory marketing as "marketing that engages the consumer's senses and affects their perception, judgment, and behavior." Krishna says that "no other cue is as potent as a scent-based cue" and explains that the human brain's structure is responsible for the close link between memory and smell.[83]

Other experts have similarly suggested the extraordinary impact of odor on our memory could be related to the proximity of our olfactory bulb, which helps us process smells, and the amygdala and hippocampus brain regions, which control emotion and memory.

A well-known idea called the "Proustian Phenomenon" proposes that distinctive smells have more power than any other sense to help us recall distant memories. Everyone has a library of smells that trigger memories, like fresh-cut grass, hot apple pie, vanilla ice cream, someone's perfume or after-shave, baked bread, coffee, balsam fir tree, rosemary, or a dirty diaper. Pew!

While scents call up memories, they also affect our moods. Research has shown that scent branding can enhance our experiences and boost sales. Neurologist Alan Hirsch showed that Nike customers' intent to purchase increased 84 percent with a floral scent in the store compared to a control group. A Washington State University study found that a simple scent, as opposed to a complex blend of smells, was easier for customers to create an association with, and thus would potentially make them spend more—on average, 20 percent more.[84]

Scent branding is composed of two specific categories:

- Ambient scenting, which uses pre-existing smells, such as movie theater popcorn, to help recall consumer memory.
- Olfactive branding, which is about creating signature scents based on a brand's qualitative traits and specific clientele.

Ambient Branding

Bloomingdale's uses ambient scenting throughout its stores. In the infant department, the soft scent of baby powder triggers a parent's memory. In the intimate apparel department, you'll find the soothing scent of lilac and coconut. Sugar cookies, chocolate, and evergreen aromas entice shoppers during the holiday shopping season. At Walt Disney World along the Main Street USA you will notice the wonderful smell of freshly baked chocolate chip cookies to make their guests' visit more pleasant and memorable. We all know the first thing we smell when we walk into a movie theater. Unsurprisingly, most theaters' profits come from selling artificial butter-flavored popcorn and other treats. If you ever sold a house, you always made sure the kitchen smelled like a freshly baked apple pie with hints of cinnamon in the air.

Any business that has control over the customer's environment can use ambient branding.

Olfactive Branding

High-end retail chains, hotels, airlines, stores, banks, and cruise ships use signature scents to build their brands.

Touring a mall with my nose front and center, I personally found that the most prominent and somewhat irritating use of distinctive fragrances was the musky, masculine colognes pumped through the ventilation systems at Abercrombie & Fitch and Hollister. It's intentional, though—it attracts their target audience of youth aged twelve to twenty-four, while the heavy-duty stimulus of scent and loud music repels adults.

I found that other brands like Anthropologie, Aritzia, American Eagle Outfitters, Urban Outfitters, and Old Navy had more subtle, unique fragrances that resonated with their environments. Standing out for me was the fashionable Hugo Boss store with its signature scent of citrus, tamboti wood, and tonka bean; Lululemon with its grass and rosemary fragrance; and the posh Tiffany& Co. jewelry store with its festive cotton candy scent. Sugar is a surprising choice for a luxury brand; maybe it helps with the sticker shock. Love can be such sweet sorrow.

Ed Burke says the upscale hotel chains have embraced scent branding in a big way. The Westin hotels use the scent of white tea and the Kimpton Hotel Monaco chain uses a blend of soft citrus, green tea, black pepper, and cloves.[85] Good enough to drink.

Carnival Cruise Line, Qantas Airways, and home-builder Jayman Built in Calgary, Alberta, all profess to use unique fragrances specifically chosen and designed to enhance their customers' brand experience. Jayman's former director of marketing, Careen Chrusch, says, "It doesn't take away from the visual experience and helps solidify the positive memories [consumers] have when they think of our brand."[86]

A study conducted by Chicago's Smell & Taste Treatment and Research Foundation found that the amount of money gambled at a Las Vegas casino slot machine increased by 45 percent when the site was odorized with a pleasant aroma.[87]

Scent Advantage

Today, brand identity is more critical than ever before. Businesses and products compete for consumer attention across an ever-increasing variety of channels. Our senses play a vital and complex role in forming our thoughts, impressions, and behaviors. By targeting the senses, brands establish a more potent and enduring emotional connection with their consumers. As online shopping continues to skyrocket, it becomes vital that every face-to-face brand experience become more memorable.

Many brands fail to make use of their customers' sense of smell. Harnessing the power of scent is an excellent opportunity to differentiate your brand from your competitors. Our memories are closely tied to smell. The longer you build your olfactive brand, the more positive memories will be associated with it down memory lane.

Stop and smell your brand. Does it smell like a successful one?

12 | BRAND TASTE

Where does a brand's taste fit in? You guessed it, in the mouth. However, if your brand can't fit into your customer's mouth, this chapter may still provide you with wisdom about this unique portal to human consumption. That is to say, the taste of any brand is more about what you think a brand is than what you believe you experience. Hold that thought, as I explain that the best way for a brand to taste great isn't necessarily orally.

The Tongue

Let's start with the tongue, which does all the heavy lifting when it comes to taste. It moves food and liquid around our mouths, if it's not busy articulating a verb or a noun. The tongue has over 10,000 taste buds. These little bumps help distinguish between sweet, sour, salty, bitter, and savory (umami). But on its own, it can only decipher these essential elements of taste. Realizing its full potential requires other inputs like smell, texture, and temperature. Taste is the summation of the tongue and nose (if not influenced by our eyes). Our brain connects these sensations into a single emotional experience. This is the sweet spot where we know branding is ripe for manipulation and trickery. Of course, it must all be done in excellent taste.

The well-known market researcher and psychophysicist Howard Moskowitz once said, "The mind knows not what the tongue wants." He was made famous by author Malcolm Gladwell in his *New Yorker* article "The Ketchup Conundrum" and his TED Talk called "Choice, happiness and spaghetti sauce."[88] The talk is a perfect video to watch on a Friday night with truffle butter popcorn. Gladwell recounts how Moskowitz reinvented spaghetti sauce through his research, where he discovered there were three main sauces: plain, spicy, and extra chunky. Yet the marketplace only offered plain and spicy spaghetti sauce at the time. Moskowitz's customer, Campbell Soup Company, used this information and introduced Prego's extra chunky spaghetti sauce, which made over $600 million in the first ten years. Moskowitz certainly understood the secret to that sauce. It wasn't the taste that made the difference but the extra chunky texture.

Taste Test

Probably the most memorable and successful taste test is the legendary Pepsi Challenge campaign, which started in 1975. This simple demonstration put Pepsi on the map and kicked Coca-Cola off its game, leading it to the New Coke blunder. Years afterward, scientists continued to ponder taste's role in building a brand.

We believe the ultimate criterion for liking a drink or food is its taste. However, we are positively influenced throughout the experience by extrinsic cues like packaging, labels, the brand story, our environment, and intrinsic product attributes like texture, smell, appearance, and perceived quality (which is tied to price).

A 2013 blind Coke-versus-Pepsi taste test research study conducted by Dr. N. Ramanjaneyalu found that only 37 percent of respondents could successfully identify Coca-Cola through taste or a lucky guess.[89] The conclusion was that building the right brand image and positioning is just as important as the taste.

In his book *Blink*, Malcolm Gladwell echoes this conclusion when he explains that people prefer a sweeter drink (a characteristic of Pepsi) in a sip test but not necessarily in a full glass. He also discusses the importance of "sensation transference," a phrase coined by scientific researcher Louis Cheskin. He said people's perceptions and emotional attachments to the product's aesthetics go beyond just the product's taste.

Cognitive neuroscience research by neuroscientists Lauren Atlas and Tor Wager concluded that expectations and beliefs play a pervasive role in the brain's workings.[90] This means that expectations can influence those things we are unaware of, like our loyalty and familiarity with a brand. Consciously and unconsciously, we collect information, analyze our surroundings, and assess what we think we like and don't like.

Tasteless

Gil Morrot, a wine researcher at the National Institute for Agronomic Research in Montpellier, France, found that adding an odorless red dye to a glass of white wine had a profound effect.[91] When the color was added, the panel of tasters believed the wine was actually red wine, and they started saying they tasted red wine characteristics like cherry, dark fruit, and cedar.

The top five beer manufacturers in the US spent approximately $1 billion in advertising in 2021, which seems a smart idea if beer preference is not driven entirely by taste.[92] Another excellent example is the bottled water discussed in chapter 2, where consumers chose the brand first and the (tasteless) water second.

In a Stanford and Johns Hopkins study, researchers tested the effect of branding on taste preferences in young children.[93] Ninety-five children, aged three to five, were given identical food, except one choice came in McDonald's packaging, and the other came in plain-white packaging. All of the food came from McDonald's, except for some carrots. Which one do you think the kids liked best? No-brainer. Hands down, food in McDonald's wrappers was selected, including the carrots, which McDonald's doesn't even sell. The preferences for McDonald's-branded food increased with both the child's frequency of McDonald's consumption and the number of TV sets in each kid's home. So, a brand image can influence taste.

Tasty Brands

However, in the early days even a McDonald's logo on the coffee cup didn't help their coffee, which tasted like *merde* (pardon my French). In 2006, McDonald's upgraded its coffee from a generic, non-descript coffee to a darker-roast, Arabica premium coffee in North America. They called it the "Full Bean Coffee." People quickly started walking around the office with their extra-large McDonald's to-go cup and commenting that the coffee tasted excellent. Within a year, McDonald's coffee sales climbed 20 percent, in a market with over $30 billion in coffee sales. During that time, they gave away a lot of free coffee. Why? They wanted to demonstrate that their coffee did taste great—because the taste does matter.

Taste is among the most important factors influencing consumers' preference for choosing one food and beverage brand over another. But we should not be so naïve to think that taste is the only discerning factor—unless it's Heinz's ketchup, the perfectly balanced condiment with the right amount of tangy-sweet tomato and salty goodness, with pleasant sour notes and a buttery umami finish. Actually, even with 62 percent market share in the US (84 percent in Canada), this brand doesn't rely only on taste. Heinz spent approximately $530 million on advertising in 2013, including securing an ad in the 2016 Super Bowl (which isn't cheap).

We understand the mouth's role within our complex sensory system. It's integral in interpreting taste and defining our likes and dislikes. We also know it has its limitations. Ultimately, it is overruled by our brain's desire to bring all the senses together. So, when positioning a brand with a substantial oral opportunity, we can't put all the pressure on the tongue to carry us through. Only by ensuring multiple sensory stimulations will the tongue feel affirmation in what it's experiencing. How you influence this experience will leave your brand tasting bitter or sweet.

13 | BRAND SOUND

Audio branding is like the icing on the cake. It provides a fantastic, rich, and memorable tone to your brand identity. Sound can stop us in our tracks and quickly engage us like no other sense can. And just like smell, music and sounds can trigger memories and emotions.

Most retailers already leverage music as a selling tool in stores. Beyond retail, the use of sound is underestimated. Few other brands strategically use music, sound, and voice to create a magical brand connection.

Before television, radio was the darling for reaching consumers, as it was the entertainment center in households. Entire families would huddle around the radio to listen to broadcasts sponsored by a brand, well before the trend of radio advertising. General Mills aired the first singing commercial in 1926 entitled "Have you tried Wheaties?" It was an instant success and made Wheaties a national brand.

The art of building brands through jingles peaked during the economic boom of the 1950s. Many product categories jumped onto the trend—breakfast cereals, candy, snacks, soft drinks, tobacco, beer, automobiles, personal hygiene products, household products, and especially detergent. But like epic musical films, branding jingles began losing their appeal by the 1970s. Just about any boomer can sing a number of advertising jingles, which are lying dormant in their brains, like "Plop, plop, fizz, fizz" (Alka-Seltzer), "Oh, I wish I were an Oscar Mayer Wiener," "Ai, Yi, Yi, Yi, I am the Frito Bandito," and "I'd like to buy the world a Coke."

To be memorable and enduring, according to Linda Kaplan Thaler, former chair of Publicis Kaplan Thaler advertising agency, "[a jingle] has huge sticking power. A jingle is not successful if you listen to it once but like it. You must listen to it and want to sing it. Essentially, you become the advertiser for the brand." She also thinks today is a perfect time to build a brand through a jingle due to the many social channels to share it. Meanwhile, Martin Puris, past chair and CEO of Ammirati & Puris, thinks jingles are passé. "In a marketing wary world, a jingle seems oddly out of place. Too slick, too contrived."[94]

The "Master of Suspense," filmmaker Alfred Hitchcock, understood the importance of sound in telling a story. He said, "When we tell a story in cinema, we should resort to dialogue only when it's impossible to do otherwise." He brilliantly manipulated his audience's emotions using sound design to enhance the situation. In his 1963 movie *The Birds*, he combined real bird sounds and electronically synthesized noises, creating an auditory assault that brought the vicious bird attacks to life.

Great sound design is fully appreciated through good-quality sound systems and speakers. Since the 1960s, we have seen significant innovations concerning sound systems, from the bulky multi-unit stereo systems and the iconic boombox to putting our entire music library into our pockets with the iPod. Add a set of good-quality headphones, and you are in another world.

Brand Music

Eric Sheinkop, co-author of *Hit Brands: How Music Builds Value for the World's Smartest Brands*, says, "Music brings value to a brand in three ways: identity, engagement, currency. Specifically, using music to establish an emotional connection with a brand increases brand recognition, creates excitement and buzz beyond its core products or services, and can empower consumers, giving them valuable content to discover and share. Music creates the value brands need to win the war for attention and develop a genuine connection with their consumers. When used correctly, music not only creates loyalty but true advocacy."[95]

Music has played an essential role for automotive and aviation brands, where brand building is all about the emotional state. Music is a universal language that crosses cultural, national, and linguistic borders. It creates a personal connection to the brand. Yet, most brands use sound and music only in specific campaigns, instead of relating them to the brand overall.

United Airlines has taken a brand-oriented approach. Since 1976, United has used the familiar George Gershwin tune "Rhapsody in Blue" as a foundation for its brand. The music is played in its television ads, in airport terminals, and even in pre-flight announcements. United uses this piece of music to strategically create a distinct audio identity that expresses its value at all necessary customer touchpoints. Incredibly, they cramped the London Symphony Orchestra into a plane to play the tune. The company's onboard safety video creatively incorporates the distinctive "Rhapsody in Blue" music in various interpretations to emphasize each cultural destination—brilliant.

Sonic Branding

The sonic logo links your brand logo with a unique sound that becomes synonymous with the brand. The key is to use it everywhere the brand communicates. It takes years of reach and frequency to link a sound firmly to a brand. But, once that happens, the sound becomes timeless, like NBC's three-tone chimes, Intel's five-note bong, and the THX sound system's "deep note," as it's called. Brand strategist Kevin Perlmutter explains that because sound bypasses the rational part of the brain and reaches the most intuitive level, sound can be the fastest way to heighten brand engagement.[96] Therefore, a brand identity is incomplete without sound or music to help develop an emotional connection, even if your brand is as unemotional as a computer chip. Using a multisensory approach, you can better position a brand into the customer's mind.

Product Sound

Some products make actual sounds that can help differentiate them from the competition, like Kellogg's Rice Krispies' *snap, crackle, pop,* Alka-Seltzer's *plop, plop, fizz, fizz,* Snapple's *pop* when it's opened, Dyson's unique vacuum sound, Infiniti's engine sound, and the *scritch-scratch* sound of a Sharpie marker on paper. The sound of your product can be as unique as its look, feel, and smell. Rachael Pink, an acoustic engineer at Dyson, says, "People now expect products to sound good— not just sound quiet, but have a nice quality."[97]

Frito-Lay, part of PepsiCo Inc., introduced a compostable bag for its SunChips brand to become more environmentally friendly. However, the bag was noisy, drastically changing the customer experience. Sales fell, and consumers complained about the sound. Frito-Lay went back to the old bag. Don't underestimate the customer's relationship with your product's sound.

Today, visual branding remains the focus of many marketers and branding experts. However, you can't rely solely on visuals even with the increased number of touchpoints we have today. The trend toward digital channels (social media, bloggers, podcasts, voice assistants, video) is only intensifying.

Digital media has many channels to reach the consumer, but it can lack personality and emotional attachment. Perlmutter says the strategic use of music and sound "can dramatically improve a digital interaction by placing a brand's unique identity and personality front and center to provide clear navigation with proprietary sounds that are simultaneously functional and emotional."[98]

In our chaotic and over-stimulated communications world, brands must engage all senses to create a powerful emotional impact that transforms brand experiences. Audio branding could be the magic your brand needs to be believed. Start turning up the volume.

14 | EMOTIONAL BRANDING

The philosopher Aristotle started determining how many emotions there were in the fourth century BCE. Later, Charles Darwin continued this work. Psychologists have recently concluded that there are four to eight basic emotions.

In 1978, Dr. Paul Ekman, with the help of W. Friesen, developed the first and only comprehensive tool for objectively measuring facial movement—the Facial Action Coding System (FACS). Since then, over seventy other studies have confirmed their results for seven universal facial expressions of emotions: anger, contempt, disgust, fear, joy, sadness, and surprise.

Psychologist Robert Plutchik developed the famous Wheel of Emotions, which identifies eight basic emotions—joy, sadness, trust, disgust, fear, anger, surprise, and anticipation.[99] His theory starts with these basic emotions and then blossoms out to multiply, creating a broad spectrum of emotions with opposing relationships.

In *The Everything Psychology Book*, author Kendra Cherry says, "The basic emotions, however many there are, serve as the foundation for all the more complex and subtle emotions that make up the human experience."[100] Some compelling evidence shows that consumers use emotions rather than information to evaluate brands. Emotions also create more profound and visceral impressions that impact long-term memory.

Emotions are complex, but we can use Plutchik's eight basic emotions to build an emotional brand, dividing them into negatives and positives.

Negative Emotions

Most brands try to avoid associating their brand with negative emotions. However, some brands have successfully differentiated their emotional branding by using contentious feelings of disgust, sadness, anger, and fear.

DISGUST

Disturbing graphic images of thick, green mucus, smelly and rotting garbage, clogged drains and sewage, dirty and grimy dishes, plaque and bacterial germs, and pimples and blemishes create a perfect backdrop for building a brand based on disgust.

The famous Canadian cough medicine Buckley's serve up a spoon of disgust with the slogan "It tastes awful. And it works." The deodorant brand Rexona (Degree in some countries) has used visuals of sweat stains and body odor to promote the effectiveness of their antiperspirants. Vicks and Mucinex, cold and flu medicines, have used visuals of mucus, phlegm, and congestion to promote their brands. And brands such as Cillit Bang, Drano, Liquid-Plumr, and Febreze have successfully used disgusting slug, grime and mold to eliminate clogged pipes and odors.

But the most disgusting advertising for a brand has to go to Oxy face wash with its series of zit-popping videos from 2012. Say no more; the image of popping a pimple speaks for itself—gross!

SADNESS

Is sadness the new happiness? Does it leave a mark deeper than joy? Making people cry seems to be one of many brands' objectives these days. Look at all the epic holiday ads depicting lonely and sad people. The UK retailer brand John Lewis knows something about pulling consumers' heartstrings with their annual Christmas advert based on a tear-jerking tale of Yuletide loneliness. However, some would say we can't always be happy, so there is authenticity in using sadness to try to get deeper brand engagement. Several insurance companies, for example, have cornered the market for "sad advertising." Thai Life Insurance's ad "Unsung Hero" tells the story of a man who helps people, animals, plants, and the world. MetLife's "My Dad's Story" depicts the sacrifice a father makes to give his daughter the best life possible. And Nationwide's Super Bowl tear-jerker "Dead Boy" features a young boy listing the things he will never get to enjoy... because he's dead.

ANGER

Making people mad seems counterproductive to getting them to buy a brand, but when used correctly, it can create decisive action or a strong statement. Anger can be a potent tool to change a perception or get people to take action. We get angry when we see a person or helpless animal hurt or a significant injustice enacted.

Sadly, terrorist groups like ISIS have used this emotion effectively to build their brand. "They're very good at branding," says J.M. Berger, co-author of the book *ISIS: The State of Terror*.[101] They have a complete visual look with a black flag, distinctive clothing, black masks, and identical weapons. They use brutal violence against innocent people and public executions to generate widespread anger, which also appeals to a small niche of supporters who want to take up their cause.

After the Great Recession of 2008–2009, many brands began trying to exploit frustrated and angry consumers affected by hard times by emulating further antagonism. Eastman Kodak ranted about overpriced inkjet printer ink (full disclosure: I bought a Kodak printer based on this fact). Post's Shredded Wheat Cereal declared, "Innovation is not your friend." Miller High Life supported blue-collar customers, and Harley-Davidson condemned "The stink of greed and billion-dollar bankruptcies" to align with its customers.

A unique brand campaign that successfully angered its target audience was a simple billboard advertisement saying "TEXT AND DRIVE"—with a company logo for Wathan Funeral Home. When outraged viewers went to the funeral home's website to voice their anger, they were surprised to find a public service announcement to get people to stop texting and driving—mad with a happy ending.

FEAR

Brands' efforts to grab consumers' attention often imbue a sense of urgency, compelling us to respond swiftly. Brands typically strive to cultivate positive experiences, steering clear of risk. Yet, a cadre of brands exists for which fear is a strategic cornerstone, effectively harnessed to drive consumer behavior. Anti-smoking campaigns, drunk driving prevention messages, automobile and personal safety products, insurance and financial services, home security systems, healthcare offerings, political movements, and environmental causes all leverage fear to elicit visceral, often profitable responses.

The World Health Organization (WHO) exemplifies this approach with its stark warnings: "Our health is under siege by climate change. Diseases such as malaria, asthma, encephalitis, tuberculosis, leprosy, dengue fever, and measles are predicted to surge in prevalence." This tactic of transforming potential threats into fear-inducing proclamations has proven potent.

Donald Trump's political success has been partly attributed to his adept use of fear. *Time* magazine's Washington correspondent Alex Altman remarked, "No president has weaponized fear quite like Trump." Sociologist Barry Glassner echoed this sentiment, labeling Trump a "master" at fear generation.[102]

Research published in the *Journal of Consumer Research* reveals that fear can forge a strong bond between consumers and brands. Viewers who experienced fear while watching a film reported a higher affinity for a brand than those who experienced happiness, sadness, or excitement. This ties back to our primal survival instincts.

However, using negative emotions for brand building must be executed with care. Marketing expert Graeme Newell advises that while negative emotions can amplify a brand's impact, they should be employed delicately, ensuring audiences are left with a positive resolution.[103] Overuse of fear, such as Greenpeace's tactics, can have a diminishing impact over time.

Fear is profoundly primal and can be a significant motivator. It can cut through life's clutter and leave an indelible mark on the psyche, persuading us to take action and make purchases that promise safety and peace of mind. Fear can stem from various sources: the fear of missing out, pain, failure, loss, uncertainty, the unknown, or death.

Fear manifests in physical responses (fight or flight) characterized by physiological changes like increased heart rate and adrenaline levels. Emotionally, fear is highly personal, and responses to it can range from thrill-seeking behavior to complete avoidance.

Neuroscience supports that our brains are hardwired to seek safety and avoid threats. Studies suggest that the fear of loss is a more potent motivator than the promise of gain.[104] This is evident in consumer behavior and stock market dynamics.

Given fear's persuasive power, it's hard for brands to resist employing it in a world saturated with messages. Fear has long been a tool for religions, politicians, advocacy groups, media outlets, and brands to exert influence.

Brands aim to capture attention by triggering an alert state in consumers. Research from the 1960s indicates that the right amount of fear can spur action, while too much can provoke denial. The effectiveness of fear-based messaging hinges on its relevance to an individual's experiences and anxieties.

Advocacy groups often employ fear to deter harmful behaviors like smoking or drunk driving. Sociologist Frank Furedi notes that such groups use research to stress the worsening nature of these issues.[105]

Society has become increasingly risk-averse, evidenced by protective parenting styles and an aging population that naturally gravitates toward safety. Millennials exhibit this aversion, beginning their savings efforts earlier than previous generations, which is a good thing.

Despite living in one of the safest eras in human history, Americans' fear levels remain high.[106] The media's focus on events like shootings contributes to this climate of fear. Comparatively speaking, while heart disease consistently claims more lives annually than crises like COVID-19, media coverage disproportionately amplifies pandemic fears.

On the flip side of fear are those who embrace it—the adrenaline seekers who find joy in confronting their fears through extreme sports and high-risk activities. Research suggests that these individuals often experience transformative self-confidence and identity shifts.[107]

In summary, fear is a powerful force that brands can harness to engage consumers. It can motivate protective behaviors and drive purchases to secure peace of mind. While the overuse of fear can desensitize or overwhelm consumers, leading to disengagement or denial, when used judiciously and relevantly, it remains an influential tool in shaping consumer behavior and preferences. Healthy fear draws our attention and breaks through the noise, but it must come with a sustainable solution.

Positive Emotions

In one episode of *Mad Men*, the character Don Draper said, "Advertising is based on one thing: happiness." Indeed, many brands focus on using the emotions of trust, joy, and humor.

TRUST

Without trust, the financial industry doesn't work. A five-dollar bill is the same simple piece of paper as a hundred-dollar bill, just with different numbers on it, but its buying power is significantly different, thanks to trust. Unsurprisingly, the business and financial services industries need trust to operate. Trust is integral to the success of all brands but foundational for those brands built on faith and intangible, complex components.

And the emotion of trust becomes particularly essential for a brand if it has broken this bond with the customer.

The British Brands Group's 2015 *Consumer Trust in Brands* report states that food brands have one of the highest trust levels—it's important to have repeat customers who aren't sick or dying from eating your product. In 2008, Canada's Maple Leaf Foods Inc. sold listeria-tainted luncheon meats that killed twenty-two people and sickened thirty-five others. Sales dropped by 50 percent—but two months later, they were only down 15 percent.

"The very first thing that must happen in these incidents is acknowledgment, apologies, and action from the CEO," says Hamish McLennan, CEO of Young & Rubicam.[108] Maple Leaf Foods' CEO Michael McCain says the company's transparency and immediate reaction to the crisis helped win back customers. A *Financial Times* article agrees that "the trust built in the days after the onset of the crisis laid the foundation for its eventual turnaround."[109] Today, no trust issues face Maple Leaf Foods, thanks to McCain's conviction for making things right and not listening to his lawyers.

Humanizing your brand helps build trust, but you must foster an authentic and lasting connection with your customers to get there.

JOY

What brand do you immediately think of when you hear "joy"? I think of joy as a sudden burst of happiness on a high. Does "Open Happiness" ring a bell? Coca-Cola has long been associated with spreading joy and happiness.

Many people are keen to find more joy in their lives and are looking for those small indulgences of pleasure. Many brands have found the joy sweet spot to capitalize on this consumer desire:

- Disney: From its theme parks to its movies and merchandise, Disney is all about creating magical experiences and bringing joy to people of all ages.
- Skittles: The candy brand's slogan "Taste the Rainbow" and its vibrant, colorful branding are designed to evoke a sense of joy and playfulness.
- M&M's: The anthropomorphized M&M's characters, with their playful personalities and humorous advertisements, aim to bring joy and laughter to consumers.
- Airbnb: With its tagline "Belong Anywhere," Airbnb promotes the joy of travel and of experiencing new cultures and communities.
- Starbucks: The coffee chain's cozy atmosphere, personalized service, and seasonal offerings aim to create a joyful and comforting experience for customers.

HUMOR

Building your brand on humor is no laughing matter. This choice can be a high-risk (but high-reward) branding option. Laughter is the apparent outcome, but humor creates a positive emotional relationship between a brand and its customers. Humor can cut through the clutter and go viral in seconds—because funny attracts eyeballs. People reward clever, creative, and witty humor by watching and sharing it. Humor can revitalize an old brand or make an everyday brand extraordinary overnight—and it can make you into a brand that people want to be associated with.

Finding the secret sauce of what *makes* things funny, however, isn't much fun. E.B. White had it right when he said, "Analyzing humor is like dissecting a frog. Few people are interested, and the frog dies of it." Frog or no frog, Peter McGraw and Joel Warner wrote the book *The Humor Code*. In it, they explain their benign violation theory, which states that two simultaneous conditions are needed to make something funny.[110] First, it must violate the way we think the world should work, and second, it must be benign enough that it does so in a way that's not threatening. This is the fine line between what is funny and what is in downright lousy taste.

A master of benign violation is comedian Jerry Seinfeld, who has the innate talent of pointing out outrageous funny things (violation) in everyday life (benign). A favorite example is in the episode where Mr. Pitt eats a Snickers bar with a knife and fork.

Psychologist and professor Jack Schafer says, "Laughter releases endorphins, which make us feel good about ourselves and others. This good feeling creates a bond between two people and imbues a sense of togetherness."[111] Brands that incorporate humor in their branding strategy can increase their likability.

Unfortunately, no significant research supports this claim except to say that intrinsically, we all do business and build relationships with people we like. Rohit Bhargava, the author of *Likeonomics,* says we live in a world where brand believability is low.[112] Consumers are bombarded daily with corporate speech, half-truths, or biased messages. For survival, they are ambivalent or hostile to these messages as a default—Bhargava calls this the "likeability gap." To bridge this gap, brands must build trust, be relevant, and be unselfish in a timely and straightforward fashion. Doing something different, like using humor, can make a brand relevant and significantly impactful.

Humor generates big dollars in the entertainment industry. From 1995 to 2017, Statista movie revenue data shows that the comedy genre raked in $42 billion, second only to adventure movies. According to a recent study by Statista, comedy is the preferred genre for films and shows in America.[113] Comedy and music videos topped YPulse's list of what gen Z and millennials watched in 2022.[114] The attractiveness of humor also applies to marketing. A quarter of television commercials are classified as humorous.

The central reason humor is used to build a brand is two-fold: humor can attract attention quickly and it can enhance brand likability overnight. But this doesn't guarantee success. Ace Metrix put out an extensive research report called "Is Funny Enough? Analysis of the Impact of Humor in Advertisements," and it showed that the "keys to effectiveness are relevance and information."[115]

There are seven primary ways humor can be used to build a brand:

Bonding: Humor can be used to bring together like-minded people under a halo of fun. It can bring out the unique club mentality present in celebration without the fear of elitism. Harley-Davidson is an excellent example of a brand that has effectively built a strong bond with its customers based on fun and an adventurous lifestyle. By embracing the biker culture, fostering a strong sense of community, encouraging personalization, and promoting an adventurous lifestyle, Harley-Davidson has successfully built a bond with its customers that goes beyond just selling motorcycles. The brand has become a symbol of freedom, rebellion, and fun, resonating deeply with its loyal customer base.

In addition to conveying emotional information about oneself, laughter elicits similar emotions in others and, therefore, serves a bonding function. If laughter serves a social bonding function, it should be no surprise that it also increases a person or brand's likability.

Releasing Tension: Humor can quickly address a problematic conversation or sensitive subject like insurance, banking, or personal hygiene. Somehow, the toilet tickles many a brand's funny bone. Humor, when used with sensitivity, can be very successful, and even potty humor has a time and place outside of a locker room).

GEICO is an excellent example of a brand that takes a sensitive subject (insurance) and transforms it into must-watch TV ads. One of GEICO's most iconic and long-running campaigns features the GEICO Gecko, a CGI-animated gecko lizard with a British accent. The Gecko was initially introduced in 1999 and quickly became a beloved mascot for the brand. The commercials often feature the Gecko in humorous situations, such as trying to explain how to pronounce "GEICO" or dealing with mistaken identities. The Gecko's witty one-liners and charming personality have made these commercials highly entertaining and memorable.

Then there is Aflac's famous quacky and wacky duck, who helped to elevate the Aflac brand to one of the top twenty-five brands in 2015.[116]

Attraction: How do you take the seventy-year brand heritage of Old Spice and make it relevant to young men and the women who purchase products for the men in their lives? Women are responsible for over 50 percent of body wash sales, so hooking them as a demographic is vital. Eric Baldwin, executive creative director at Wieden+Kennedy, the agency behind the Old Spice brand, said they wanted to promote the company's body wash and deodorant by entertaining the hell out of them. And they did, with a perfect blend of humor, self-awareness, and sheer ridiculousness. The brand released a series of now-famous ads featuring the comedic, deadpan delivery of actor Isaiah Mustafa, a well-muscled, usually towel-clad man with a deep voice, coupled with rapid-fire editing and surreal visuals, which created a sense of controlled chaos that kept the viewer engaged and entertained. Whether he was riding a horse on a beach or floating in a boat in the middle of the ocean, the commercials constantly surprised and delighted with their absurdity. Old Spice has been doing "The Man Your Man Could Smell Like" since it debuted in 2010.

Rivals: How does the little brand take on Goliath, who has more market share, brand awareness, brand recognition, and deep pockets to keep it that way? Create a cult phenomenon using humor! It's easier said than done, but many brands have succeeded. Humor can also be used to avert potential detractors.

If used correctly, humor can be a clever and original way to communicate tons of information playfully and entertainingly. One great example is the Dollar Shave Club. By embracing a humorous and irreverent tone in its ads, which debuted in 2012, Dollar Shave Club was able to stand out in a crowded market and connect with consumers who were tired of the traditional, overly serious marketing tactics of established razor brands. The company's use of self-deprecating humor, absurd analogies, and parody allowed them to position themselves as a refreshing and relatable alternative, ultimately contributing to the viral success of their launch video and the rapid growth of their brand.

Entertainment: For those brands looking to capture younger audiences, entertaining and keeping them engrossed can come down to creating nonsensical brand stories. In a study, published as "How Humor in Advertising Works," Dr. Martin Eisend showed that humor may help overcome weaknesses in advertising messages. Skittles's "Taste the Rainbow" campaign, which launched in 1994, is an excellent example of a brand showing its humor. By embracing the absurd, the surreal, and the nonsensical, Skittles created a unique and memorable brand identity that stands out in the crowded candy market as playful and whimsical.

To wrap your brand with humor, you must understand what type fits your brand. Are you looking for a giggle like a school kid? The nervous and uncomfortable chuckle? The derisive snort? The joyous cackle? The big contagious hearty belly laugh? Or the soft, suppressed chortle?

The bigger the laughter, the higher the risk and the higher the potential of being divisive, but sometimes the reward is worth that risk. Sometimes, though, being too funny can have the opposite effect to the one you intend. For example, Burger King's "Subservient Chicken" campaign generated immense viral buzz in 2004, the disconnection between the wacky humor and Burger King's brand identity was glaring. The chicken's sole purpose was to mindlessly follow users' commands, no matter how absurd. As a result, the humor overshadowed the brand because it lacked a cohesive tie-in to what Burger King actually stands for as a brand. While wildly popular, the campaign is an example of humor running amok if not carefully linked back to a brand's central values and positioning.

There is always a brand that crosses the line and takes funny to a non-benign place. In 2015 Bloomingdale's ran a holiday advertisement in a Christmas catalog that featured a woman laughing and looking away as a male model looked suggestively at her back. The headline on the ad said: "Spike your best friend's eggnog when they're not looking." I'm not sure anyone found this funny. Bloomingdale's apologized and quickly removed the ad.

In the fall of 2018, luxury Italian brand Dolce & Gabbana (D&G) faced backlash for a series of videos promoting its Shanghai fashion show, which were deemed racist and offensive toward Chinese culture. The ads featured an Asian model struggling to eat Italian food with chopsticks, accompanied by a stereotypical male voiceover mocking Chinese speech. The incident sparked outrage, with protesters appearing at D&G stores, online retailers removing their products, and Chinese celebrities terminating contracts with the brand. The fashion show was eventually canceled. Almost six years later, D&G is still struggling to recover in the Chinese market, with fewer stores and lower sales than before the misstep.

There are also those brands that are so funny and outrageous that the consumer only remembers the joke but has no idea who or what the brand was. In his book *Production and Creativity in Advertising*, Robin Evans coined "the vampire effect" to describe the scenario when humor or a spokesperson overshadows the brand message. The moral of this story is to keep your humor on message to help build up instead of detract from your brand.

Surprise: Consumers appreciate a pleasant surprise, and if done right, a surprise can be leveraged across all consumer touchpoints (social, events, in-store, advertising, mobile, etc.).

A social listening study conducted by Draftfcb (now known as FCB or Foote, Cone & Belding), found that "surprise" came a distant sixth place behind anger, love, sorrow, joy, and fear when association with a brand. So, there is room for brand differentiation when using this emotion.

Mastercard has been running its "Priceless" campaign for over seventeen years. In 2014, the company introduced "Priceless Surprises" with the goal of surprising cardholders when they least expected it—getting to meet Justin Timberlake or Gwen Stefani, for example, or receiving VIP tickets to special events. A solid emotional element exists in watching a fan connect with a star, and Mastercard #PricelessSurprises made it happen. Raja Rajamannar, CMO of Mastercard, said, "The success of Priceless is the campaign's ability to create emotion, influence behavior, unite people and touch upon consumer passions."

On a smaller scale, GoPro ran a campaign called the "Million Dollar Challenge," where GoPro fans submitted inspiring video clips captured on GoPro's latest flagship camera. From 2019 to 2023, they gave away $5 million in prize money. In 2023, the contest generated a record 42,446 total video clips representing a 66% increase in submissions year-over-year.

Anticipation: Researchers have found that people experience more intense emotions around planning future events or opportunities than when they remember those events in the past. High-end cruise liners have perfected the art of creating holiday anticipation, offering cruise planners and exclusive updates long before the travelers embark.

Sandals Resorts understands the importance of anticipation, enticing customers with images of stunning, natural blue and turquoise oceans and clear sky, but more importantly, keeping the excitement growing on their social media channels. Tiffany Mullins, the company's social media manager, says Sandals's "strategy is to evoke an emotion with every single social media post." The idea is to humanize the brand, using its social media presence to create a virtual vacation experience before the actual vacation. Brilliant.

The Apple brand is an expert in contemplating the future and engaging customers in anticipation of the next generation of technology. Each version is a stepping stone to further brand loyalty or a stronger cult-like following. Apple is notorious for its pre-launch hype, limited availability reorders, and long lineups on launch day, only to repeat it within another twelve to eighteen months.

Summary

Harvard Business School professor Gerald Zaltman says that 95 percent of purchase decision-making occurs in the subconscious mind, where emotions are king.[117] If you are going to engage in emotional branding, understand how and where you want to connect to your customers so you can consistently build on every touchpoint.

As the former chief creative officer for the creative agency 180LA, William Gelner, explains, "We live such digitally switched-on, always-plugged-in lives, and yet we still somehow feel disconnected from people. As human beings, we're looking for true human connection, and I think that emotional storytelling can help bridge that gap."[118]

Pick your emotion(s) and start building your emotional branding story today, every step of the way.

15 | THE COOL FACTOR

The concept of "cool" has long been a subject of fascination, both in popular culture and academic circles. It's that almost magical quality that makes something stand out, draws people in, and inspires loyalty, emulation, and desire. But what exactly is the cool factor, and how can brands harness it?

The cool kids in school set the trends. They seem effortlessly in sync with the latest fashions and social currents. They have a way of being that others aspire to, a way that seems to put them years ahead of their peers. This phenomenon is not limited to individuals; it also extends to brands. Some brands have "it"—that indefinable quality that elicits an "OMG, that's so cool!" reaction.

Coolness is elusive, but the rewards can be substantial for brands that capture it. A cool brand can command premium pricing, inspire insatiable demand, and benefit from an enhanced image that seems to grow organically beyond the reach of controlled marketing efforts. It sets a high barrier for competitors to clear. Researcher and blogger Harsh Verma describes "cool" as "a scarce resource capable of bringing about value transformation."[119]

Stephen Cheliotis, chair of the CoolBrands Council, suggests that innovation, originality, authenticity, and desirability are critical components in making a brand cool.[120] However, this isn't a one-size-fits-all proposition. Coolness often matters most to those who see their identity reflected in the products they use. For a brand to become an integral part of someone's identity, it often requires a community aspect—a way for users to interact with the brand and each other.

It's easy to see how high-tech companies like Tesla, Apple, Google, Samsung, and Sony, and luxury brands like Gucci, Rolex, Prada, and Tiffany have become cool. But what about everyday items like deodorant or food? How do they achieve cool status? According to Wikipedia, "cool" began as a term of admiration or approval among Black American jazz musicians in the 1940s—those original "cool cats." Today, cool things or practices are seen as superlative, excellent, exclusive, exceptional, original, unique, rare, exciting, and desirable.

To understand coolness scientifically, we can look at research by Alan Tapp and Sara Bird, who describe it as the best term to encapsulate that "elusive, exclusive quality that makes behaviors, objects so hip, desirable and symbolic of 'being in the know.'"[121] Marketing researchers Clive Nancarrow, Pamela Nancarrow, and Julie Page define cool as a laid-back, selfish, and indulgent attitude combined with insider knowledge.[122]

A study by Datamonitor found that perceptions of cool vary by age.[123] Young consumers often emulate celebrities deemed cool, while teenagers and adults view cool as an expression of individualism. For older customers, cool may be synony-mous with quality.

Cool Brand Wheel

Eleven Cool Brand Characteristics

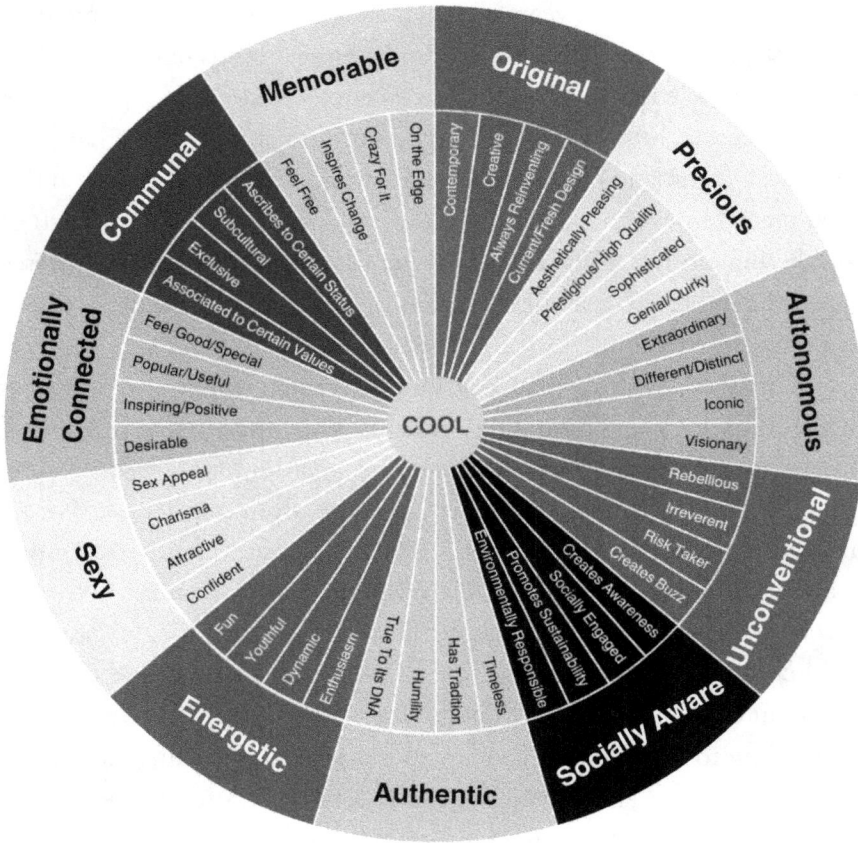

Memorable · Original · Precious · Autonomous · Unconventional · Socially Aware · Authentic · Energetic · Sexy · Emotionally Connected · Communal

On the Edge · Contemporary · Creative · Always Reinventing · Current/Fresh Design · Aesthetically Pleasing · Prestigious/High Quality · Sophisticated · Genial/Quirky · Extraordinary · Different/Distinct · Iconic · Visionary · Rebellious · Irreverent · Risk Taker · Creates Buzz · Creates Awareness · Socially Engaged · Promotes Sustainability · Environmentally Responsible · Timeless · Has Tradition · Humility · True To Its DNA · Enthusiasm · Dynamic · Youthful · Fun · Confident · Attractive · Charisma · Sex Appeal · Desirable · Inspiring/Positive · Popular/Useful · Feel Good/Special · Associated to Certain Values · Exclusive · Subcultural · Ascribes to Certain Status · Feel Free · Inspires Change · Crazy For It

COOL

Sources: Research studies "Characteristics of Cool Brands: The Development of a Scale" and "Brand Coolness"; author's input

The Cool Brand Wheel was inspired by two research papers—a conference paper entitled "Characteristics of Cool Brands: The Development of a Scale," by Sandra Maria Correia Loureiro and Rui Lopes, and a journal article called "Brand Coolness," by Caleb Warren, Rajeev Batra, Richard P. Bagozzi, and Sandra Maria Correia Loureiro.[124] I took the liberty of updating and consolidating some of the terminology in these papers to formulate the Cool Brand Wheel. The purpose of the wheel is to outline the factors such as behavioral tendencies, state of mind, aesthetic appeal, social distinction, and autonomy that have come to define "cool" for a brand. Beyond the research , I've discovered that an important cool factor was missing: sexy. So, here are the eleven cool factors.

Autonomous: Cool brands either lead their product category or create an entirely new one. Tesla has marketed itself as the electric car company, owning that new category even though other automakers also make electric vehicles. Studies show that appropriate autonomy (i.e., not going too mainstream) helps brands seem cool.[125] Apple is an example of a brand that achieved autonomy early on by aligning itself with the graphic design community and powerful software tools. Over time, Apple has maintained its coolness through continuous innovation.

Memorable: In an age where attention is scarce, creating memorable campaigns that stick with consumers long after their initial exposure is vital. Embracing humor, self-awareness, and a willingness to take risks, Old Spice has successfully transformed itself from a staid, heritage brand into a relevant and engaging presence in the minds of younger consumers and their partners. So, cool. Still, too much sappiness isn't considered cool.

Precious: Exclusive, expensive brands seem cool. People are drawn to beauty and luxury; sleek modern designs can elevate a product's appeal. Apple's clean, iconic product design makes its electronics feel high-end and natural. Brand prestige is less about high prices and more about invoking pride and aspiration through mythical storytelling.[126]

Socially Aware: In the age of heightened environmental and social consciousness, brands that demonstrate a commitment to making a positive impact resonate strongly with consumers, particularly millennials. This demographic tends to support companies that align with their values and proactively address global issues such as climate change. For instance, Toms's one-for-one model, which donates a pair of shoes for every pair sold, has inspired other brands to follow suit with similar initiatives, like providing eyewear, clean water, or maternal health aid for every purchase. Patagonia stands out for its environmental and social responsibility, embedding these principles into its mission statement and business practices.

Communal: The concept of "communal" in branding refers to the balance between inclusivity and exclusivity. A "cool" brand cultivates a sense of belonging while maintaining an aura of exclusivity that keeps admirers aspiring to join its ranks. Apple exemplifies this by creating a loyal following with its ecosystem of products and frequent updates. At the same time, Harley-Davidson has fostered a dedicated clan through the Harley Owners Group (H.O.G.), rallies, and branded merchandise. These brands have created more than just customer bases; they've built a community.

Authentic: Authenticity in branding means staying true to one's heritage and core values while continually evolving to exceed customer expectations. Luxury brands like Louis Vuitton and Chanel capitalize on their storied histories and craftsmanship to maintain their cool factor. Similarly, Coca-Cola has remained relevant by sticking to its classic branding while subtly updating itself. Authenticity is about being genuine and consistent, which in itself is cool.

Original: Being original involves continuous reinvention in line with the brand's vision while staying true to its purpose. Apple's evolution from the iMac to iPhone exemplifies this trait. Old Spice rejuvenated its brand by updating its image and targeting a younger demographic without losing sight of its nautical theme and original appeal. The brand maintained its fundamental elements while successfully navigating the line between timeless and contemporary.

Unconventional: Cool brands often break the mold with their unique approaches. Ben & Jerry's ice cream flavors (Cherry Garica, Chucky Monkey, Phish Food, The Tonight Dough, and Americone Dream) and unconventional business strategies, like selling company shares door-to-door and bold marketing campaigns, showcase how deviating from the norm can build a strong brand identity. Their commitment to social causes further cements their cool status.

Emotionally Connected: An emotional connection with customers can significantly influence purchasing decisions, often subconsciously. Brands that understand and tap into customers' emotions can build stronger relationships. However, missteps like Pepsi's controversial ad with Kendall Jenner show that not all attempts to connect emotionally are successful.

Energetic: Brands that exude energy and excitement are often seen as cool. They're dynamic, actively engaging with cultural moments and conversations in ways that resonate with younger demographics. Brands like Apple, Nike, and Coca-Cola are consistently seen as energetic because they're not just part of the conversation, they often lead it.

Sexy: Last but not least is sexy. Sex appeal can be a potent element of a brand's coolness, drawing on deep-seated human instincts for attraction and desire. Brands like Calvin Klein have leveraged sex appeal to create an edgy image. However, using sex in branding comes with risks and can sometimes backfire if it overshadows the brand's other attributes or crosses the line into controversy.

Staying Cool

The journey from mere functionality to the allure of coolness for a brand can be navigated using the Cool Brand Wheel. A product may be a bundle of features, but a brand transcends that—it's a story people yearn to become a part of, to purchase. A *cool* brand, however, is much more; it's a mythology, a belief system, an object of desire. Cool brands infuse our lives with meaning. They are the architects of our happiness and pride. They don't just sell products; they bestow the essence of cool upon us.

Genuine coolness appears natural and uncontrived. It's not merely the result of clever or alluring marketing. Many brands that are considered cool began as outsiders, often controversial or rooted in subculture, acquiring an almost cult-like status. However, as such brands grow and, as often happens, become absorbed by larger corporations, maintaining that edge of coolness can become challenging.

What is deemed cool is not static—it evolves with cultural and demographic shifts. There was a time when smoking cigarettes, particularly Marlboros, was seen as the epitome of cool. The Hummer vehicle was once a symbol of cool excess, and Krispy Kreme donuts held a cult-like fascination, with one enthusiast proclaiming them as "the food of the gods." But what of the brands that have lost their sheen? Gap, MTV, Nokia, Dr. Martens, and Playboy were once icons of cool that didn't quite keep up with the times.

Brands are not simply manufactured but nurtured and grown through community engagement. It's the consumer who crowns a brand as cool. Brands can sustain their cool status by skillfully managing the eleven cool factors and continuously innovating to transform customer desires into necessities. The rewards for being a cool brand are substantial—fame and fortune await those who can master this balance.

These "cool factors" are not standalone elements but intersecting facets that contribute to a brand's overall image and appeal. Each factor shapes how consumers perceive a brand, influencing their purchasing decisions, their advocacy, and, ultimately, their loyalty.

Is Your Brand Cool?

- Does your brand exhibit autonomy by leading its product category or creating a new one?
- Are your marketing campaigns memorable, humorous, and self-aware?

- Does your brand invoke a sense of exclusivity, luxury, and prestige?
- How does your brand demonstrate social and environmental awareness?
- Have you cultivated a sense of community and belonging around your brand?
- Are you staying true to your brand's heritage and core values while evolving?
- Are you continuously reinventing and innovating your brand while staying true to its purpose?
- Does your brand break the mold with unconventional approaches and strategies?
- Are you effectively building emotional connections with your customers?
- Does your brand exude energy, excitement, and dynamism?
- Have you leveraged sex appeal in an appropriate and effective way to enhance your brand's coolness?

BRAND CONSTRUCT SUMMARY

Constructing a brand identity is a multifaceted endeavor that transcends visual aesthetics. It is a sensory symphony that orchestrates the tangible and intangible elements to create a coherent and impactful brand experience. The "what" of a brand is not just its name or logo but the cumulative effect of the sensory signals it emits, the emotional resonance it generates, and the personality it projects. As we saw in Prince's experiment with an unpronounceable symbol, even a solid personal brand can face challenges without a clear and communicable identity.

The essence of a brand lies in its ability to be recognized, remembered, and revered. The name is the foundation upon which all other branding elements are built. It must be protectable, distinctive, and scalable to support the brand as it grows and evolves. From the practicality of descriptive names to the aspirational allure of image and experience names, the approach to naming is as diverse as the brands themselves.

Whether leveraging a family name's legacy, capturing the essence of an experience, or creating new meaning through acronyms, the ultimate goal remains consistent: to forge a connection with consumers that is as enduring as it is endearing. The perfect brand name is out there, waiting to be discovered or created. It requires due diligence, creativity, and strategic thinking to ensure that it captures the essence of the brand and propels it forward into the hearts and minds of consumers.

In the ever-evolving branding landscape, where competition is fierce and consumer attention spans are fleeting, standing out is not just an advantage but a necessity. The "what" of your brand is your battle cry in the marketplace, a declaration of your presence and promise. Choose it wisely, protect it fiercely, and let it resonate deeply. This is how you construct a brand that not only exists but thrives in the collective consciousness of your audience.

To begin the process of constructing a brand's "what," consider the following list of questions:

- What is the brand's origin story, and how does it inform the brand's name and identity?
- Which core values and beliefs should the brand embody?
- What are the key physical attributes of the brand, such as products and services?
- How can the brand's essence be encapsulated in a memorable, meaningful, and protectable name?

- What visual elements best represent the brand, including colors, fonts, and logo?
- How can sensory experiences like sound, smell, taste, and touch be integrated into the brand image?
- What emotions and feelings should be evoked through the brand's touchpoints?
- How does the brand's personality differentiate it from competitors?
- What tonality should the brand voice have, and how can it be communicated consistently across all channels?
- How can you ensure the brand name and identity will resonate with the target audience?
- What legal considerations, such as trademark availability, must be taken into account when selecting a brand name and logo?
- How will the brand's identity scale and evolve as the business grows?
- How can the brand's "what" be cohesive across various platforms and mediums?
- How will the effectiveness and impact of the brand identity on the audience be measured?
- What story does the brand want to tell, and how will it be expressed?

Part Three

BRAND COMMUNITY
THE WHO

"If people believe they share values with a
company, they will stay loyal to the brand."

—HOWARD SCHULTZ, FOUNDER OF STARBUCKS

This quote from Howard Schultz is perfect because he uses the word "people,"
not "customer." People means everyone associated with the brand, such as suppliers, employees, distributors, stakeholders, customers, and advocates. In a broad
sense, a brand community encompasses all individuals and groups affiliated with
or impacted by the brand in some way—it's your people. It's not just the customer
who needs to believe in the brand; everyone associated with it must buy in, not just
today but into the future.

The idea is to create a network of individuals and organizations committed to
the brand's success and willing to support it in various ways. By building a solid
and engaged brand community, a brand can improve customer loyalty and tap into

a wealth of resources, ideas, and insights that can help drive innovation, growth, and long-term success.

Building a solid brand community requires a strategic approach centered around your audiences' needs, interests, and values, also known as the "who" of your brand. In this chapter, I'll walk through how to define your target audiences by identifying the individuals and groups most likely to be interested in your brand, and who will benefit the most from being part of the community. The starting point is aligning your brand commitment with your community to offer a clear and compelling reason why they should join your brand vision. Once you have a community, it is essential always to remember who owns the brand. Ultimately, the brand is owned by the people who consume it. The accumulation of all branding C's makes the brand reside in their minds. They hold trust, loyalty, and commitment to the economic relationship and bond.

To create a successful brand, it's important to avoid transactional relationships and move toward a more collaborative, engaging partnership by consciously working to do these key things:

Foster Interaction and Engagement: Encourage members of your community to engage with each other and your brand. This could be through social media, forums, live events, or other channels.

Nurture Relationships: Build strong, personal relationships with members of your brand community. Respond to their questions, address their concerns, and celebrate their successes.

Encourage Co-creation: Involve members of your brand community in creating and evolving your brand. This could be through crowdsourcing, beta testing, or other forms of collaboration.

Create a Sense of Belonging: Make members of your brand community feel like they are part of something bigger than themselves. Celebrate their achievements, recognize their contributions, and create a sense of belonging and community.

Continuously Listen and Learn: Stay attuned to the needs and preferences of your brand community. Always gather feedback to improve your brand and the experiences you offer to your community.

By following these principles, you can create a strong brand community that is engaged, loyal, and committed to your brand and its success. Let's examine the various audiences that can make or break your brand.

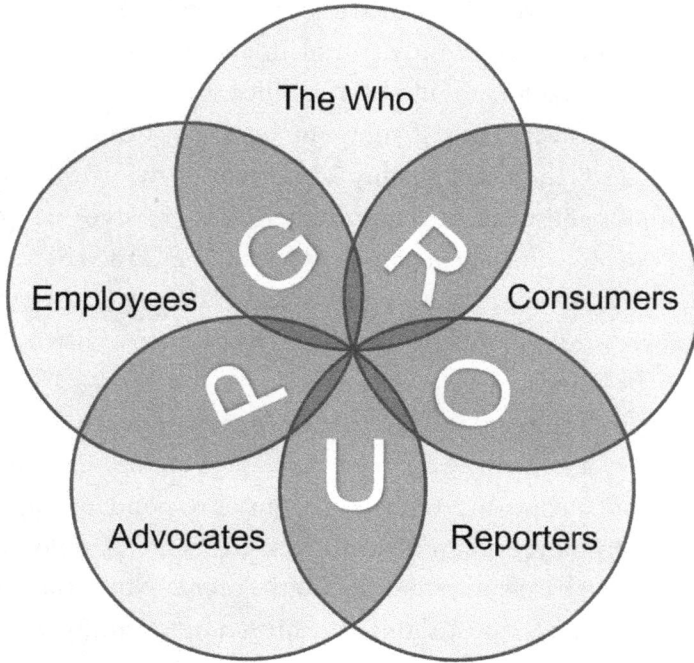

16 | EMPLOYEES

Your greatest brand asset is your employees. What are they saying about your brand? Are they inspired to share your brand virtues with friends and family? Do they tell incredible brand stories or constantly complain about work? Turning employees into advocates or ambassadors should be a significant priority for any brand.

Why should any customer care if your employees don't care about your brand? According to a 2023 Gallup report, only 23 percent of the world's employees are engaged in their jobs and work.[127] That means 77 percent aren't happy. Employee engagement is a big problem. The report showed that the United States and Canada had the highest level of employee engagement, but that 69 percent of North American employees are still unhappy at work. Disgruntled or disengaged employees spell trouble for brands.

If an employee isn't engaged in your brand, why should a customer be any different? According to a study by Edelman, employees are the most trusted source of information about a company, with 41 percent of respondents saying they trust information from employees more than from the CEO.[128] Employees can play a critical role in building trust and credibility for the brand. Not surprisingly, engaged employees are most brands' most significant missed opportunity. Another Gallup study found that engaged employees are more likely to be brand ambassadors, with 67 percent of engaged employees reporting that they advocate for their company. Creating a culture of engagement can help foster employee advocacy and contribute to a positive brand reputation. Hinge Research Institute has similar findings, that brands with a formal employee advocacy program generate five times more web traffic and 25 percent more leads than brands without one.[129] Another study by Weber Shandwick reinforced the importance of employee advocates by showing that brands with high levels of employee advocacy have customers who are 2.5 times more likely to recommend their products and services.[130]

With the prevalence of social media, every employee can be a brand advocate or destroyer. But as Jay Baer, author and president of Convince & Convert, says, "If your employees aren't your biggest fans, you've got problems WAY bigger than social media."[131]

Building a brand culture that employees can embrace and amplify requires a comprehensive approach that prioritizes purpose, engagement, development, recognition, and transparent communications.

Culture

The first step to building a vibrant culture and collaborative environment for employees starts with the first branding C—Commitment. When employees clearly understand the organization's mission and purpose, they are likelier to be engaged and motivated and feel a sense of connection and purpose in their jobs. This can increase collaboration, productivity, and innovation as employees work together toward a shared vision. Engaged employees feel empowered, trusted, and valued; those who lead them show confidence, provide feedback, and demonstrate appreciation.

Employee expectations are changing. Gone are the days of using the carrot and/or the stick to motivate employees. Today, employees are looking for companies that will pay them well and provide a job with a purpose. Daniel Pink, author of the book *Drive: The Surprising Truth About What Motivates Us*, says today's employees are seeking more autonomy with a clear sight of goals that matter in the big picture of life. That's not asking for much, is it?

Numerous studies suggest there are six key elements to building a brand culture that employees can embrace and amplify. By investing in purpose and values, employee engagement, training and development, recognition and rewards, communication and transparency, and diversity, equity, and inclusion (DE&I), brands can create a culture that inspires employees to advocate for the brand, driving financial success passionately. Let's look at each element to build a culture that customers love.

PURPOSE AND VALUES

A clear purpose and set of values can help to align employees around a joint mission and inspire them to work toward a shared vision. By communicating the brand's purpose and values to employees and empowering them to live those values in their work, companies can create a culture of purpose-driven employees who are passionate about the brand. In a study, Deloitte found that brands with a strong sense of purpose and values outperform their peers by a factor of 12.[132]

Zappos (now owned by Amazon), located in Las Vegas and having roughly 1,500 employees, is one of the most massive online shoe and clothing retailers. Its campus-style-meets-frat-house environment allows employees to make their space their own. If you wanted privacy, this wouldn't be the place for you. Every new employee undergoes five weeks of extensive training, including call center support and shipping. Once completed, they are offered $3,000 to quit. The company does this to ensure new employees are willing and ready to support the Zappos customer value culture.

Former Zappos CEO Tony Hsieh said, "We believe that your company's culture and brand are just two sides of the same coin. The brand may initially lag the culture, but eventually, it will catch up. Your culture is your brand."[133] Zappos's number one core value, "Deliver WOW Through Service," is driven by its employees, who are ambassadors of delivering a customer-centric experience.

ENGAGEMENT

Employee engagement is critical to building a brand culture that employees can embrace and amplify. By creating opportunities for employees to provide feedback, collaborate with colleagues, and contribute to the brand's mission, companies can foster a culture of engagement that empowers employees to take ownership of their work and advocate for the brand. While the pandemic brought new complexities and hybrid working styles, the foundation of employee engagement remains the same.

Employee engagement refers to the degree to which employees are invested in and committed to their work and the organization they work for. Engaged employees are passionate about their work, have a strong sense of purpose and belonging, and are motivated to go above and beyond.

Engagement is not the same as job satisfaction, which refers to an employee's level of contentment with their job. Engaged employees may still face challenges and frustrations in their work but remain committed to their jobs and the organization's mission and goals.

You can measure employee engagement through various methods, including surveys, interviews, and other feedback forms. Organizations can use this feedback to identify areas for improvement and develop strategies to build a more engaged workforce. A meta-analysis of 263 research studies concluded that higher levels of employee engagement are associated with lower levels of employee turnover, higher levels of customer satisfaction, and higher levels of profitability.[134]

A cornerstone of employee engagement is creating a psychologically safe environment where employees can speak up, share ideas, and take risks without fear of negative consequences. A study conducted by Harvard Business School professor Amy Edmondson and her team found that high-performing teams had a high level of psychological safety where open communications, respectful interactions, and a willingness to admit mistakes and ask for help were evident.[135] The study found that these teams were more likely to be innovative, to learn from their mistakes, and to perform well on tasks. In addition, members of these teams reported higher levels of satisfaction and engagement with their work.

Google goes to great lengths to create an environment for employees with perks such as free gourmet food, beach volleyball courts, mini-golf courses, and adult playgrounds. The goal is to create an environment that lets employees feel relaxed and comfortable in vocalizing creative, even wacky, ideas. More importantly, Larry Page, former CEO of Google's parent company, Alphabet Inc., said their employees believe in their actions. In an interview, he explained, "We have somewhat of a social mission, and most other companies do not. I think that's why people like working for us…"[136]

TRAINING AND DEVELOPMENT

Providing employees with training and development opportunities can help to develop their skills, knowledge, and understanding of the brand's values and mission. By investing in employee development, companies can create a culture of continuous learning and improvement, which can help to drive innovation and growth.

One of the largest online learning platforms, LinkedIn, found that companies that invest in employee development have 34 percent higher employee retention rates and 53 percent faster growth than those that do not.[137]

It also discovered that employees who spend time learning are 47 percent less stressed at work and 39 percent more likely to feel productive. The same companies also have higher retention rates.

The world's largest coffee chain, Starbucks, is another company dedicated to building a culture where its employees matter. Historically, the retail industry isn't known for employee engagement or retention strategies—Starbucks is the exception. Former Starbucks CEO Howard Schultz has said that its culture and employees, referred to as "partners," were the company's most sustainable competitive advantage. Starbucks doesn't leave its employees to become brand ambassadors magically. It invested millions of dollars into a "Leadership Lab" where store managers are trained to better understand the Starbucks brand and culture. The program is designed to create a leadership culture, and to empower employees to make decisions and take ownership of their work. In Schultz's book *Onward: How Starbucks Fought for Its Life without Losing Its Soul*, he explains that "[Employees] are the true ambassadors of our brand, the real merchants of romance and theater, and as such, the primary catalysts for delighting customers."[138]

RECOGNITION AND REWARDS

Recognizing and rewarding employees who embody the brand's values and mission can help to reinforce those values and create a culture of excellence. By acknowledging and celebrating employee achievements, brands can develop a culture of positivity and recognition that inspires employees to go above and beyond in their work. Recognition can come in many forms, such as public recognition, bonuses or promotions, personalized notes or messages from supervisors, or opportunities for growth and development. Ultimately, the most impactful recognition makes the employee feel valued, respected, and motivated to continue contributing to the organization.

COMMUNICATION AND TRANSPARENCY

Effective communication and transparency are essential to building a brand culture that employees can embrace and amplify. By keeping employees informed about the brand's goals, challenges, and successes and involving them in decision-making processes, companies can foster a culture of trust and collaboration that empowers employees to advocate for the brand.

Stever Robbins, a personal coach and podcaster, says, "Transparency and authenticity build a trusting relationship in which people are more likely to bring their full creativity, commitment, and motivation to work. How you treat your employees will be mirrored in the way your employees treat your customers. Treat your employees poorly, and they'll pass that treatment along to your customers."[139]

DIVERSITY, EQUITY, AND INCLUSION

DE&I has become critical in developing a positive and productive workplace culture that provides a variety of perspectives, experiences, and talents. Winning brands understand the importance of diversity of thinking, which helps them make more creative, innovative, and better and more informed decisions. The Society for Human Resource Management (SHRM) examined the impact of the pandemic on DE&I initiatives and found that brands with strong DE&I cultures are more likely to have engaged, committed, and productive employees.[140]

The German software company SAP has quantified what employee engagement means to its bottom line. Its annual *Integrated Report* estimated that for every percentage point on its employee engagement index, the impact on its operating profits goes up between € 35 million and € 45 million.[141] The secret ingredient? Its employees understand the "why" behind their jobs and how their inspiration ties to a bigger vision—it's why they come to work each day.

Southwest Airlines has been around for over forty years in an industry that sees many airlines fail. As Herb Kelleher, founder of Southwest, explains, any airline can buy all the material things and copy a company's business model, but "the things you can't buy are dedication, devotion, loyalty—the feeling that you are participating in a crusade."[142] In 2013, Southwest updated its vision and purpose, and Southwest CEO Gary Kelly said, "Southwest is a great place to work and brings the greatest joy because we have such meaningful purpose." The purpose is to "connect people to what's important in [customers'] lives through friendly, reliable, and low-cost air travel."[143]

Brand Advocates

Unsurprisingly, the strong brands we know and love are also strong within their company's walls. Employee brand advocacy is a competitive advantage. Engaged employees can make it hard for competitors to replicate and for customers to ignore.

Here are eight key aspects that help turn employees into brand advocates, and some actions you can take to drive each one:

Strong Understanding of the Brand's Big Picture and Purpose

- Hold regular brand education sessions to ensure employees understand the company's history, mission, values, and long-term goals.
- Connect the brand's purpose to the more significant industry or societal context to make it more meaningful for employees.
- Provide brand guidelines, mission statements, and success stories to reinforce the brand's identity and purpose.

Linkage Between Their Aspirations and Those of the Brand

- Foster conversations between employees and leadership to identify and align personal goals with the company's objectives.
- Develop individualized career paths that show how employees can grow within the organization while contributing to the brand's success.
- Encourage employees to share their personal stories and how their journey intersects with the brand's story.

Freedom to Speak and Share Their Brand Experiences

- Establish an open and transparent communication culture where employees feel comfortable sharing their opinions and experiences.
- Create formal channels for feedback, such as suggestion boxes, surveys, or regular town hall meetings.
- Recognize and reward employees who promote the brand through storytelling and sharing their experiences.

Autonomy to Enhance a Customer Relationship or Fix a Problem

- Empower employees with the authority to make on-the-spot decisions to resolve customer issues, enhancing their satisfaction and loyalty.
- Provide training that focuses on problem-solving and conflict resolution, enabling employees to handle challenges independently.
- Celebrate and share stories of employees who have gone above and beyond to improve a customer relationship or solve a problem.
- Set up a clear framework for escalation, so employees know when and how to involve higher management in customer issues.

Tools to Help Employees Share the Brand

- Offer easy-to-use digital platforms for employees to share brand content on their social media networks.
- Provide pre-approved brand messages and graphics that employees can use to maintain brand consistency.
- Organize workshops or webinars on personal branding and how employees can align their own brand with the company's.
- Implement an employee advocacy program that rewards staff for sharing brand messages and engaging with content online.

Trust that the Company Is Protecting Their Well-Being

- Prioritize employee well-being through comprehensive health and wellness programs.
- Communicate the company's commitment to safety, security, and work-life balance.
- Regularly gather feedback from employees and take action to address their concerns and needs.

Appreciation and Support

- Implement recognition programs that celebrate employee achievements, both big and small, within the organization.
- Provide regular, constructive feedback that guides performance and acknowledges effort and dedication.
- Offer support through mentorship programs, where more experienced employees guide newer team members, fostering a sense of belonging and community.
- Organize team-building activities and social events that promote camaraderie and show appreciation for the team's collective work.

Knowledge that Their Contribution Is Supporting the Brand Purpose

- Highlight specific examples of how individual roles and contributions directly impact the brand's mission and strategic objectives.
- Share success stories where employee actions have led to positive outcomes for the brand, reinforcing the value of their work.
- Involve employees in decision-making processes and idea generation, emphasizing that their input is crucial for the brand's growth and success.
- Regularly communicate the company's achievements and milestones, ensuring employees understand how their work contributes to these successes.

First, brand advocates don't appear overnight. Second, building a solid brand culture takes time and trust. Finally, and most importantly, it must start with the leadership at the top of an organization, followed by all other levels. Building a robust employee culture is worth the effort. It will help create a durable brand cult and many happy customers.

Start by keeping a pulse on your employee culture and engagement. If you have a strong customer brand, you already have a dedicated employee culture. Ensure you give them the tools and support to help them amplify your brand. You only rent your employees if you don't build a culture supporting your brand vision. The same will then go for your customers.

May the employee brand force be with you!

17 | CUSTOMERS AND CONSUMERS

There is a big difference between a customer and a consumer. A customer is someone who has already purchased a brand's product or service. A customer has experienced the brand and, depending on their number of transactions, has built a relationship with it. A consumer represents a broader audience, someone who is shopping for products and services for various wants and needs—this includes your *potential* customers. All brands start by attracting consumers and converting them into customers. Eventually, you have two distinct target audiences: one with whom you're building a strong relationship, and the other whom you are still trying to entice to make the first purchase. Of course, you also have those who came and went for many reasons.

Your first goal is to determine who your potential customers are. One way to determine your prospective customer is to conduct target audience research to see who needs or wants your product or service. You could also find out what they like and don't like and how much they would be willing to pay. The more extensive the sample study, the better you can see if there are any similarities based on demographics (such as age, gender, race, income, and education), the awareness level of the problem or need, psychographics (such as lifestyles, values, attitudes, interests, personality traits, and behaviors), and other relevant characteristics or experiences.

According to Pew Research, which specializes in generational research, "An individual's age is one of the most common predictors of differences in attitude and behaviors."[144] While no generation is a homogeneous group, each one has unique characteristics and preferences shaped by its environment. Social ideology and political events (wars, communism, dictators), crises (climate change, epidemics, financial collapse), technological advancements (GenAI, machine learning, blockchain, robotics, 3D printing), economic conditions (prosperity, inflation, credit, banking), cultural movements and events (civil rights, #metoo, art, music, movies), education and parenting (knowledge, guidance, and influence) can all influence how we think, feel, and act.

Layered on top of these events is culture, which is a collection set of values, beliefs, behaviors, practices, and social norms. What was deemed acceptable fifty years ago might not be permitted or tolerated today. Brands that predict or create the future can see a shift in emotions, behaviors, and beliefs. These shifts generally reside in a subculture of people who can shape and influence society over time. Subcultures or outliers are distinctly different from the mainstream and from one another, based on various factors such as music preferences, fashion, hobbies, lifestyle, attitudes, and political ideologies. Social media has allowed people, more than ever, to find their unique community. Three examples of brands that started in a subculture are Patagonia outdoor clothing and gear, initially popular mainly with devoted environmentalists; Burt's Bees, with their Earth-friendly and antichemical followers; and Harley-Davidson and its H.O.G (Harley Owners Group) freedom riders. Our perceptions, beliefs, and behaviors evolve as our environment changes. However, when predicting future trends and impacts, the most dependable starting point is to analyze age groups and generational mindsets. Statisticians and economists can provide accurate forecasts of the future size and influence of these demographic segments. In contrast, cultural shifts and subcultures are more challenging to predict, as they are constantly in flux and evolve in new, non-linear directions, making them less reliable indicators of future trends.

The Population Pyramid

The perfect population pyramid is a theoretical situation where the number of people entering the workforce, those exiting the workforce, those having children, and those dying is balanced. The ideal scenario is a broad base of young people entering the workforce, a smaller middle portion of working-age individuals, and a narrow top of older people retiring—creating a pyramid shape.

Following the silent generation, the baby boomers created a sizable historical population foundation for the perfect pyramid. But the next generation, generation X (not to be confused with X, formerly known as Twitter), which grew up with birth control, higher education, and extensive career opportunities for women and men, didn't match the boomers' birthrate, so the "pyramid" looks a bit more like a cupcake. As the boomers got older, they had the highest level of disposable income and the most significant purchasing power ever seen. They were influential in driving new trends and innovations in all sectors of consumer products and services. Generation X lived in the shadow of baby boomer consumers and continue to bear the burden of their predecessors' environmental impact. However, the baby boomers' children, the millennials (also called generation Y), are another reckoning force that created the second wave of imposing consumers with their own unique beliefs and values, followed by gen X's children, generation Z.

Looking into the future, by 2050 we see the baby boomers fading into the sunset and a more traditional pyramid shape appearing. But we don't know what the fertility rate of millennials and generation Z will be, nor the migration policies, so we don't know if the future will be a cupcake or a pyramid.

US Population Pyramid 2020

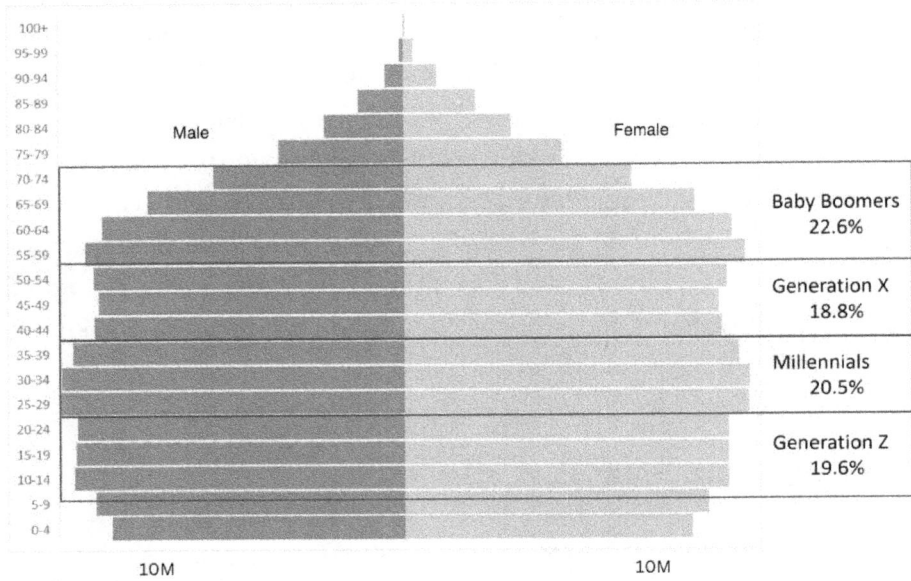

Source: United States Census Bureau, International Program Center, International Data

US Population Pyramid 2050

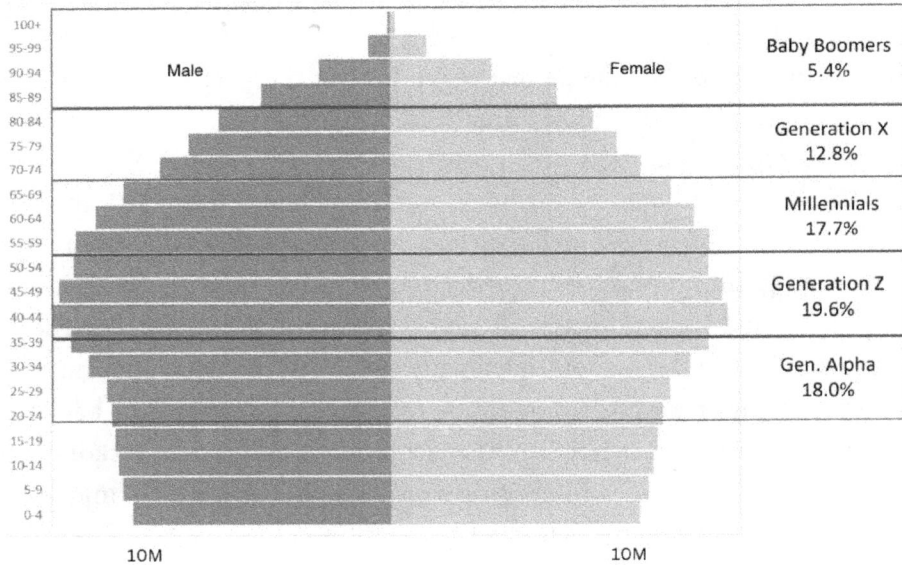

Source: United States Census Bureau, International Program Center, International Data

Nevertheless, today, there are some startling imbalances concerning wealth, social status, and ethnicity between the generations. For example, half of America's wealth is currently held by rich boomers, who are primarily white. The top wealthiest 1 percent of households have accumulated as much wealth as the bottom 90 percent. When viewed by race, white households hold a disproportionate share of the wealth. David Kelly, chief global strategist at J.P. Morgan Asset Management, believes that rather than focusing on why some are rich, we should shift the conversation to examining why poverty persists and how we can alleviate it.[145] Not only are brands impacted by these facts, but the smart brands will play a role in addressing these inequalities.

American Wealth Distribution by Generations

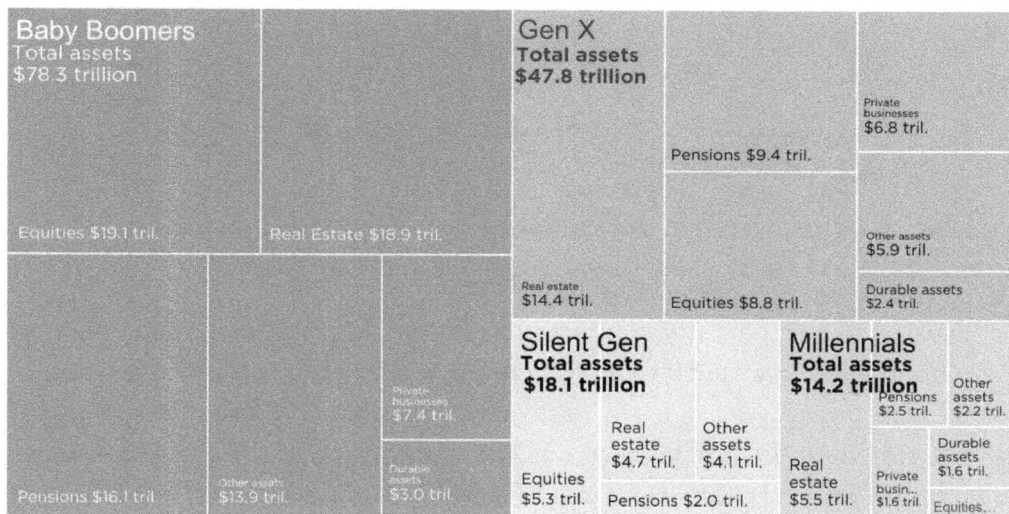

Baby Boomers Total assets $78.3 trillion		Gen X Total assets $47.8 trillion	
Equities $19.1 tril.	Real Estate $18.9 tril.	Pensions $9.4 tril.	Private businesses $6.8 tril.
			Other assets $5.9 tril.
		Real estate $14.4 tril. / Equities $8.8 tril.	Durable assets $2.4 tril.
Pensions $16.1 tril. / Other assets $13.9 tril.	Private businesses $7.4 tril. / Durable assets $3.0 tril.	Silent Gen Total assets $18.1 trillion / Millennials Total assets $14.2 trillion	

Silent Gen — Total assets $18.1 trillion: Equities $5.3 tril.; Real estate $4.7 tril.; Other assets $4.1 tril.; Pensions $2.0 tril.

Millennials — Total assets $14.2 trillion: Real estate $5.5 tril.; Private busin... $1.6 tril.; Pensions $2.5 tril.; Other assets $2.2 tril.; Durable assets $1.6 tril.; Equities...

Note: Based on Q4 2022 wealth data - assets and liabilities adjusted for inflation.

Source: US Federal Reserve, Board of Governors of the Federal Reserve System

American Median Wealth by Race/Ethnicity

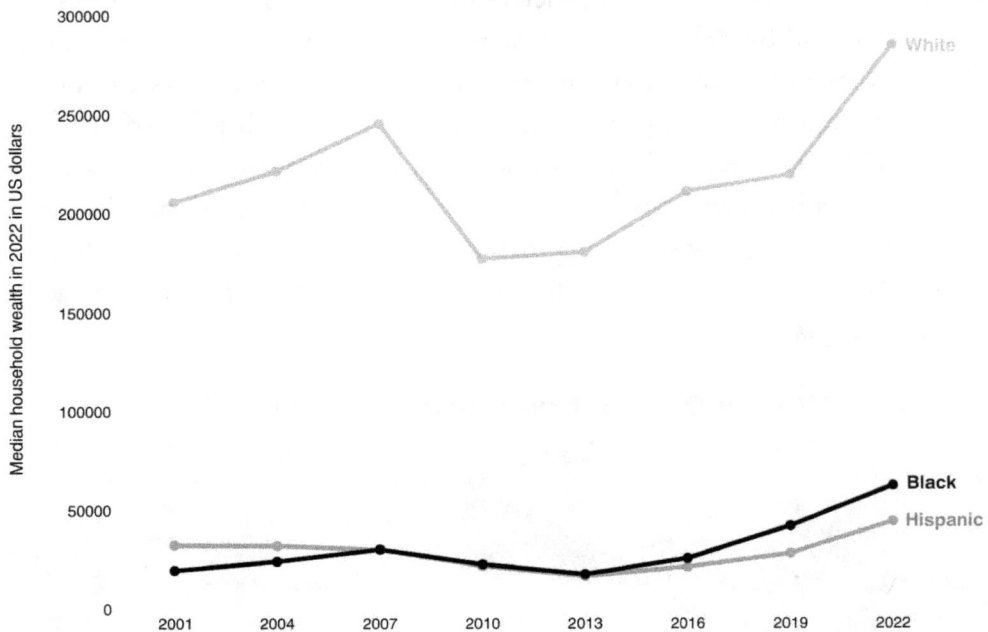

Note: Based on Q4 2022 wealth data - assets and liabilities adjusted for inflation in 2022 dollars.

Source: US Federal Reserve, Board of Governors of the Federal Reserve System

Consider the age-old question: can money buy happiness? It would seem so if you contrast the wealth of the generations against the University of Oxford's *World Happiness Report*, now in its twelfth year. The 2024 report shows that overall happiness in North America has declined since 2012, with Canada falling from fifth happiest country to fifteenth of 143, and the US from eleventh to twenty-third. If you dig deeper into the numbers, you will see that young people are less happy than their parents. Canada ranks a sad fifty-eighth in the world in happiness for people under thirty, and those over sixty rank an impressive eighth.[146]

Similarly, the US ranks sixty-second for happiness among the young and tenth for those over sixty. According to the research, this wasn't always the case, but over the last twelve years, the young person's happiness score keeps sliding, increasing the gap as the boomers' happiness stays relatively consistent.[147] Australia and New Zealand have seen the same trend. Reporter Ian McGugan attributes the decline to unaffordable housing, political upheavals, and economic uncertainty.[148] I would add wars, AI, and climate-change disasters to that list; the future doesn't look so bright and sure.

Understanding how spending patterns differ across generations provides valuable consumer insights that can inform branding and marketing approaches. Generation

X currently makes up the largest share of overall consumer spending. Having reached the stage of raising families, their expenses predominantly revolve around housing, transportation, personal insurance and pensions, food, education, and increasing healthcare. Consequently, family-focused brands and financial services have a strategic opportunity with this demographic.

Meanwhile, baby boomers and the silent generation are allocating more of their budgets to categories like housing and healthcare, and leisure travel. Companies in these sectors would do well to target these groups. For their part, millennials tend to mimic the spending habits of generation X, dedicating funds to housing, transportation, groceries, and fashion, albeit on a somewhat tighter budget. Brands that promote aspirational yet affordable lifestyle offerings could connect well with this cohort. Finally, as dependents are still primarily supported by their parents, generation Z spends mostly on essential necessities like housing, transportation, food, and education. Still, they represent an early chance for youth-oriented brands to establish affinity. Overall, evaluating consumption patterns by life stage grants helpful context for brands seeking to appeal to consumers across age brackets.

American Consumer Spending Type by Generation

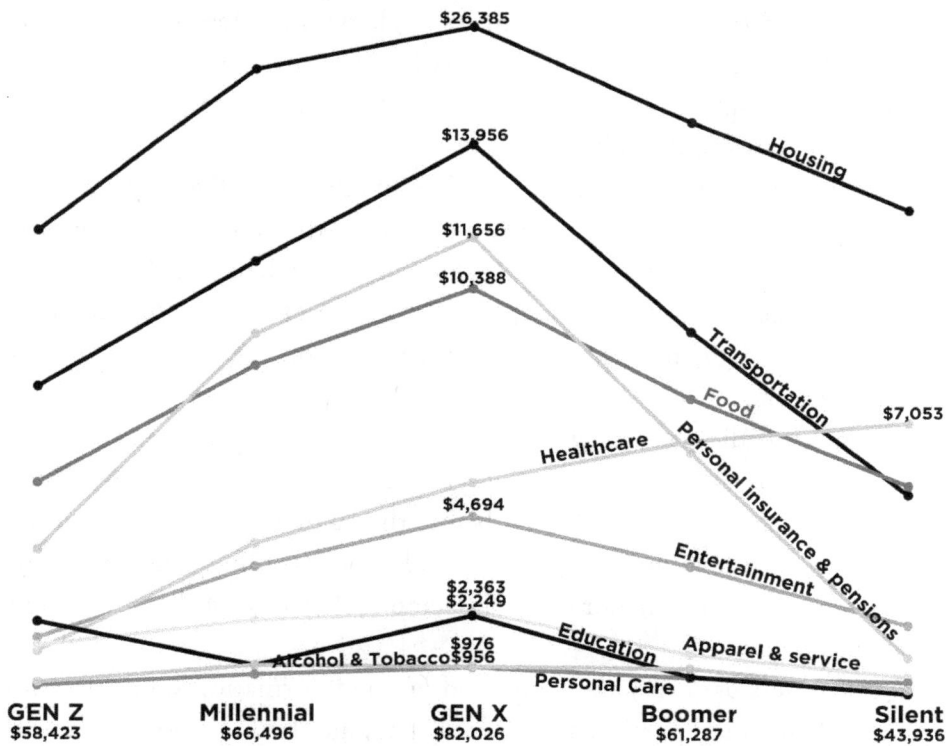

$26,385				
$13,956			Housing	
$11,656				
$10,388		Transportation		
	Food		$7,053	
	Healthcare	Personal insurance		
$4,694				
$2,363 $2,249		Entertainment	& pensions	
$976	Education	Apparel & service		
Alcohol & Tobacco $956				
Personal Care				
GEN Z $58,423	Millennial $66,496	GEN X $82,026	Boomer $61,287	Silent $43,936

Source: US Bureau of Labor Statistics (2021)

Generation Z

The youngest consumers are gen-Z individuals born between 1997 and about 2012. Gen Z can be a lot like their gen-X parents. Stanford scholar Roberta Katz's research describes the typical gen Z as "a self-driver who deeply cares about others, strives for a diverse community, is highly collaborative and social, values flexibility, relevance, authenticity and non-hierarchical leadership, and, while dismayed about inherited issues like climate change, has a pragmatic attitude…"[149] What made them this way? They are the first truly digital native generation, having grown up with the internet, social media, and mobile technology as an integral part of their lives. They don't know a world without these things. Over 56 percent of American gen Z prefer online shopping than in-store shopping.[150] Social media is their primary source of product information, trends, and news, including recommendations, guidance, and how-to. They use it daily for work, shopping, dating, entertainment, connecting with friends and family, and making new friends. With the constant flow of information, they have a shorter attention span than any other generation and expect short-form content to be entertaining and concise.

Many of them grew up in a world shaped by the terrorist attacks of September 11, 2001. The Great Recession in 2008 was perhaps their first introduction to the financial world, and they saw their parents struggle with job loss and economic insecurity. They saw years of cheap credit, inflation, and high-interest rates. They saw firsthand the struggles of being financially secure, creating a conservative pragmatism seeking security and stability.

Gen Z has grown up with the most racially and ethnically diverse generation in history, and they have grown up in an environment that values and celebrates diversity. They are the most diverse generation, with nearly half gen-Z Americans identifying as a racial or ethnic minority.[151] They saw the first Black president in the USA and legalized gay marriage, shaping their views on race, gender, and sexuality. Diversity is the norm.

As active social media users, they are the socially conscious generation who are politically aware and engaged in issues they care about; 67 percent are concerned about climate change issues.[152] Still, even before the pandemic, gen Z earned the title of the "loneliest generation" by spending endless hours online. Unsurprisingly, mental health has become a major concern facing society during these turbulent and unpredictable times.

Gen-Z consumers use every tool, app, and online information source to help them make the best ethical purchasing decisions. They are also the most visually oriented generation, growing up amid the explosion of video games, YouTube content, streaming movies and shows, and continuous social media video clips. Not only are they consumers of content, but they are significant content producers. Sixty-eight percent believe self-expression is crucial as they share their personal lives online using new tools for digital creativity.[153] A survey by the McCann Worldgroup advertising agency found that 80 percent of gen Zs believe it's vital for brands to be honest and transparent, and that 75 percent believe brands should try to improve the world.[154] This view also translates into their personal lives, as they are more health conscious than previous generations, for example choosing to drink less alcohol (spurring growth in the non-alcoholic beverages industry).

Gen Z is known for their preference for experiences (travel is prevalent) over material goods, and they are more likely to support companies and brands that align with their values and beliefs. They expect speed, flexibility, and convenience with their brand transactions, which mainly take place within their smartphones. Just ask Uber, Uber Eats, Amazon Prime, DoorDash, Airbnb, Netflix, and HelloFresh, who have gen Z figured out. To build long-term brand engagement, Matt Kleinschmit, gen-Z research expert, says brands must create an emotional connection, be virtually shareable, and align with gen Z's values.[155] They also protect their work-life boundaries and prefer working from home if they can.

So, what do you need to do if gen Z is your brand's target audience?

Purpose: Be a purpose-driven brand that is authentic, transparent, and aligned with gen-Z values and interests.

Video and Images: Prioritize visual and entertaining content optimized for mobile devices in your marketing and communications strategy.

Social Media: Have a strong and relevant presence on social media and engage with gen Z.

Influencers: To promote your products or services, partner with genuine and relatable micro-influencers with a strong following among gen Z.

Real-Time Solutions: Use technology to provide flexible and convenient real-time solutions, information, and customer care.

Personalization: Create personalized experiences that engage gen Z and leverage personal data to develop unique offers and promotions.

Micro-Content: Build bite-size, visually appealing content like short videos, memes, and interactive content.

Generation Y (Millennials)

Gen Y, the millennial generation, is defined as people born between 1981 and 1996. There are approximately 1.8 billion millennials worldwide, representing 23 percent of the global population. Millennials are the first generation to grow up with technology as an integral part of their lives, and they are known for being highly proficient with computers, smartphones, and other devices. In addition, they were the first to grow up with the idea of an online social network, using start-ups SixDegrees, Friendster, and MySpace, followed by Facebook, YouTube, Twitter (now called X), and Tumblr; therefore, they are heavy users of social media. They were also a highly diverse generation with diverse ethnic, racial, and cultural backgrounds. Their parents were boomers who invented the term "helicopter parent," overprotecting and obsessing over the lives of their millennial children. Even so, they grew up prioritizing their personal lives and well-being over their careers, focusing on work-life balance and flexible work arrangements, which made them more likely to start businesses or pursue alternative career paths. With their parents' support and encouragement, they also place a high value on education and are more likely to have followed higher levels of education than previous generations. So millennials are the most educated generation in history, with many having advanced degrees. This also means they are the generation with the most student loans, with over 15 million Americans owing an average debt of $32,800 per borrower.[156]

They had a fair share of significant events to shape their views and beliefs, having witnessed in slow motion the September 11 attacks, the Great Recession in 2008 and subsequent economic downturns, the Arab Spring in the Middle East, and the increasing urgency surrounding climate change and global warming. These events have made millennials conscious of security risks and terrorism, more financially cautious, and more focused on stability and security in their career. In addition, they are more socially active, and they advocate against social injustices and the environmental consequences of an increasingly consumerized population.

All of these world-changing events that have shaped the lives of millennials were experienced in a media-saturated environment. Consequently, millennials are known for their frugality and preference for experiences over material goods. They are also more likely to support companies and brands that align with their values and beliefs.

In 2022, they spent nearly $75,000 on household expenditures in the United States.[157] They will comprise about 44 percent of the US workforce by 2030.[158]

This generation has been researched to death—everyone is trying to figure them out from every possible business and marketing angle.

Millennials have lived most (or at least half) of their lives with a cell/smartphone around them, staying connected 24/7 with friends and family. Their ability to consume digital content (emails, texts, tweets, video chats, websites, apps, videos, and images) and also produce their own is admirable, but what is truly remarkable is they do this while sitting in meetings, visiting with friends, eating, running, walking, and driving a car. They sleep with their cell phones. Three-quarters of millennials have accounts on social networking sites like Facebook, X, Snapchat, TikTok, YouTube, or Instagram. This was the first generation to have tech-savvy parents, who were always in contact with them via texting and online chat throughout the day.

As they consume services, products, food, beverages, and entertainment, millennials share their experiences, good and bad, via social media as photojournalists, comedians, critics, advocates, and just plain participants. Boston Consulting Group reports, "The vast majority of millennials report taking action on behalf of brands and sharing brand preferences in their social groups."[159] Not only do millennials like to share, but they like to feel informed, involved, and in control, not just marketed to.

Millennials have high expectations for brands, leaning toward those that are working to improve the world, like Toms shoes and Soapbox Soaps, which have one-to-one giving models, Starbucks with its Coffee and Farmer Equity (C.A.F.E.) sustainable coffee-production practices, and Ben & Jerry's fair-trade ingredients and farm sustainability program.

This generation didn't (or isn't about to!) leave home soon. Gen Z isn't much different. Even now, at the average age of 35, 17 percent of millennials still live "at home" with their aging parents.[160] The book *How Cool Brands Stay Hot: Branding to Generation Y* says that 85 percent of teens name one of their parents as their best friend rather than naming a peer.[161] More than a third of millennials of all ages say they influence what products their parents buy, what shops and restaurants they visit, and what trips they take.

However, they also face the economic reality of being unable to afford to live independently because of the high cost of living, inflation, and rising rental rates. Home-cooked meals, laundry, and maid services are also benefits, if they're lucky.

They grew up with Facebook and many pride themselves on having a lot of Facebook friends or X (formerly Twitter) followers—or better yet, getting a lot of "likes" on a post. They want to surround themselves with brands they can think of as friends, like Nike, Apple, Samsung, Sony, and Walmart. "This is a group that will adopt brands," says Norty Cohen, founder of Moosylvania. "If you can create a friendship with these consumers, you really take it to the next level. They will go to great lengths to support you."[162]

This generation entered the workforce during the most pronounced downturn since the Great Recession. During the darkest period in 2013, the unemployment rate for millennials in the US was over 13 percent. Millennials have been labeled "the cheapest generation" for their propensity to avoid large-scale purchases such as cars and houses. While this generation might be price-conscious shoppers, technology has allowed them to research every purchase and presents them with more options and pricing models than ever before. Millennials love loyalty programs, with over 61 percent claiming membership in at least one.[163] Millennial shoppers depend on ratings and reviews to make informed purchase decisions, regardless of the channel. Over 99 percent read reviews when shopping online and 63 percent when shopping in-store.[164]

They can also see value in non-traditional business models, such as Uber, which connects riders to drivers and replaces taxicabs, or Airbnb, which provides travelers with unique accommodations around the world and replaces hotel chains. Other examples of disruptive marketing are the very popular Dollar Shave Club, who introduced the subscription business model into men's personal grooming products (like razors), and Netflix, which has changed how movies and TV series are consumed.

Millennials grew up on entertainment from the early days of VCRs, maybe watching and rewatching the entire library of Walt Disney movies and sneaking in the odd National Lampoon reel. Then there were the hilarious physical, slapstick comedies (starring Jim Carrey, Mike Myers, Adam Sandler and Ben Stiller) the Harry Potter and Twilight franchises, and endless video games. They had instant access to be amazed and distracted. World-renowned game designer Jane McGonigal estimates that a twenty-one year-old has spent 10,000 hours gaming—about the same amount of time he spent in school from fifth to twelfth grade.[165]

Tanya Giles, formerly the general manager at Comedy Central, says comedy is intrinsically intertwined with millennials' identities.[166] A study by Edelman confirms that 80 percent of millennials like to be entertained by advertising—that is, if the brand is current and the offering is appealing or relevant.[167]

Procter & Gamble's Old Spice has been around for seventy years. It was a very popular brand for the men of the silent generation. Boomers saw it as an older man's product. However, that changed in 2010 when the company launched one of the most successful rebrands for young men, featuring the "Old Spice Guy." Its hilarious video "Mom Song" has had over 3 million views on YouTube.

Millennials want to be loved and appreciated as individual customers, and if they have a problem, they want the brand to fix it. In an Edelman study, over 70 percent of millennials said they would return to brands they love.

So, what do you need to do if millennials are your brand's target audience?

Don't Bore Them: Be entertaining. Allow them to co-create and share in the experience.

Create an Experience: Consider creating an immersive brand experience online and physically by hosting live events and podcasts, engaging partners and influencers, creating interactive virtual reality content, and using gamification (contests, quizzes, etc.).

Build a Community: Create and nurture online communities, forums, or social media groups where millennials can connect, share, and learn from their brand experiences.

Deliver Instant Gratification: They enjoy instant gratification, so make use of messaging/texting apps like WhatsApp, Messenger, and chatbots.

Provide Real-Time Access: Use technology to provide flexible and convenient real-time solutions, information, and customer care.

Personalize: Provide personalized experiences that engage millennials to provide personal data in exchange for unique offers, discounts, and promotions.

Don't Generalize: Segment your marketing campaigns to target specific subgroups within the generation based on demographics, lifestyle, interests, and behaviors.

Generation X

Generation X is defined as people born between 1965 and 1980. Their name, or letter, came from the novel *Generation X: Tales for an Accelerated Culture* by Douglas Coupland. Their parents were from the tail end of the silent generation and the first boomers. This generation, often called the "latchkey generation," grew up in households where both parents worked, fostering a sense of self-sufficiency and independence. However, they are also seen as the "neglected middle child" between the two largest generations—the boomers ahead and the millennials behind. They witnessed the emergence of personal computers and video games, laying the foundation for today's tech-centric world.

Generation X experienced increasing cultural diversity, rising divorce rates, and evolving societal norms. They embraced alternative music genres like grunge and hip-hop, leaving a significant mark on the pop culture of the 1980s and 1990s. Raised during periods of economic uncertainty, they tend to be pragmatic, adaptable, and entrepreneurial.

As a transitional generation, gen X bridges the idealism of the baby boomers with the digital native characteristics of millennials and generation Z. They value work-life balance, often prioritize family life, and have exhibited resilience in navigating changing technology and economic landscapes. As parents, they've adopted more involved parenting styles and maintain strong family bonds.

Older gen Xers have tended to be more conservative than boomers and millennials, often supporting the Republican party and being more pessimistic about their future, especially their retirement financial security.[168] Unsurprisingly, they have a similar work ethic as the generation above them, as they had to compete with workaholic boomers for jobs and promotions their whole lives.

Another uniqueness of this generation was the growth of Hispanic people in America, who brought their values, culture, food, and traditions, transforming America. During this generation, the working class experienced job losses as good-paying manufacturing work disappeared to Asia. The most brutally hit were Black and Hispanic people, who had limited job opportunities and stagnant wages.[169]

While this generation never got the media headlines or the endless research studies about them, generation X's identity is marked by independence, adaptability, skepticism, and a unique cultural imprint reflecting their era's challenges and opportunities.

So, what do you need to do if gen X is your brand's target audience?

Integrated Marketing: Use an omnichannel approach of synchronous and asynchronous communication tactics, including traditional advertising, online channels, emails, and social media, with a particular emphasis on Facebook and Instagram.

Efficiency Marketing: Focus on highlighting the value and practicality of products or services to simplify and enhance the efficiency of customers' lives.

Peer Influence: Capitalize on reviews and testimonials, leveraging the power of peer recommendations and user-generated content that customers highly trust.

Informative Engagement: Provide in-depth content that educates and informs, including how-to videos, discussion boards, forums, webinars, infographics, and visual storytelling to aid purchasing decisions.

Retro Connection: Engage with nostalgia marketing that triggers positive memories of the 1980s and 1990s to resonate with the target demographic's youth.

Direct Interaction: Offer face-to-face customer support and direct assistance for inquiries or issues, acknowledging the preference for personal interaction.

Trust-Building Resources: Maintain an informative and user-friendly website complete with FAQs, blogs, podcasts, and articles to establish your brand as a knowledgeable authority and build trust with customers.

Baby Boomers

Baby boomers took the world by storm. North America saw over 84 million babies arrive between 1946 and 1964. In fact, during that period, the entire Western industrialized world saw the number of babies born explode. In Diane Macunovich's book *Birth Quake: The Baby Boom and Its Aftershocks*, she describes the baby boom as an initial major event with an ongoing ripple effect that followed ("aftershocks"), which we still experience today.[170] Demographers and social scientists of the day were blindsided, and ill-prepared to explain what had happened. The extraordinary birthrate lasted for less than twenty years. Researchers are still trying to determine what triggered such a huge global event.

Peace reigned around the world after World War II. In 1944, the Bretton Woods system was designed to ensure global economic stability, promoting growth and economic prosperity. This led to the emergence of a vast middle class in the western world that allowed families to own homes in the suburbs and save for their kids' college tuition. The "perfect family" had two to three children and a lovable dog, emulating the idealism portrayed by the popular sitcoms of the time, such as *Father Knows Best*, *Leave It to Beaver*, and *Ozzie and Harriet*.

Little did we know, at the time, that we had created the largest generation ever to inhabit the Earth at one time. This generation would significantly impact everything they touched, consumed, acquired, developed, and influenced. In 1966, *Time* magazine named its "Man of the Year" as "the man—and woman—of 25 and under." From the moment they arrived, boomers were a force that couldn't be contained. They were the start of a social and cultural phenomenon.[171]

What came to be known as the "Me" generation had a significant impact on culture, society, and the economy. They are known for their strong work ethic and commitment to their careers. Consequently, they had high levels of disposable income. They were the biggest consumers in the world with insatiable consumption habits and a desire for new trends and innovations in consumer products and services, which helped to shape the digital landscape. Baby Boomers value quality products and are loyal to brands they come to trust.

As of July 2019, American millennials surpassed baby boomers as the largest generation; gen Y is projected to stabilize at about 75 million, while the boomers at that point had declined to 71 million. However, the accumulated wealth of American boomers today still exceeds $78 trillion in assets, about half of the country's total wealth. About $16 trillion will be transferred to millennial and generation X heirs within the next decade.[172] This period will mark the first time in recorded history that older adults—aged 65 and older—will make up almost 20 percent of the US population, putting enormous pressure on the healthcare system and government budgets.

By 2030, all baby boomers will be over 65, with the oldest in their mid-80s. The current boomer population is estimated to be below 60 million and will drop dramatically over the next twenty years.

Until then, baby boomers will continue to be a significant consumer group with considerable purchasing power, and brands that understand their needs, preferences, and values are well-positioned to build lasting relationships with this demographic.

So, what do you need to do if the baby boomer is your brand's target audience?

Classic Outreach: Prioritize traditional media channels such as television, radio, and print publications to reach the boomer audience effectively.

Sentimental Marketing: Use nostalgia marketing to evoke the 1960s, 1970s, and 1980s memories, tapping into boomers' fondness for their youth's iconic moments and cultural references.

Generational Values: Emphasize themes of family, legacy, and meaningful relationships, which resonate deeply with boomers as they reflect on their impact and heritage.

Ease of Use: Offer simple, secure solutions that minimize risk and complexity, ensuring easy adoption without requiring intricate instructions or log-in requirements.

Direct Assistance: Recognize boomers' appreciation for face-to-face customer support and provide direct assistance for any questions or issues they may encounter.

Reliable Excellence: Highlight the quality, craftsmanship, and time-tested nature of products or services, underscoring traditional values and the reliability that boomers value.

Expertise Online: Maintain an informative and user-friendly website with FAQs, blogs, podcasts, and articles to reinforce your brand's knowledge and build trust with the boomer audience.

The Cycle of Life

Beyond the various cohorts, there is a natural progression of life stages and events that an individual goes through from birth to death. The "cycle of life" is a concept that describes that natural progression and encompasses the various phases and transitions during a person's lifetime. While the specifics may vary between cultures and individuals, a simplified representation of the cycle of life typically includes the following stages:

Birth: No surprise; this is the starting point for any life cycle.

Infancy: This stage includes the earliest years of life, typically from birth to around age two. Infants are entirely dependent on caregivers for their basic needs. This is where brands like Procter & Gamble, The Children's Place, Johnson & Johnson, and OshKosh start their brand journey.

Childhood: Childhood encompasses the period from early infancy to adolescence, usually from age two to around twelve or thirteen. It's a time of rapid physical, emotional, and cognitive development, marked by milestones such as learning to walk, talk, and attend school. This is when consumption increases for clothes, educational materials, entertainment, toys, and sports equipment. At the same time, most of these expenditures are the responsibility of the children's parents, who significantly influence brand choices.

Adolescence: Adolescence is the transitional period between childhood and adulthood, typically spanning the teenage years. It involves significant physical changes, identity development, and increased independence. In terms of purchasing power, we see more of the same, except that price points and variety continue to rise, encompassing more expensive electronics, entertainment sources, and new technologies. While most of the brand decisions are in the hands of the adolescent's parents, they can influence the decisions.

Early Adulthood: This stage generally includes the late teens through the twenties and even into the thirties. It's characterized by pursuing education, establishing careers, forming relationships, and potentially starting families. These young adults are beginning to consume more fashion, accessories, health and wellness products, cosmetics, transportation, banking products, and housing. For many, this is the first time they go into debt with student loans.

Adulthood: Adulthood is the most prolonged phase of the life cycle, typically quantified as lasting from the thirties or forties into the sixties or seventies. It involves building a career, raising a family, and contributing to society. After testing various brands, lifestyle choices, and work options, adults are slowly settling down into full-time jobs, careers, life partners, and homes, and potentially having children. More debt is accumulated.

Middle Age: Middle age is typically described as the late thirties or forties through the early sixties. It may involve reflection on life's achievements, changes in career or family dynamics, and physical changes.

Old Age: Old age is the later stage of life, usually beginning in the sixties or seventies and continuing into one's eighties and beyond. It's often marked by retirement, potential health challenges, and reflection on life's accomplishments.

End of Life: The final stage of the life cycle, the end of life, involves facing mortality and dying. It's a time of reflection, closure, and, potentially, preparing for the afterlife or addressing one's legacy.

It's important to note that the life cycle is not a one-size-fits-all model. People experience these stages differently based on culture, individual circumstances, and personal choices. Additionally, some individuals may experience unique life events or challenges that do not fit neatly into this linear progression. Nevertheless, the cycle of life provides a broad framework for understanding the typical phases of human existence and the transitions that occur throughout a person's journey.

The Cycle of Spending by Age and Generation

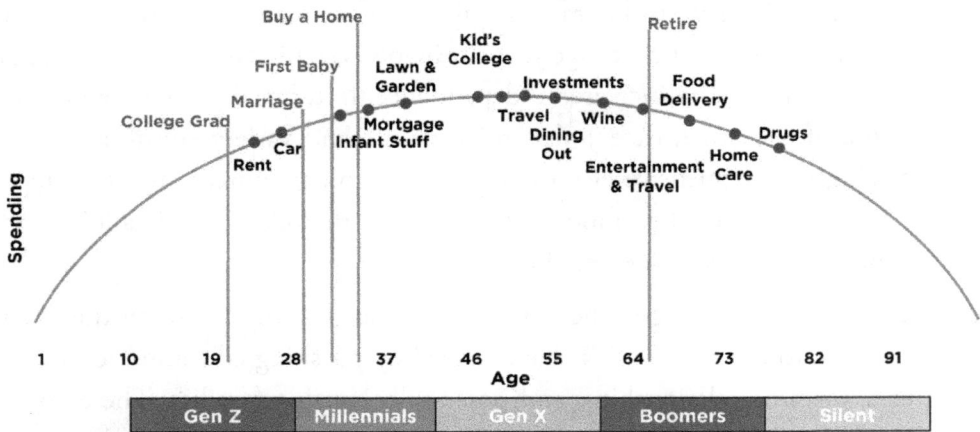

Source: Visa Business, Economic Insights, US Department of Labor

Work and Living

To be a consumer, you need some income. Generally, most people work to earn an income, unless they win the lottery or acquire funds through an inheritance or other means. In recent years, we have dramatically changed how we live, work, and consume.

While the number of hours worked on average hasn't seen a dramatic shift over the past twenty years, the nature of work has changed considerably. Work structure, content, and context have evolved due to technological advancements, economic shifts, and changes in worker preferences.

Technological progress, especially the rise of the internet, has led to digitizing many jobs and tasks that were previously manual or analog. This has resulted in significant changes in job content, with increased demand for tech-savvy professionals and a decrease in routine manual roles. Since the early 2000s, there has been a notable rise in digital entrepreneurship, with individuals leveraging platforms like Shopify to start online businesses, and the use of social media for marketing and influencer-driven income streams has become mainstream.

The work context has also shifted, with more people working remotely or from home, a trend that was already on the rise but was dramatically accelerated by the COVID-19 pandemic. This has altered where people work and how they work, with greater emphasis on flexible hours and work-life balance.

Furthermore, the gig economy has grown, characterized by short-term contracts or freelance work instead of permanent jobs.[173] While this has offered workers more autonomy and flexibility, it has also led to discussions about job security and benefits. Upwork's annual freelance study shows that 38 percent of the American workforce performed freelance work in 2023, up from only 20 percent in 2014.[174] Over 52 percent of all generation Z professionals performed freelance work.

Globalization has increased the interconnectedness of the world economy, leading companies to outsource and offshore various functions to different countries. This means that businesses are increasingly relocating their operations, such as manufacturing, customer service, and IT support, to regions where labor and production costs are lower. As a result, economic shifts in one part of the world can have a significant impact on businesses and consumers in another, creating a more complex and interdependent global economic landscape than ever before. This has changed the types of jobs available in various regions and has profoundly impacted manufacturing and service industries.

Despite these changes in the type of work, average work hours in many developed countries have remained relatively stable, partly due to labor regulations and cultural norms that limit the working week.[175] However, there's been an increase in "overwork" among certain professions, due to connectivity enabling constant access to work-related communications.[176]

Today, we live in a hybrid world with a blend of physical and online activities like shopping, communicating, working, learning, and socializing. Unsurprisingly, the hybrid experience is more pronounced among gen Z and millennials, who will continue to drive the global economy as they age.

Online shopping, digital banking, remote work, and virtual events have become the norm. A report from IBM indicates that the pandemic has accelerated the shift toward e-commerce by roughly five years.[177] Online shopping saw a massive surge during the pandemic, and this trend continues in our hybrid environment.

The pandemic also heightened awareness of how we live physically and psychologically. Consumers today are more conscious of their physical health, mental health, and hygiene practices. Safety and security have become a priority in how and where we live as we appreciate and value outdoor spaces.[178] We have become "mindful" consumers, with wellness products and services surpassing $450 billion in America and set to grow by 5 percent annually. Six significant trends continue to grow: health, fitness, nutrition, appearance, sleep, and mindfulness. It's fair to say that wellness starts to feel important as we age, but millennials are currently driving health and wellness trends.[179]

The pandemic and climate change have also heightened awareness about the world we live in. More consumers are considering the environmental impact of their purchases and favoring brands that demonstrate commitment to sustainability. According to a report from Capgemini Research Institute, 79 percent of consumers are changing their purchase preferences based on social responsibility, inclusiveness, or environmental impact.[180]

The disrupted supply chains and distribution channels during the pandemic alerted consumers to our global interdependencies and the need to seek new brand alternatives from anywhere and locally. For example, over 52 percent of consumers purchased from new brands during the pandemic because of inventory issues, prices, and greater convenience.[181] Brand loyalty is not what it used to be. Younger generations in particular aren't as brand loyal as they switch to other brands that offer better value and better service, and are more experience-based than transactional.

There's been a surge in support for local businesses as consumers recognize the impact of their spending on their local economy. This trend might continue as communities work together to recover from the economic effects of the pandemic. In a survey by Nextdoor, 91 percent of participants said they support small, local businesses, and 78 percent shop at, patronize, or hire a local business at least once a month.[182]

Before the pandemic, over 87 percent of employers had most or all employees working from an office. In 2022, the EY Future Workplace Index showed that just 29 percent of companies have employees working exclusively from the office.[183] This means 70 percent of employees work in a hybrid model. Educational institutions have also followed a similar pattern of offering a combination of in-person, face-to-face classroom instruction and online learning. The convenience, accessibility, and quality of online classes have continued to grow. Coursera, a central online learning platform, has seen online enrollment surge since 2016 from 26 million students to 189 million in 2021.[184] The highest growth rate in new learners came from emerging economies like those in Paraguay, Lebanon, Philippines, Guyana, and Indonesia, where face-to-face education opportunities are often too expensive or not readily available. Access to high-quality online learning is a game-changer for many people, especially in a fast-changing world where technologies, AI, automation, and e-commerce continue to disrupt labor markets.

More than ever, brands must be faster, agile, digital, innovative, and customer-centric. Emerging customer-centric business models provide ongoing value, personalizing experiences or facilitating user connections. They require a deep understanding of customer needs and behaviors based on data and the ability to adapt quickly to behavior and attitude changes. Here are a few examples:

Direct-to-Consumer (D2C) Models: Brands like Warby Parker, Dollar Shave Club, and Casper have bypassed traditional retail channels to sell directly to consumers. This allows them to control the entire customer experience, from product creation to post-purchase service.

Subscription-Based Models: Brands like Netflix, Dollar Shave Club, and Spotify offer their services on a subscription basis, providing continuous value to customers. This model is designed around understanding and catering to customers' ongoing needs.

Freemium Models: Brands like Dropbox, Canva, and LinkedIn offer essential services for free, with the option for users to pay for premium features. This model centers on attracting a large user base and converting some into paying customers.

Personalization Models: Brands like Stitch Fix and Spotify use data and AI to personalize their offerings. By understanding individual customer preferences, they can tailor their products or services to each user.

Community-Based Models: Brands like Airbnb, TikTok, and Etsy are built around communities of users. They facilitate exchanges between users and rely on user-generated content or services.

Service-Dominant Logic Models: Brands like IBM, Michelin, and Rolls-Royce have shifted from selling products to selling solutions or outcomes. For example, IBM works closely with its clients to understand their needs and provide customized solutions rather than off-the-shelf products. Instead of selling jet engines, Rolls-Royce sells "engine hours," and Michelin charges customers per mile driven rather than selling them tires outright.

18 | ADVOCATES, AMPLIFIERS, AND BELIEVERS

The roles of advocates, amplifiers, and believers are pivotal in creating a strong brand identity. These groups form the backbone of any successful brand strategy, driving customer engagement, loyalty, and brand growth. Understanding their differences, their importance, and how to cultivate these relationships is crucial for any business aiming to build a robust and influential brand.

Advocates

Advocates are individuals or entities that actively promote your brand. They are loyal customers who use your products or services and speak positively about them to others. They can be employees, influencers, or satisfied customers who voluntarily endorse your brand. Advocates are essential because they provide authentic and credible endorsements that can enhance your brand's reputation. They also help attract new customers through word-of-mouth, which is considered one of the most effective forms of advertising.

Providing excellent customer service and quality products or services that exceed expectations is essential to cultivating advocates. Encourage customer reviews and testimonials, reward loyal customers with exclusive offers or loyalty programs, and engage with them regularly through social media or newsletters. Here are some tangible examples of how you can create brand advocates:

Customer Service: Zappos, the online shoe and clothing retailer, is famous for its exceptional customer service. The company goes above and beyond to ensure customer satisfaction, and there have been instances where customer service representatives spent hours on the phone with a customer. This level of dedication turns customers into advocates who willingly promote Zappos to their networks.

Loyalty Programs: Starbucks's rewards program is a perfect example of turning customers into advocates. By offering free drinks, birthday rewards, and exclusive member events, Starbucks incentivizes customers to make repeat purchases and share their experiences with others, thus promoting the brand.

User-Generated Content: GoPro encourages customers to share videos captured with its camera. The best ones are shared on GoPro's social media channels and even in its advertising. This enables customers to interact with the brand and turns them into advocates as they share their GoPro-created content with their networks.

Product Development: Some companies involve customers in new product development. Lego Ideas, for example, is a community-based platform where fans can submit designs for new Lego sets. If a design gets enough support from the community, it can be turned into an actual product. This involvement in product development creates a sense of ownership among customers, turning them into strong advocates for the brand.

Recognition: Dropbox has a referral program that rewards users with extra storage space for every friend they refer who signs up for the service. This incentivizes users to share Dropbox with others and recognizes and rewards their advocacy efforts.

Community: Harley-Davidson has cultivated a strong community of brand advocates through its Harley Owners Group (H.O.G.). Members of H.O.G. receive exclusive benefits and the opportunity to connect with other Harley-Davidson enthusiasts, fostering a sense of belonging and advocacy for the brand.

Amplifiers

Amplifiers, however, *magnify* the reach of your brand's message. They may not necessarily use your product or service, but they share, retweet, or repost your content, increasing its visibility. Amplifiers can be social media influencers, bloggers, or individuals with a significant online presence and following. Amplifiers play a crucial role in improving your brand's visibility and reach. In our digital world where information overload is common, amplifiers help your brand stand out and reach potential customers who may not have been accessible through traditional marketing channels.

Amplifiers can be fostered by creating engaging, shareable content. This includes high-quality blogs, infographics, videos, or social media posts that provide value to the user. Collaborating with influencers or bloggers can also help in reaching a larger audience. Here are some actual examples of how to build brand amplifiers:

Influencer Partnerships: Fashion Nova, an online clothing brand, has built a massive following by partnering with influencers on social media platforms like 21.6 million followers on Instagram and 4 million followers on TikTok. The influencers wear Fashion Nova's clothing in their posts and tag the brand, amplifying its reach to their large followings.

Social Media Contests: Airbnb runs a successful contest called "Airbnb Experiences," where hosts share unique stories about their experiences. By asking hosts to share these stories on their social media with a specific hashtag, #Airbnb significantly amplifies its brand reach.

Employee Advocacy Programs: Dell's employee advocacy program, "Dell Champions," encourages employees to share brand content on their personal social media accounts. With training and guidelines provided by Dell, employees become trusted brand amplifiers.

Believers

Believers are individuals who trust in the value and promise of your brand. They may not actively promote or amplify your brand, but their belief in your product or service is unwavering. These are typically long-term customers who have a deep emotional connection with your brand. Believers are the bedrock of your customer base. Their steadfast faith in your brand provides stability and consistent revenue. They also contribute to building a positive brand image, as their belief often stems from positive experiences with your brand.

Believers can be nurtured by consistently delivering on your brand promise and maintaining a robust customer-centric approach. Regular communication, personalized services, and acknowledgment of their feedback can help strengthen their belief in your brand. Here are some examples of cultivating brand believers:

Consistent Quality and Innovation: Apple has built a legion of brand believers through consistently delivering high-quality, innovative products. Customers trust that every new product will be cutting-edge and reliable, reinforcing their belief in the brand.

Transparent Practices: Clothing company Everlane has committed to "Radical Transparency," providing detailed cost breakdowns (materials, hardware, labor, duties, transport) and information about the factories where its clothes are made. It also includes a robust review section with proper sizing and verified comments and scores. This transparency builds trust and turns customers into believers.

Community: Fitness company Peloton has built a strong community of believers through its interactive platform, where users can join live classes, compete with others, and share their progress on social media. This sense of community fosters a strong belief in the brand.

After-Sales Service: Amazon has won the trust of millions of customers worldwide through its hassle-free return policy and responsive customer service. This commitment to customer satisfaction post-purchase builds belief in the brand.

Purpose: Patagonia, an outdoor clothing company, is well-known for its environmental activism as a purpose-driven brand. By staying true to its mission and values, Patagonia has built a base of believers who align with the brand's purpose.

Actionable Steps

Advocates, amplifiers, and believers contribute to brand visibility and credibility and provide a stable customer base that can drive consistent growth. By understanding customers' differences, recognizing their importance, and implementing strategies to cultivate relationships with them, businesses can build a robust and influential brand that resonates with its audience. Here are some tactics you can apply to start cultivating your brand advocates, amplifiers, and believers:

Loyalty Rewards: Implement a loyalty program that rewards brand advocates with exclusive benefits, encouraging continued support and promotion of your brand.

Influencer Collaborations: Partner with influencers who share your brand's values, leveraging their reach to engage with potential amplifiers and broaden your audience.

Social Media Planning: Develop a social media content calendar to consistently publish engaging content that resonates with amplifiers and encourages them to share your message.

Customer Feedback Loop: Conduct regular surveys to understand customer needs and preferences, using insights to improve your products or services and reinforce the commitment of your believers.

Tailored Engagement: Personalize your communications with customers to make them feel uniquely valued and appreciated, fostering a deeper connection with your brand.

19 | REPORTERS, PODCASTERS, AND ASSOCIATIONS

Reporters

Building a relationship with a media reporter can be a strategic move for a company seeking free publicity. While everyone wants to see their brand projected positively on ABC's *Good Morning America* or the *Wall Street Journal* newsfeed, this expectation might be unachievable for most brands. Still, many smaller news outlets and channels are always seeking new and fresh stories, especially local ones.

Even if you have an incredible story to tell, it might not be easy to grab the attention of a local reporter. First, start by doing your homework to better understand the reporters who might be interested in your industry and product or service area. Read their past articles to understand their interests and style.

Once you have narrowed down a list of potential reporters, find a way to connect with them. Sending a cold email isn't generally the most successful route. Seek them on social channels like LinkedIn and X (formally Twitter). Follow and engage with them by sharing their articles, providing thoughtful comments, and joining conversations they're interested in. Check your network to see if anyone is directly connected with them and if they are willing and able to introduce you directly.

If possible, arrange to meet with them for a quick coffee chat or phone call. Be prepared to share your expertise and relevant story ideas that are newsworthy and would benefit your audience. Do not try to sell your product or service. (We'll talk more about news releases and media pitches in Part Four: Brand Content).

Like in any relationship, you must build credibility and trust, which takes time. Remember, building relationships with reporters is about providing value and being a reliable source. Don't expect to see results overnight. Be patient and keep working at it. Eventually, you will start to see results.

It's not just about getting publicity for your brand; it's about establishing a mutually beneficial relationship that can result in positive coverage over time. If a reporter does write about your business, be sure to thank them. This will show that you appreciate their time and effort and make them more likely to write about your business again.

Podcasters

Podcasts have become a popular medium for content consumption. Being a guest on a popular podcast that caters to your target audience is an excellent and free way to promote your brand. Like when you pitch a media reporter, you need to hone in on specific topics, offering valuable information or expert insights that interest the audience. Here are three examples of business leaders sharing their brand stories on a podcast:

Second Life **podcast with Hillary Kerr:** In 2019, Kendra Scott, founder of Kendra Scott LLC, a jewelry company, shared her brand story. Scott discussed how she started her business with just $500 in her spare bedroom and grew it into a billion-dollar company. The exposure from the podcast helped increase brand recognition and drive sales for her jewelry line.

How I Built This, **hosted by Guy Raz**: In 2016, Spanx founder Sara Blakely was a guest on NPR's *How I Built This*, where she shared how she built her company from scratch. Her appearance helped to promote the Spanx brand and inspire other entrepreneurs.

The GaryVee Audio Experience: This popular podcast, hosted by entrepreneur Gary Vaynerchuk, has featured a multitude of founders and CEOs across various industries, such as Mark Zuckerberg, co-founder and CEO of Facebook; Jack Dorsey, co-founder and past CEO of Twitter (now called X) and Square; Satya Nadella, CEO of Microsoft; and Daniel Ek, co-founder and CEO of Spotify. Their appearances helped promote their brands, position their innovations, and put a human face to them.

Partnerships

More and more companies are partnering with other brands to leverage each other's customer base. Brand partnerships can be a very effective way to reach new customers, increase brand awareness, and generate sales.

There are many reasons that brand partnerships are so prevalent. First, they can help brands reach a wider audience. When two brands partner, they combine their customer bases, giving them both access to a new group of potential customers who might not have been aware of their brand.

Second, brand partnerships can help to increase brand awareness. When two well-known brands partner, it creates a lot of buzz and attention, providing more awareness and making them more memorable.

Third, brand partnerships can generate sales. When two brands partner, they can offer their customers something they might not be able to provide on their own, creating a sense of urgency and excitement and increasing sales.

Such partnerships can take the form of co-marketing initiatives, product collaborations, or long-term strategic alliances. Here are some tangible examples:

Spotify and Starbucks: In 2015, Spotify and Starbucks entered a multi-year partnership. Spotify curated Starbucks's music, allowing Starbucks customers to influence in-store playlists through the Starbucks Mobile App. This allowed Spotify to reach Starbucks's extensive customer base and gave Starbucks an innovative way to enhance its in-store experience.

GoPro and Red Bull: GoPro, the action camera company, and Red Bull, the energy drink brand, have a long-standing partnership based on their shared interest in extreme sports. They co-sponsor events and athletes, and GoPro provides the equipment to capture high-adrenaline moments. This partnership allows both brands to reach each other's audiences and reinforces their shared brand message of adventure and high performance.

ASOS and GLAAD: Online fashion retailer ASOS partnered with GLAAD, an LGBTQ+ advocacy group, to collaborate on a clothing line. Sales from this line support GLAAD's initiatives. This partnership allows ASOS to reach GLAAD's audience and aligns both brands around a message of inclusivity.

If you're considering partnering with another brand, choosing a partner that's a good fit for your brand and can help you achieve your goals is essential.

Associations

Joining a well-respected industry organization can enhance your brand's credibility and reputation. It signals to customers, competitors, and suppliers that your company adheres to the standards and best practices set by the association. It also provides networking opportunities at conferences, meetings, events, and seminars with other industry professionals, leading to partnerships, collaborations, talent acquisition, and new business opportunities. Associations can provide resources like research reports, webinars, and training programs to help your company stay informed about industry trends, regulatory changes, and innovative practices. Industry associations often advocate for the interests of their members at the local, state, or national level. They can influence policies and regulations that directly affect your business. Associations often feature their members in directories, newsletters, on their website, or at their events, which can increase your brand's visibility within the industry and lead to new business opportunities.

For example, a tech start-up joining an association like the Technology Services Industry Association (TSIA) can benefit from networking opportunities with potential partners or clients, access the latest industry research, and enhance its credibility by aligning with a recognized organization. Similarly, a food company joining the National Restaurant Association could benefit from advocacy efforts around food regulations, participate in significant industry events, and gain visibility among potential clients in the restaurant industry.

Suppliers

Suppliers and distributors can play an essential role in helping to build a brand. Here are a few ways they can help:

Quality Control: Suppliers and distributors can help maintain the brand's reputation by ensuring the quality of the products or services they supply and giving customers a consistently positive experience.

Inventory Management: Suppliers and distributors can help minimize disruptions and maintain the brand's availability to customers by carefully managing inventory levels and ensuring that products are always in stock.

Marketing Support: Suppliers and distributors can help promote a brand by providing marketing materials, participating in joint marketing initiatives, and leveraging their marketing channels to reach new customers.

Customer Service: Suppliers and distributors can help build a positive reputation for the brand and foster customer loyalty by providing excellent customer service and responding to customer inquiries and complaints promptly and effectively.

Logistics Support: By efficiently managing logistics and ensuring that products are delivered to customers in a timely and cost-effective manner, suppliers and distributors can help minimize operational costs and enhance the overall customer experience.

Communities

Beyond everyone associated with your business, products, and service, there is a physical community where your brand calls home. It could be brick-and-mortar retail space, a manufacturing center, a warehouse, an office, or a mailing address. How a brand treats its hometown reflects its values and can significantly impact its public image and reputation. It also shows how much you value your employees, families, and neighbors. Like a customer strategy, you need a community strategy that actively engages with the local community by listening to their needs, investing and collaborating with local organizations, and supporting community events and initiatives. Your community involvement should be compatible with your business footprint based on economic contribution, environmental and social impact, applicable laws and regulations, and cultural and social needs.

Overall, a brand's responsibility in a community goes beyond profit-making. It involves being a good corporate citizen, making positive contributions, and aligning its actions with the values and needs of its community. Remember, a brand's reputation in a community can significantly impact its success. By fulfilling these responsibilities, a brand can build trust and loyalty with consumers, improve its public image, and ultimately enhance its bottom line.

BRAND COMMUNITY SUMMARY

In essence, a brand community lies not merely in the transactional exchanges between a company and its customers but in the shared values and beliefs that bind all stakeholders together. A truly inclusive brand considers and involves all stakeholders in its ecosystem, including employees, suppliers, distributors, partners, and advocates. A brand that successfully cultivates a sense of belonging and purpose among these groups can expect a robust and enduring loyalty that transcends generational divides.

To forge such a community, a strategic approach is paramount—one that prioritizes the needs, interests, and values of the "who" in the brand equation. This strategy must be rooted in a commitment that resonates with the community's ethos, offering compelling reasons to align with the brand's vision. The role of employees is particularly pivotal; they are not just workers but the foremost ambassadors of your brand. Their engagement and advocacy can significantly amplify your brand's reputation and reach.

Studies have repeatedly shown that employees who are engaged and believe in their company's mission are more likely to become powerful brand advocates. Conversely, disengagement can lead to negative perceptions and diminished brand value. Therefore, brands need to foster a culture that nurtures engagement through recognition, empowerment, and opportunities for growth and development.

In practice, this means creating interactive platforms for engagement, building personal relationships with community members, encouraging co-creation and innovation, fostering a sense of belonging, and continuously seeking feedback to refine and enhance the brand experience.

Ultimately, the strength of a brand community is a testament to the company's commitment to its people—recognizing that the brand is genuinely owned by those who believe in it and advocate for it. By investing in these relationships and cultivating a culture of trust, collaboration, and shared purpose, brands can achieve temporary success and enduring greatness.

Avoid transactional relationships and create more collaborative and engaging partnerships by focusing on the following actions:

Foster Interaction and Engagement: Encourage members of your brand community to engage with each other and your brand. This could be through social media, forums, live events, or other channels.

Nurture Relationships: Build strong, personal relationships with members of your brand community. Respond to their questions, address their concerns, and celebrate their successes.

Encourage Co-creation: Involve members of your brand community in creating and evolving your brand. This could be through crowdsourcing, beta testing, or other forms of collaboration.

Foster a Sense of Belonging: Make members of your brand community feel like they are part of something bigger than themselves. Celebrate their achievements, recognize their contributions, and create a sense of belonging and community.

Continuously Listen and Learn: Stay attuned to the needs and preferences of your brand community. Always gather feedback to improve your brand and the experiences you offer to your community.

By following these steps, you can create a strong brand community that is engaged, loyal, and committed to your brand and its success.

To begin developing a strategic framework for cultivating a strong, engaged, and loyal brand community, consider these thought-provoking questions:

- Who are the core members of the brand community, including customers, employees, suppliers, distributors, stakeholders, and advocates?
- What shared values and beliefs does the brand embody that can resonate with the community?
- How can you effectively communicate the brand's values and mission to all community members?
- In what ways can you encourage interaction and engagement among community members?
- Which platforms are most suitable for fostering community engagement? (Refer to Part Four for more on content)
- How can you nurture strong and personal relationships with each brand community member?
- What feedback mechanisms can you implement to ensure your brand is responsive to the community's needs and concerns?
- How can you involve community members in the co-creation and evolution of the brand?
- What incentives can you offer to motivate community members to participate and engage actively?
- How can you measure the success of the brand community in terms of loyalty, advocacy, and growth?
- What strategies can you employ to ensure the long-term sustainability of the brand community?

- How can your approach to community building be adapted as the brand and its audience evolve?
- What potential challenges exist in managing a diverse brand community, and how can you address them?
- How can you leverage ideas and insights from the community to drive innovation within the brand?
- What are the best practices for recognizing and celebrating the contributions of community members?

Part Four

BRAND CONTENT
THE WHERE

"Content is king."
—Bill Gates, co-founder, Microsoft

Content is only king if you know "what" you will communicate and "where," to ensure you have the right message for the right customer or client at the right time. This isn't a single moment but multiple touchpoints. A customer or client touchpoint is anytime a customer engages with your brand, which can come through advertising, "out-of-home" signs and billboards, a retail environment, media or news articles/broadcasts, emails, apps, social media, word-of-mouth, a call center or helpline, a sales call, product packaging, giveaways, sponsorships, partners, blogs, podcasts, forums, influencers, employees, websites, bots, and reviews. That's a long list and I've surely missed some, but you understand the point I'm trying to make. While these touchpoints have various degrees of influence, collectively they help define your brand experience. To better understand and manage these touchpoints, it is essential to understand the various communication channels by exploring their unique branding opportunities, and evaluate their effectiveness in reaching and engaging your target audience.

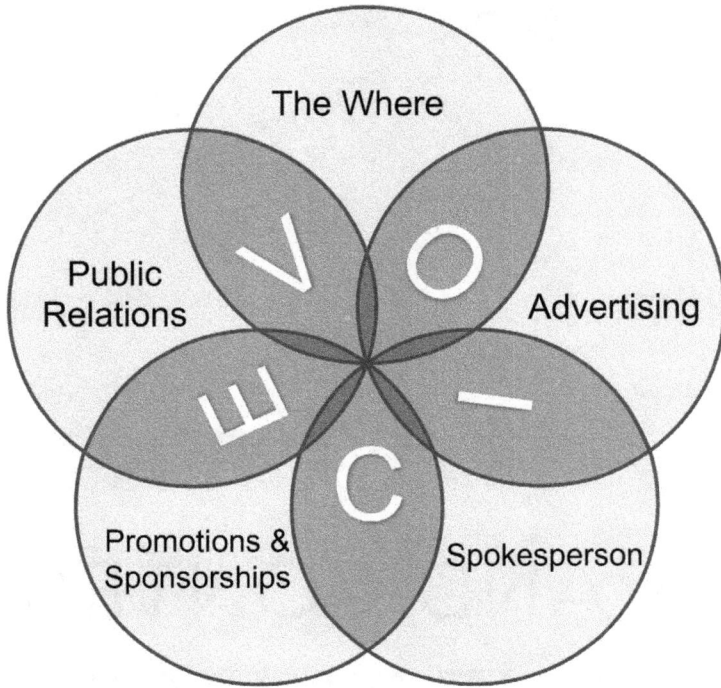

20 | BRAND VOICE

YOUR VACATION STARTS BEFORE THE VACATION

You decide to go on a vacation. You're considering a winter escape to the Caribbean, because you fondly recall an advertisement that showed a sand snowman on a pristine beach with emerald waters and a sunny blue sky. Naturally, your first step is to go online to explore your options. You visit travel websites like Expedia, American Airlines Vacations, Kayak, or Hotels.com, where you peruse various destinations, hotels, and beaches. You view photos, read reviews, and compare prices.

While researching, you remember a podcast where the host raved about Cancun's incredible sandy beaches and friendly people, drawing your attention to this destination and its associated travel deals. You start bookmarking a few places of interest and travel deals that expire by the end of the month.

The next day, during your train ride to work, you browse TikTok and Instagram using #Cancun to watch videos and photos. You eventually close the app, not wanting others around you to think you have a foot fetish (you've been viewing an awful lot of beach feet!). During a break at work, you excitedly share with your colleagues that you're considering a winter trip to Cancun. A respected colleague across the boardroom table shares her recent experience at a fantastic place in Cancun, praising the friendly and helpful staff and the lost earrings they found in her room. She enthusiastically offers advice on where to find cool Mexican art, discusses the excellent restaurants, and even suggests an affordable Mexican wine at the hotel's Italian restaurant. You leave the conversation eager to check out the hotel she spoke of.

On your subway ride home, there's a large banner ad enveloping the entire interior of the car. It features pale yellow sand, blue-green waves, a brilliant deep blue sky, and a festive CANCUN logo. Your social media feed shows you more feet on beaches and vacation options. Your excitement intensifies, and you can't wait to get home to start packing!

That night, you discover that your colleague's suggestion is one of the hotels you had already shortlisted. You feel like it's meant to be. You delve deeper into the reviews, examining the descriptors, costs, flight schedules, and fine print. You're thrilled to share with your colleague that you are officially booked and seek more insights.

In the following weeks, you receive several emails from the travel company and the hotel to help you prepare for your trip, including a link to an exclusive mobile app for the hotel. This app offers a list of things to do at the resort, including a calendar of daily activities like beach yoga at 7:00 a.m. (though you're skeptical about that). It also features an enticing selection of day trips and adventures you can conveniently book through the app, even making reservations at the Italian restaurant. You're growing fonder and fonder of the place, and you haven't even set foot on the property yet.

Word-of-Mouth

Word-of-mouth or word-of-social is one of the most potent forms of marketing because it is based on personal recommendations and experiences. People are more likely to trust and believe in recommendations from friends, family, and other people they know and respect rather than advertisements and other forms of traditional marketing.

From a marketing perspective, word-of-mouth refers to the informal, personal communication between individuals about a product, service, or brand. This can include face-to-face conversations, phone calls, text messages, online forums, social media, blogs and podcasts, and other communication channels. Satisfied customers eager to recommend their experiences can drive brand awareness and consideration, generate leads and sales, and help build a positive brand reputation. Unsatisfied customers can also do the opposite, even faster.

Word-of-mouth is also vital because it can have a multiplier effect, as one person's recommendation can lead to many others being exposed to the product, service, or brand. Additionally, it can be a cost-effective form of marketing, as it relies on the collective efforts of a brand's customers and fans rather than on paid advertising. Jay Baer, in his book *Talk Triggers,* says no brand should leave word-of-mouth to chance, that it's important to understand the psychological triggers that influence people to talk about your brand. Think about it. When do you talk about a brand? When it disappoints you, yes, and also when it over-delivers—especially when someone goes out of their way to help you when you least expected it. Word-of-mouth is very often driven by delivering something extra to make someone feel special. Baer calls these moments *talk triggers*, and says they must be remarkable, relevant, reasonable, and repeatable. He points out several natural triggers that generate positive conversation, like a brand being extra human and likable, delivering more value than expected, going out of its way, and being responsive and quick with an infectious, optimistic attitude.[185]

Another great way to get people talking about your brand is through accessible media, which includes influencers, bloggers, podcasters, journalists, and anyone with an audience—preferably your target audience—who reads, listens, or watches them. This is the power of public relations. All you need is to get Oprah Winfrey to "like" your brand, and your brand will become a bestseller in no time. Reporters might showcase your business, product, or service locally, regionally, nationally, or internationally, depending on your unique story.

While word-of-mouth and public relations are still the most influential ways to create brand awareness, you can't rely on others to always say nice things that will resonate with your branding goals. A comprehensive branding strategy should include a mix of marketing channels and tactics, such as advertising, content marketing, social media marketing, and customer service, to ensure that your brand message is consistently communicated across all touchpoints.

By leveraging the power of word-of-mouth and public relations, while also investing in other marketing channels, you can build a strong, recognizable brand that resonates with your target audience and drives long-term success for your business.

Brand Voice Channels

TRADITIONAL   DITITAL

Brick & Mortar   Packaging   Website
Television   Social Media
Word-of-Mouth   Search Advertising
Print & OOH   Social Media Advertising
                    BRAND
                    VOICE
Events & Promotions   Other Digital Media
Sponsorships   Online Audio
Spokesperson   Reviews
Awards & Recognition   Radio   Influencer

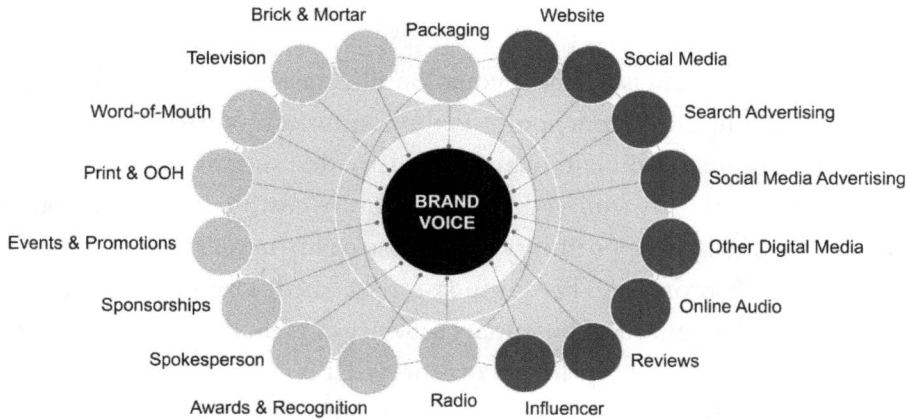

While the extent of the channel options can hurt your head, it's the message that's critical—tell a story that resonates with your audience and makes a memorable emotional connection. To help navigate this jungle of channel opportunities, let's start with a simple formula to demonstrate the brand value of each touchpoint and channel to build brand loyalty successfully. It's called the Brand Loyalty Formula.

21 | BRAND LOYALTY FORMULA

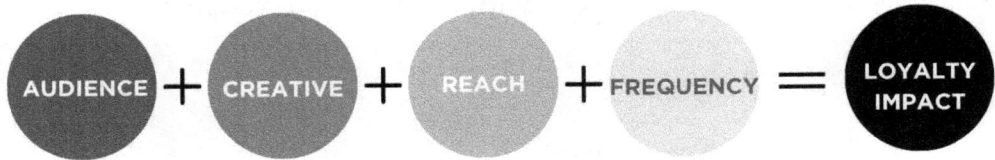

AUDIENCE + CREATIVE + REACH + FREQUENCY = LOYALTY IMPACT

The Brand Loyalty Formula is a simple equation illustrating the essential components of every communication touchpoint in the consumer's journey. While advertising and marketing are prominent, many other activities, such as word-of-mouth, must be considered from a branding perspective. Every customer communication touchpoint or channel is an opportunity to increase or maintain brand loyalty and reconfirm the brand's promise. This formula can be used with every channel to remind you to consider your ideal potential customer or archetype (AUDIENCE), then captivate them with compelling content (CREATIVE) that emotionally attaches the brand to their lifestyle by leveraging various communication channels (REACH) over some time (FREQUENCY) to create positive brand awareness. It's important to treat this as a living formula, conducting continuous measuring and analysis of the effectiveness of your brand awareness efforts, and refining the various components continuously based on insights and feedback. Let's break down the formula and look at each component.

Audience

Your target audience is the specific group of individuals you aim to reach with your communications, such as public relations, advertising, or promotional efforts. These individuals are identified as the most likely to be interested in your product, service, or message, and therefore the most likely to become customers or users.

The target audience is often defined using a variety of parameters, which can be categorized into four main types:

Demographic Parameters: These are statistical aspects of a population, such as age, gender, income level, education level, marital status, occupation, and ethnicity. For example, a men's athletic deodorant brand might target males between the ages of sixteen and thirty-five who live in urban and suburban areas across the country with middle- to upper-middle-class income levels.

Psychographic Parameters: These involve the personality traits, values, attitudes, interests, and lifestyles of your audience. For instance, the men's deodorant might target young men who value an active, fitness-conscious lifestyle, sports enthusiasts, and outdoor adventurers.

Geographic Parameters: These involve the physical location of the audience. This can be as broad as targeting an entire country or as specific as targeting a neighborhood within a city. For example, the men's deodorant brand could target young men in all US cities that have an NFL football team.

Behavioral Parameters: These involve understanding the audience's behavior in terms of their purchasing habits, usage rates, brand interactions, and other actions related to the product or service. For instance, the men's deodorant brand might target young men who are willing to pay a premium for products that meet their needs and enhance their active lifestyle. These men might shop online or at sports/health stores. They might frequently use social media channels like Instagram, TikTok, and YouTube. They are likely heavy consumers of sports channels and TV networks like ESPN and Fox Sports.

Understanding the target audience is crucial in building brand loyalty because it informs your selection of channels, your creation of messages and content, and the timing and frequency of your advertising efforts. The goal is to optimize reach and engagement with your target audience while maximizing the efficiency of your marketing spend.

Creative

Creating a positive brand impression that is memorable, compelling, and deeply personal is the ultimate goal of any message. Artists, sculptors, and film directors can struggle for years before they create a masterpiece that speaks to an audience. The creativity required to communicate a brand's essence is almost equal to that of any other art form.

It doesn't matter what medium you use, whether visual, audio, or print; creating something extraordinary takes creativity and effort. A study by Project Apollo discovered that 65 percent of a brand's sales lift from advertising came from the creative.[186] In 2017, NCSolutions, a data-driven consulting firm that helps brands optimize their advertising campaigns, developed *5 Keys to Advertising Effectiveness,* which they updated in 2023. "Creative" was the most significant key in the original study, driving nearly 50 percent of incremental sales.[187]

Creativity is essential because it allows us to deliver messages in new and innovative ways. It can also help us to connect with others on a deeper level. A creative message can be as simple as a few words (e.g., "Just Do It"), a pervasive sound (such as the Intel inside chime), a color (like a pink ribbon), or a captivating image that connects to a human need or want. It's the sweet spot where the brand becomes relevant.

A well-crafted and innovative message can generate buzz, word-of-mouth, and social media sharing, further amplifying brand awareness. The creativity of the message is essential in building brand awareness. A creative and compelling message can capture consumers' attention, differentiate the brand from competitors, and leave a lasting impression. It helps to create a strong brand identity and build an emotional connection with the target audience. Don't underestimate the power of creativity and effort. Creativity is crucial in effectively communicating the brand's values, offerings, and personality to increase brand recognition and recall among consumers.

Reach

Without reaching your target audience, you have little hope that your creative work will impact them. Reach is the total number of unique individuals or households exposed to a branding message over a specific duration. In a campaign, a particular communications channel or multiple channels could create a cumulative reach. The better your understanding of your target audience, determined by demographics, interests, behaviors, geographic location, etc., the more effective and efficient the reach. The more precise your targeting, the easier it becomes to determine the best channel(s) based on your budget. While mass television has the most potential reach, social media has the most significant *targeted* reach. The perfect reach is achieved through a multi-channel approach that combines a variety of touchpoints with a relevant creative message at the right time.

Everything a brand does and says that reaches a customer adds to the brand experience positively or negatively. This includes interactions with employees, advertising, packaging, websites, retail/office spaces, and word-of-mouth. When you reach out to consumers, you do so for several reasons:

- Build on customer relationships and transactions
- Improve customer engagement and retention
- Reinforce brand image and share of voice (SOV)
- Reach potential new or lapsed customers

Reach is a function of your budget. A small budget means a smaller potential reach. With a smaller budget, the creative becomes critically important—the more compelling the content, the greater the chance that the creative will drive the reach. Consumers love to share great creativity. Having a campaign go viral is golden. However, it's truly an exception, and not something you can plan for when determining the reach of a campaign.

The association between potential brand reach and budget size can vary depending on several factors. In general, having a larger budget can often provide more opportunities for a brand to reach a wider audience through marketing and advertising efforts. A larger budget allows for more extensive and frequent campaigns through a multi-channel approach, which is beneficial and necessary in today's fragmented media landscape. It enables companies to reach their target audience more effectively and efficiently, leading to better engagement, higher conversion rates, and increased loyalty.

However, it's important to note that a smaller budget doesn't necessarily mean a brand can't succeed in reaching its target audience. In fact, having a limited budget can often lead to more creative and innovative marketing strategies. Startups and smaller brands with tight budgets can leverage cost-effective channels such as social media, content marketing, and grassroots campaigns to build brand awareness and engage with their audience.

By focusing on creating high-quality, shareable content and fostering genuine connections with their customers, smaller brands can generate organic word-of-mouth marketing, which can be just as powerful as paid advertising. Additionally, by targeting niche audiences and leveraging influencer partnerships, startups can maximize their budget's impact and reach the right people with their message.

Ultimately, while a larger budget can provide more opportunities for brand reach, a smaller budget can still be effective when coupled with creativity, authenticity, and a deep understanding of the target audience.

Frequency

Frequency is the optimal number of times a consumer should see, hear, or interact with a message for it to be effective. The number of times can vary widely depending on the context, the relevance, the complexity of the message, the target audience, and the specific branding objectives. If the creative is brilliant, maybe only one time is enough, as with the infamous "1984" Apple commercial that ran once during Super Bowl XVIII. However, a long-standing rule in advertising is the

"Rule of 7," which suggests that a consumer needs to be exposed to a message at least seven times before it is firmly set in their mind. This is generally referred to as message awareness, where the consumer is aware of an advertisement and has formed an impression—hopefully a positive one.

This rule isn't universally applicable, especially in the digital world where consumers are exposed to overwhelming amounts of content daily. Some studies suggest that even a lower frequency, like three to five impressions, can be effective for brand recall.

The consumer's mindset and context are critical factors in the effectiveness of a marketing message. The environment in which the consumer receives the message, whether passive or active, can significantly impact how they perceive and act on it.

It is also essential to consider the type of product or service you're selling. You might sell a high-involvement product that requires significant thought, research, and consideration from the consumer before making a purchase decision. These products are usually expensive, complex, or have a significant impact on the buyer's life or self-image, such as cars or houses. For this type of product, consumers need to see your message multiple times before they make a purchasing decision. On the other hand, if you're selling a low-involvement product, such as a candy bar or a soda, consumers may only need to see your message once before purchasing.

In a passive environment, such as when consumers are casually browsing social media or watching TV, they may not actively seek products or services. In this context, higher frequency can reinforce the message and keep the brand top-of-mind, as the consumer might not be fully attentive or receptive to the message at first glance.

On the other hand, in an active environment where the consumer is specifically seeking a solution or product, such as searching online for a book about branding, they are already in a receptive mindset. Here, the quality and relevance of the message become more important than the frequency. A well-targeted and compelling advertisement seen once at the right moment can prompt immediate action.

Monitoring engagement metrics and adjusting the frequency based on the response rate and other feedback is crucial in digital marketing. Overexposure can lead to ad fatigue and negative brand perception, so it's important to strike a balance.

The key is to balance frequency and relevance based on the consumer's mindset and the context of their interaction with the message.

Loyalty Impact

Brand loyalty starts with the first interaction with the brand, which could be the purchase transaction. Or, returning to the vacation example, the brand experience could start months before the actual purchase (and vacation) takes place. We often hear that it's the journey that matters, not the destination. The consumer's total experience determines their brand loyalty, which then manifests through active engagement, repeat business, positive recommendations, advocacy, and price insensitivity.

The essence of the Brand Loyalty Formula lies in its strategic orchestration of every communication touchpoint to build and maintain consumer allegiance. By intricately understanding and targeting the right audience with demographic, psychographic, geographic, and behavioral precision, you can craft resonant and emotionally compelling content. When disseminated through carefully selected channels to reach the audience with the right frequency, your creative messaging ensures that the brand captures attention and secures a place in the consumer's lifestyle and routine. The continuous cycle of measuring, analyzing, and refining based on feedback solidifies the relationship between your brand and your consumers, reinforcing brand promises and driving growth through unwavering loyalty.

22 | STOREFRONT

To have a brand presence, you need, at minimum, a webpage or social media profile. A brand needs a place to own its story, present why it exists, and allow customers to learn more or buy its products and services. Having just a brick-and-mortar store isn't enough (in fact, it's often not required at all), especially for younger generations who live in the digital universe.

Website

If you aren't online, your brand will be invisible. At a minimum, be sure to create a free Google Business Profile, which will allow you to manage the business listing that appears in Google Search and Maps, so customers can easily access your address, email address, phone number, website, hours of operation, and even photos.

A proper website, however, should be a no-brainer. Every brand needs a web presence, even if you are a brick-and-mortar brand. Beyond showcasing your products and services, a website allows you to tell your brand's story, generally on a "Who We Are" or "About Us" page. For many companies, the "Careers" section is the most viewed by potential new talent in determining whether your brand might be a good place to work. This is where you can tell them about your great culture, or better yet, have your employees tell them. Use that space to sell them on the benefits of working with your brand, and talk about what DE&I means for your organization. Include a "Sustainability" section and explain your environmental, social, and governance (ESG) strategy and corporate giving program, including concrete examples and results. You can also keep your audiences informed with a transparent "What's New" section with the last announcements, stories, and perspectives.

In today's market, a website is an essential tool for any business, digital or not. It serves as your brand's digital storefront, providing legitimacy and access to your brand. A social media presence is also important, but it isn't enough. Your brand doesn't own your followers and connections on social media platforms. The platform owns those contacts. A website is your business's online foundation, offering a controlled environment where you can present your brand narrative, showcase products or services, tell your brand story, and engage with customers. It's accessible around the clock, broadening your reach beyond local boundaries and traditional business hours.

To determine the type and complexity of your website, address the following questions:

- What is the primary purpose of the website?
- Who is the target audience?
- What content will be most effective in reaching and engaging this audience?
- How will the website design reflect the brand's identity?
- What functionality is necessary for meeting both business and user needs?
- Will your brand offer e-commerce, now or in the future?
- How much are you willing to spend on a website?

At a minimum, a website must provide clear information about the business, its products or services, contact information, and a user-friendly navigation system. The site should be either mobile-first or mobile-friendly.

Beyond the minimum requirements, you may also want to include other features on the site, such as a blog, a social media feed, or a customer support forum. Use a blog to share news and updates about the business and provide helpful information to the target audience. Connect a social media feed to the page, to connect and participate in a two-way conversation with current and potential customers. A customer support forum can help answer customer questions and provide support.

For the site to grow into a lead generator and sales funnel, it must incorporate search engine optimization (SEO) strategies to attract organic traffic, include lead-capture forms, integrate e-commerce capabilities, and offer valuable content that addresses customer needs and pain points.

You can hire a professional web designer/developer or do it yourself using website builders like Wix, GoDaddy, Shopify, Squarespace, or WordPress.

Social Media Profile

Having a social media presence is the bare minimum. A brand's presence on social media is not merely an extension of its identity; it is a vital conduit to its audience. Social platforms offer the ability for a brand to weave its narrative, engage in real-time dialogue, and foster a community around its ethos and offerings. The immediacy and interactivity of social media provide an unparalleled opportunity to build brand awareness, loyalty, and even advocacy without the traditional barriers of geography and time. Remember, no matter what social media channel or channels you decide to use to showcase your brand, it's only rented space and followers. Social media platforms come and go, and their algorithms are constantly changing. Building a brand presence on social media takes work, and your follower network can disappear in a second—ask those brands that built a following on the now-defunct Google+. With the actions taken by the US government to ban TikTok and the rebranding of Twitter as X, the future has become unpredictable for some platforms.

So, while social media profiles are indispensable in today's marketplace, they are just one facet of a comprehensive digital strategy. A dedicated website remains the sovereign territory of a brand's online presence—a hub where the controlled narrative, depth of content, and full spectrum of engagement coalesce. The digital storefront invites deeper exploration, offering a curated experience that social media alone cannot fully encompass. Thus, while social media profiles command attention and conversation, a website stands as the enduring bastion of a brand's digital existence, anchoring its presence in the vast expanse of the internet.

Brick-and-Mortar

Until Mark Zuckerberg creates a metaverse of a virtual or augmented-reality brand environment, the physical retail store will remain a considerable brand builder where the physical environment can stimulate all five senses. Within a brick-and-mortar setting, you can build a robust brand presence by creating an immersive and memorable experience that resonates with customers. The physical layout, décor, and sensory experiences (scent, sound, and lighting) can be meticulously curated to align with the brand's identity and values. Many brands like to test new retail concepts to dazzle their customers, such as Nike, which launched Nike Live, a data-driven store that catered to customer preferences, and Amazon, with its cashierless convenience store, Amazon Go.

Several years ago, retail futurist Matthew Brown identified a transformative trend, coined "me-tail."[188] This new retail philosophy emphasizes personalized, inspiring experiences over mere transactions. As online shopping threatens traditional models, innovative "clicks to bricks" brands like Amazon and Warby Parker are reinventing physical stores to create seamless integrations with their digital presence. Once doubted for its unconventional retail approach, Apple has set a global standard with its iconic store designs and customer-centric service, proving that retail spaces focusing on community, storytelling, and expert solutions can thrive. Dyson's London showroom exemplifies brand storytelling, allowing visitors to explore the company's history, engineering processes, and product innovations through various exhibits. The showroom features a "Dyson Demo" area where customers can test vacuum cleaners and learn about their features from knowledgeable staff members. Similarly, the wireless home audio company Sonos created the Sonos Studios where it hosts events, exhibitions, and performances that celebrate the intersection of music, art, and technology in a community-building environment.

Starbucks's new Reserve Roastery in New York City, Seattle, Shanghai, Milan, Tokyo, and Chicago epitomizes the evolution of retail. This innovative concept marries luxury with experience, offering an upscale environment far surpassing the traditional coffee-shop setting. By positioning itself near high-traffic, fashionable destinations, Starbucks is tapping into the experiential retail trend that's aligned with consumer desires for unique and premium experiences. The spacious Roastery serves as a coffee haven and an artisanal food hub, featuring a bakery and a bar with coffee-infused cocktails, catering to the tastes of a discerning clientele.

These Reserve Roasteries are not mere coffee shops; they are destinations offering a sensory journey through gourmet offerings and sophisticated design—a clear nod to the trend of creating memorable consumer engagements that resonate with today's experience-driven culture.

For physical retail to succeed in the future, it must offer unique, memorable, community-like experiences that leverage design technology such as virtual and augmented reality, 3D modelling and printing, and computer-aided design to foster genuine connections with customers.

Here are some questions to consider if you are interested in building a unique brick-and-mortar brand experience:

- What is the core identity and value proposition of the brand?
- Who is the target audience, and what are their shopping habits and preferences?
- How does the location align with the brand's image and target demographic?
- Which retail format, such as a standalone store, mall store, or pop-up shop, best suits the brand's product or service?
- What are the potential retail environment's traffic patterns and footfall statistics?
- What does the competition look like in the area, and how will the brand differentiate itself?
- What are the costs associated with the retail space, including rent, utilities, and design?
- Are the lease terms flexible enough to accommodate future growth or necessary changes?

- How will the retail environment support the brand's need for visibility and customer engagement?
- What technological infrastructure is available or necessary for the brand's retail operations?
- How will inventory and supply chain logistics be managed in this retail environment?
- Can the retail environment be adapted to provide an experiential shopping experience?
- Is there potential for local partnerships or community engagement through this retail space?
- How does the retail environment fit into the brand's omnichannel strategy?
- What are the security considerations for the products and customers in this area?
- What is the desired net impression and feeling that consumers should leave with after experiencing the brand's physical environment?

23 | PUBLICITY, PR, AND AWARDS

Publicity, public relations (PR), and awards form a powerful trio that can significantly impact your brand. Publicity generates initial visibility, PR nurtures relationships and shapes perception, and awards validate your brand's achievements. Together, they create a strong foundation for your brand's success by generating earned media that is free—credible visibility that can significantly impact attracting customers and building a positive reputation. And again, it's relatively *free*.

Publicity

Publicity is a powerful tool for brand building. Unlike advertising, which is paid media, publicity is earned media. It includes print and digital media coverage and social media mentions. Publicity is particularly effective because it is perceived as more credible and unbiased than advertising.[189]

Publicity can significantly increase a brand's visibility and awareness. A positive news story or a viral social media post can reach millions at no cost. Moreover, publicity can enhance a brand's reputation. For example, a positive product review from an influential blogger or a celebrity endorsement can boost a brand's credibility and desirability. Just ask any brand that has been on Oprah's Favorite Things list.

Making your story newsworthy means presenting it in a timely, relevant, engaging, and valuable way to the target audience. It's more than just sending a media release, which has about a 3 percent chance of a journalist positively reacting to it.[190] Pitching a branding story requires convincing reporters that your story is unique, newsworthy, and worth their time and attention. Journalists receive numerous pitches daily, making it crucial to stand out from the crowd and capture their interest instantly. Crafting a compelling narrative, highlighting the relevance and impact of your brand, and understanding the journalist's audience are essential elements in overcoming this challenge. It takes creativity, persistence, and a deep understanding of storytelling to successfully pitch a branding story to a reporter and secure valuable media coverage.

Start by building your credibility and authority with a local TV, radio, or print reporter, blogger, or podcaster that fits your brand's topics. Do your homework and find the perfect fit for your topics with the correct report. Connect online through various social media platforms. See if you know someone in their network who can help you get an introduction. It's not what you know but who you know to start the conversation with. Develop several stories or topics to help the journalist create new and exciting news articles. You're not trying to sell your brand; you're helping the reporter create a story that their readers value.

Like all of us, reporters are busy, so be concise and to the point, have an emotional hook, cover all the *W*'s (who, what, when, where, and why), and be human.

Here are a few examples:

Make Your Story Relevant to Current Events: If your brand is launching a new environmentally friendly innovation, you could tie your story to current events or discussions around climate change or sustainability. Try to link it to another more significant news event like a UN Climate Change Conference or other hot climate topics; you could highlight how your innovations contribute to reducing carbon emissions.

Highlight Unique or Groundbreaking Elements: Everybody loves a break-through. If your brand is the first to introduce a groundbreaking technology or innovation, it's likely to be considered newsworthy. For example, when SpaceX launched its reusable rockets, it significantly advanced space technology and garnered considerable media attention.

Share Human Interest Stories: Stories that evoke emotion or highlight the human side of your brand can also be newsworthy. For instance, if your company started a community outreach program that has significantly improved lives, sharing personal stories from this initiative can be compelling.

Celebrate Significant Company Milestones: Major company milestones such as substantial anniversaries, reaching notable sales numbers, or expanding into new markets can also make for newsworthy stories. For example, when Apple sold its billionth iPhone, it was a significant milestone that attracted media attention.

Provide Expert Opinions on Trending Topics: If someone from your company is an expert in a field related to a trending topic, their insights and opinions can be newsworthy. For instance, during the COVID-19 pandemic, many health and safety companies offered expert commentary on safety measures and procedures.

In a noisy world where competition is fierce and consumer attention is fragmented, publicity stands as a cornerstone for brands, especially new ones, striving to carve out their niche. Particularly for those without the luxury of a hefty advertising budget, generating buzz through creative and strategic public relations can be a game-changer. Harnessing the power of word-of-mouth, leveraging social media platforms, and engaging in community events are just a few cost-effective tactics that can amplify a brand's presence. By building relationships with customers, thought leaders, and the media, a brand can cultivate a reputation that resonates with authenticity and trustworthiness. In essence, publicity is not merely a substitute for traditional advertising; it is a vital artery that pumps life into the heart of a brand's identity, fostering recognition and loyalty that can sustain and propel a business even in the most saturated markets.

Public Relations

Public relations (PR) is pivotal in building and maintaining a solid brand, serving as the strategic communication bridge between a company and its stakeholders. It is essential in shaping the narrative around a brand, highlighting its successes, and managing its reputation, especially during crises. Effective PR involves reactive measures to mitigate negative press or public sentiment in times of trouble, as well as proactive strategies to promote a brand's achievements, values, and vision. A well-prepared crisis management plan is vital; it should outline clear protocols for rapid response and transparent communication to minimize damage and maintain trust with customers, employees, and the public.

PR extends beyond crisis management to cultivating positive relationships with advocacy groups and like-minded partners. Such alliances can amplify a brand's voice on social and political issues, helping to navigate legislative and regulatory landscapes that may impact the brand's operations or ethos. By aligning with organizations with similar values or objectives, a brand can bolster its image as a socially responsible entity and engage in meaningful initiatives that resonate with its audience.

Strategically, brands must consistently monitor public perception, seek opportunities to showcase their successes through various media channels, and engage in community and stakeholder dialogue to reinforce their market position. PR guidance should emphasize authenticity, consistent messaging, and long-term relationship building. By doing so, brands can ensure they not only weather storms but also emerge with a more substantial, more respected presence in their respective industries.

PR is a multifaceted beast in the world of brand management. The adage "all publicity is good publicity" is often bandied about, but is there any truth to it?

Consider the case of Target Corp., whose shares plummeted by 8 percent in the latter half of 2013 after a massive data breach during the Black Friday shopping frenzy. This breach wasn't just a minor hiccup; it affected 110 million customers.[191] The aftermath was brutal: customers shied away, profits for the fourth quarter nosedived by 46 percent, and ultimately, CEO Gregg Steinhafel stepped down. The cost to Target? At least $148 million. This is a textbook example of negative PR causing tangible harm to a brand's financial health and reputation.

In contrast, emerging brands often struggle to capture any media attention. For these newcomers, any form of PR can be beneficial. According to a Stanford Graduate School of Business study, negative book reviews can paradoxically lead to a 45 percent increase in sales for unknown authors.[192] This is because any publicity, even if not entirely positive, increases visibility, which is vital for brands trying to break into the market.

This dichotomy suggests that the impact of PR largely depends on the existing level of brand awareness. Established brands like Target will likely suffer from negative PR because it amplifies customers' doubts and fears, leading to direct financial losses. In contrast, for brands lacking recognition, even negative PR can provide a platform for discussion and curiosity they otherwise wouldn't have had.

However, all brands must remember that the strategy to handle PR should be tailored to their specific context. Unknown brands should approach negative PR as an opportunity to engage with a new audience and frame their narrative positively. For household names like Target, the focus should be on swift damage control and restoring customer trust.

Awards

Imagine going to a new restaurant that you've never heard of before. As you approach the entrance, you see a prestigious Michelin Star award in the window. What would be your immediate reaction? You would most likely be excited, anticipating a remarkable culinary experience. Even before glancing at the menu, your expectations would have already soared. This illustrates the power of business awards and recognitions.

Receiving awards goes beyond mere social proof and bragging rights. It serves to solidify your brand's reputation as a trustworthy and exceptional entity. Consider this scenario: Two new restaurants are competing for your attention, and they seem equal in every aspect except for one crucial detail—the presence of a Michelin Star. Which one would you choose? The answer becomes evident. Awards elevate your brand above the competition, attracting customers who value excellence and quality.

Business awards and recognitions not only enhance your reputation but also act as a catalyst for customer trust and preference. They set your brand apart, signaling to potential customers that you are a reliable and exceptional choice.

However, business awards can be seen as a double-edged sword. While they elevate expectations and create a sense of anticipation, they also make you responsible for consistently exceeding those expectations. Once a brand has been recognized for its excellence, customers naturally expect nothing less than exceptional products or services.

Receiving awards sets a high bar for performance and quality. It implies a commitment to maintaining the same level of excellence that led to the recognition in the first place. While achieving award status means continuous improvement, innovation, and a dedication to surpassing customer satisfaction, other rewarding benefits include boosting employee morale, increased visibility, networking, and PR opportunities.

It's impossible to pinpoint an exact number of business awards globally due to the vast number of topics, industries, countries, and awards categories. They include small local recognitions, as well as prestigious regional, national, and international awards. There are undoubtedly thousands, maybe millions of awards across the many fields like human resources, leadership, DE&I, sustainability, innovation, and entrepreneurship.

Take charge of earning recognition for your accomplishments instead of waiting to be noticed. Begin by exploring local and industry-specific awards that align with your business. Obtain a copy of their entry form and carefully analyze the qualifications they outline. Develop a strategic plan to excel in all the required areas. Consider reaching out to previous winners and requesting to see a winning entry so you understand the benchmark for success.

Once you're confident that your brand has surpassed the competition, submit your entry. Whether you win or lose, celebrate your efforts with your stakeholders, employees, and customers. Recognize the hard work and dedication that got your brand to this point, regardless of the outcome.

Taking proactive steps to pursue awards and recognition increases your chances of being acknowledged and demonstrates your commitment to excellence. So, don't hesitate—start researching and preparing to showcase your brand's accomplishments and celebrate them with those who have contributed to your success.

24 | MARKETING AND ADVERTISING

Marketing and advertising serve to craft the narrative that imbues a brand with meaning and positions it within the cultural landscape. Through strategic storytelling, creative expression, and targeted communication, marketing and advertising do not merely inform potential customers about a brand; they invite them into a relationship. They shape perceptions, build emotional connections, and engender the kind of loyalty that can elevate a brand to become a part of a consumer's identity. By consistently reflecting the brand's values and vision, these efforts cultivate a community of advocates and ambassadors who carry the brand's message forward.

As we delve deeper into the concepts of marketing and advertising, it is essential to understand their fundamental role in the brand-building process. Marketing and advertising are not merely tools for promoting products or services; they are the means by which a brand establishes its identity, communicates its values, and forges meaningful connections with its audience.

Marketing

Marketing often focuses on immediate objectives—launching campaigns that drive sales, capture market share, and deliver quarterly results. These initiatives are the tactical maneuvers that generate momentum and keep the business engine running. However, these short-term actions must be carefully choreographed to resonate with the brand's overarching narrative and values. This is where branding steps in, serving as the North Star, guiding the strategic direction, and ensuring that every marketing effort reinforces the brand's identity and promise.

The symbiotic relationship between marketing and branding is crucial; while marketing leverages promotions, advertisements, and other tactics to compel customer action now, it also contributes brushstrokes to the more prominent masterpiece that is the brand's image over time. Branding's role is to imbue these actions with deeper meaning, establishing trust and cultivating loyalty that will endure beyond any single transaction. By ensuring that short-term marketing campaigns align with the brand's long-term vision and values, companies can foster a consistent brand experience that not only persuades customers to act today but also invests in a loyal customer base for the future.

In practice, this means that while marketers may deploy urgent calls-to-action or time-sensitive offers to ignite immediate sales, they must do so in a way that does not compromise the integrity or dilute the perception of the brand. It's about finding harmony between meeting the next quarter's targets and nurturing a brand that stands the test of time—a brand that customers recognize, respect, and prefer long after the time-sensitive sale.

Marketing and selling a product or service are more important at the beginning of building a brand. The vision is short-term, transactional, and adaptable. It's about building the brand one customer at a time—conducting real-time customer research where you learn what works and what doesn't. This is a time to take risks, test hypotheses, and pivot when necessary. At this point, it's all about the product attributes and benefits and solving customers' pain points. It is through building customer relations or through the clear, steadfast vision of the founder that the brand begins to form. A brand evolves. Back in the brick-and-mortar world, there was time to nurture a brand slowly. Everything took time. Once the product niche was established, the brand followed, and so did the economizing of scale and barriers to entry. As the money started flowing, so did the marketing campaign expenditures.

In the digital world, more brand elements are front-loaded. You're looking to reach a massive market—fast. Your efforts are about disruption, filling a market gap, or a new urgent need. This shift is thanks in part to venture capitalists and angel investors who invest in high-risk, high-reward start-ups. In some cases, brand positioning and product marketing are research tested, but in many cases a brand's potential remains an unknown until it hits the real world.

Marketing encompasses all of a company's activities to promote a product or service to create a reaction from a consumer or customer, hoping for a purchase. While every tactic used to build demand for a product *contributes* to brand building, these are two separate strategies.

Product marketing focuses on driving sales for a specific product or service. It involves identifying the target customer, crafting product messaging, setting pricing, and creating promotional tactics to educate potential customers about its features and benefits. The goal is to directly boost product sales and ensure the product fits the market needs.

On the other hand, *brand marketing* (also called brand building or simply branding) aims to build and enhance the company's overall reputation and identity. It's less about immediate sales and more about creating an emotional connection with the audience, establishing brand values, and cultivating loyalty over time. Brand marketing efforts are broader, encompassing storytelling, visual identity, and consistent messaging across all touchpoints to engender trust and recognition. Ultimately, product marketing and brand marketing aim to turn consumers into loyal customers.

For instance, on July 8, 1971, Coca-Cola shifted from product marketing to brand marketing when it ran its first high-definition color TV commercial called

"I'd Like to Buy the World a Coke." The commercial featured five hundred young people from more than twenty countries singing together on a hilltop in Italy, holding bottles of Coke. It didn't focus on a forty-cent Coke bottle but on the universal value of bringing young people together. Bill Backer, creative director at the McCann Erickson advertising agency, devised the song idea while traveling from the US to London. The flight was rerouted to Ireland, where passengers had to share rooms at a hotel near the Shannon Airport. The following day, waiting for their next flight, Backer saw the once tired and cranky strangers now laughing and talking over bottles of Coke. Looking back, he recalled, "In that moment [I] saw a bottle of Coke in a whole new light... to see Coke not as it was originally designed to be—a liquid refresher—but as a tiny bit of commonality between all peoples, a universally liked formula that would help to keep them company for a few minutes."[193] This is how a brand can move from tangible benefits to emotional commitment. Remember, it's not what a brand says, but how it makes customers feel.

Advertising

What do the world's top brands all have in common? Advertising. The World Advertising Research Center (WARC) predicts that global advertising spending will surpass $1 trillion by the end of 2024. To put this into perspective, that's $125 per person on earth. More surprising is that half of the global advertising spend will go to five digital media outlets: Alibaba, Alphabet (Google and YouTube), Amazon, ByteDance (TikTok and Douyin), and Meta (Facebook and Instagram).[194]

The top twenty brands, as defined by *Forbes*, Kantar BrandZ, and Interbrand, spent about $190 billion on advertising in 2022, approximately 4 percent of their total revenue. The average advertising-to-sales ratio (which measures the percentage of income spent on advertising) can range from 2 to 15 percent, depending on the industry. Generally, business-to-consumer (B2C) products and services tend to have higher marketing spend than business-to-business (B2B) advertisers.

Almost 60 percent of advertising spend is digital, with nearly three-quarters of that focused on social media and search, with the line share of the search dollars going to the most prominent digital media player—Alphabet, which owns Google Search, Google Display Network, and YouTube.[195] This is followed by traditional broadcast TV, streaming, news channels, "out-of-home" channels like billboards, magazines, radio, podcasts, and cinema.

Average Advertising Cost Comparisons in the United States

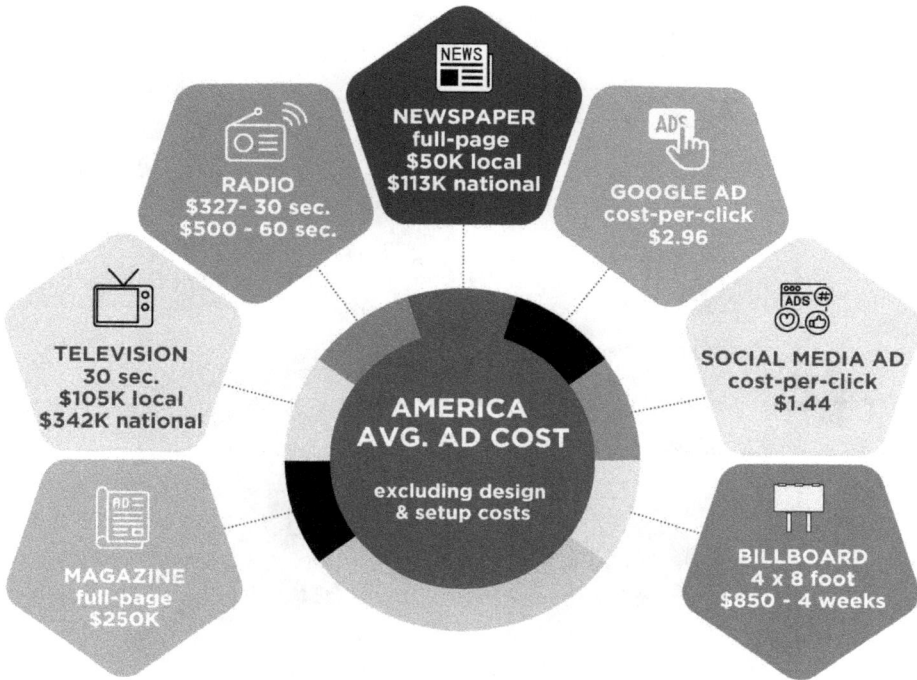

NEWSPAPER
full-page
$50K local
$113K national

RADIO
$327- 30 sec.
$500 - 60 sec.

GOOGLE AD
cost-per-click
$2.96

TELEVISION
30 sec.
$105K local
$342K national

SOCIAL MEDIA AD
cost-per-click
$1.44

AMERICA AVG. AD COST
excluding design & setup costs

MAGAZINE
full-page
$250K

BILLBOARD
4 x 8 foot
$850 - 4 weeks

Note: These are rough averages as each situation will differ based on reach, frequency, specific time and location, and ad size/duration. These costs do not include creation and production costs.

Sources: Fit Small Business, WebFX.com (2022)

When comparing traditional advertising avenues such as TV, newspapers, and radio with digital platforms like Google and social media on a cost-per-click basis, the landscape of brand building versus sales generation takes on a nuanced contrast. Expensive traditional media have long been the bastions of brand building, offering a broad canvas to paint powerful brand stories, reaching a wide audience simultaneously, and creating a shared experience that can enter the cultural zeitgeist. Their impact, while difficult to measure with precision, is often profound in terms of brand recall and establishing brand prestige. On the other hand, with their cost-per-click model, digital platforms offer a granular level of targeting and analytics that traditional media can rarely match. This allows for more efficient spending, as brands pay only for engagement, not for mere exposure.

Average Media Cost Per Mille (CPM) Comparison in the United States

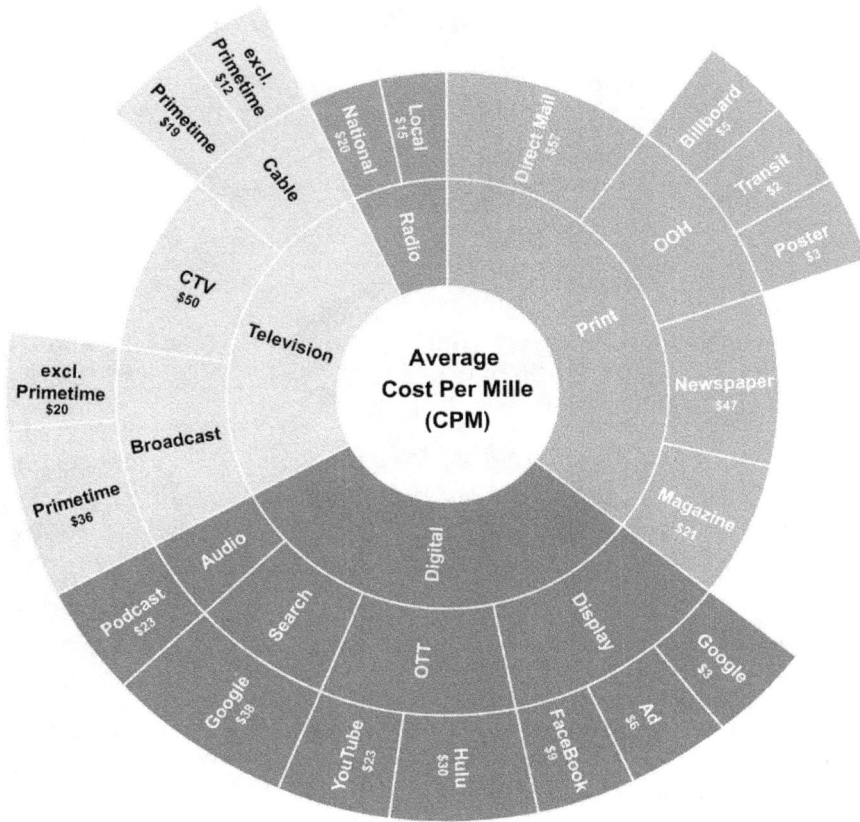

Note: These are rough averages, as each situation will differ based on the target audience, ad type, placement, timing, and competition. These costs do not include creation and production costs.

Sources: OAAA, Solomon Partners, Fou Analytics, Post Media, author's analysis (2021 & 2022)

Cost per mille (CPM) is a pricing model in which advertisers pay for every 1,000 impressions (or views) of their ad. CPM is a standard pricing model for online advertising, but it is also used for offline advertising, such as print and television advertising. Getting an accurate measurement is the hard part because actual costs may vary depending on factors such as target audience, ad placement, seasonality, and market competition.

However, the CPM for traditional advertising is generally higher than the CPM for digital advertising. This is because traditional advertising is a less targeted medium. When you advertise in a newspaper or on television, your ad is seen by a large number of people, many of whom may not be interested in your product or service. With digital advertising, you can target your ads to specific demographics, interests, and keywords. This generally makes digital advertising more efficient for reaching your target audience.

However, traditional advertising has some advantages. It can reach a large audience quickly and easily and create a strong brand image.

Digital advertising is also more measurable than traditional advertising. You can track the number of people who see your ad, the number of people who click on your ad, and the amount of money you spend on your ad.

Moreover, the interactive nature of digital platforms enables brands to engage in two-way conversations with consumers, fostering a sense of community and personal connection that can be highly effective for brand building. However, the ephemeral nature of digital interactions and the cluttered online environment can make it challenging for brands to leave a lasting impression.

Each has its strengths—traditional media offering a grand stage for brand narrative and digital platforms providing precise tools for engagement—but the ultimate effectiveness of your brand building lies in how well you harmonize these approaches to deliver a consistent and compelling brand story across all channels.

25 | DIGITAL ADVERTISING

Digital advertising is a catch-all term that captures all online advertising. In 2023, global e-commerce sales surpassed $5.7 trillion and are projected to grow well beyond $8 trillion in 2027.[196] Over 50 percent of these transactions are from mobile devices like smartphones and tablets.[197] Boston Consulting Group predicts that e-commerce will command over 40 percent of global retail sales by 2027, a significant increase since it was only 18 percent in 2017.[198] Amazon, the world's biggest e-commerce retailer, will continue to dominate the United States online retail sector.[199] To put this into perspective, its closest competitor, Walmart, trails far behind with only 6.4 online market share, which is only 13 percent of Walmart's total sales—still, lots of room for growth.

Global Digital Advertising Spend by Channel

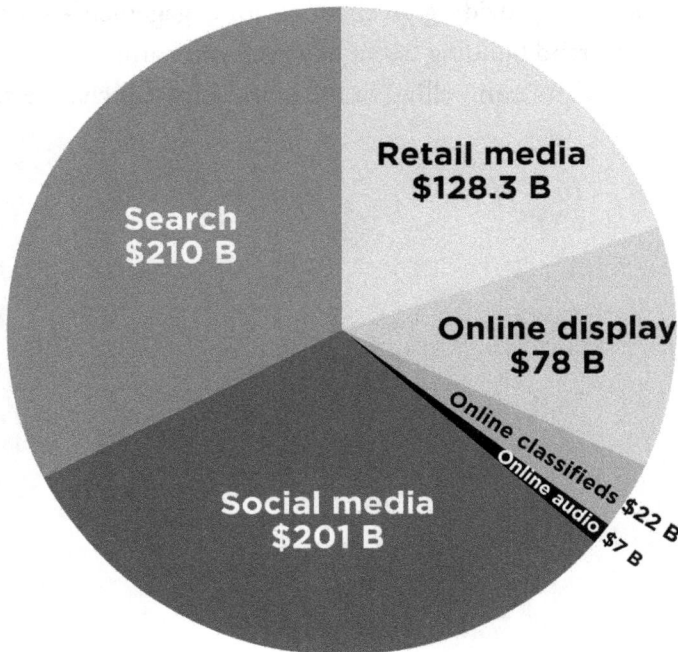

Pie chart: Retail media $128.3 B; Search $210 B; Online display $78 B; Online classifieds $22 B; Online audio $7 B; Social media $201 B

Source: WARC Media (2022)

Search Advertising

Paid search advertising is the largest global advertising channel, projected to reach over $307 billion in 2024. The lion's share of these advertising dollars went to Alphabet; in 2022, Google search revenue was $162 billion, up 9 percent from the previous year, and YouTube's ad revenue was $29 billion.[200] However, about half of online shoppers start their search on Amazon, whose search engine is tailored for e-commerce. Microsoft Bing is still trying to create a presence in the search advertising area, with TikTok sneaking into the top five.

Search advertising isn't generally seen as a brand-building tool; however, it can contribute to brand building, albeit less directly than other branding tactics. Search advertising can increase brand awareness by ensuring that a brand appears prominently when potential customers actively seek related products or services. This consistent visibility can reinforce brand recognition. Moreover, search advertising can be used to control the narrative around a brand. By real-time bidding on branded specific keywords or phrases or terms related to the brand's values and messaging, companies can guide the perception of their brand. This is particularly important when dealing with reputation management or highlighting specific brand attributes.

For example, the beauty brand L'Oréal uses search advertising to appear in a wide array of beauty-related searches. By doing so, it reinforces its position as a leading authority in the beauty space and as an innovative beauty resource. It uses search to provide unique consumer insights to reach a vast, interested audience who engage with the content they're most interested in when it matters most to them.[201]

HOW THE BIDDING PROCESS WORKS

Keyword selection: The company identifies the branded terms and related keywords that they want to target. These may include the company name, product names, slogans, or phrases that reflect the brand's values and messaging.

Bid setting: The company sets a maximum bid for each keyword, which represents the highest amount they are willing to pay each time a user clicks on their ad. The actual cost per click (CPC) is determined by factors such as ad quality, relevance, and competition.

Ad creation: The company creates ad copy that incorporates the targeted keywords and reflects the brand's messaging. The ad should be compelling and relevant to the user's search query.

Ad auction: When a user searches for a keyword that the company is bidding on, an ad auction takes place. The search engine evaluates the bids and ad quality of all competing advertisers and determines the order in which the ads will be displayed.

Ad placement: If the company's bid and ad quality are competitive enough, their ad will appear at the top of the search results, above the organic listings. This prominent placement increases the likelihood that users will click on the ad and visit the company's website.

Less-known brands must reach consumers at the beginning of their search journeys to help them solve a problem. Dominating these search results can place a brand into the consumer's initial consideration set, which can make them start associating the brand with a solution. Fifty-eight percent of TikTok users discover new brands on the platform, making it one-half times more effective than other social media platforms.[202]

Social Media Advertising

Social media refers to internet-based platforms that allow users to create and share content, exchange information, and participate in social networking. Social media platforms include Facebook, Instagram, X (formally Twitter), LinkedIn, and TikTok. Social media has become indispensable to brand building as it allows companies to interact directly with customers, build communities, increase brand awareness, and drive website traffic and sales. Statista projects the number of people using social media will be almost six billion by 2027, representing 87 percent of the global consumer population over fifteen.[203] From a generational perspective, around 90.4 percent of millennials, 77.5 percent of generation X, and over 48.2 percent of baby boomers actively use social media.[204] The typical user spends about 15 percent of their waking lives (or almost 2.5 hours a day) using social media. Given the large user base, social media presents unparalleled opportunities for companies to boost their digital marketing efforts. The 2023 annual *Social Media Marketing Industry Report* found that 86 percent of marketers agree that their social media efforts have generated more exposure for their brand. Beyond increasing traffic for their business, 56 percent agreed that social media helps build a loyal fanbase that continues to improve with consistent presence over the years.[205] By crafting social media campaigns tailored to their target audience and goals, brands can drive meaningful business impact and loyalty.

While there are numerous social media platforms available, the top five platforms —Facebook, YouTube, Instagram, TikTok, and LinkedIn—collectively boast over 9 billion active users. It's important to note that many users are active on multiple platforms, with the average social media user currently engaging with more than six different platforms.[206] While WhatsApp and WeChat are considered social networks, they are more direct messaging platforms, so they have been excluded from this analysis. As these social media channels evolve, more Asia-centric platforms might need reconsidering.

How people use each platform is also slightly different. Facebook, the grandparent of social media, started by keeping friends and family connected. Even after twenty years, 88 percent of Facebook users log on to keep up with real-life friends. This is unique, as in all the other platforms, users tend to personally know less than half of their connections and followers.

Global Social Media Platforms Ranked by Users

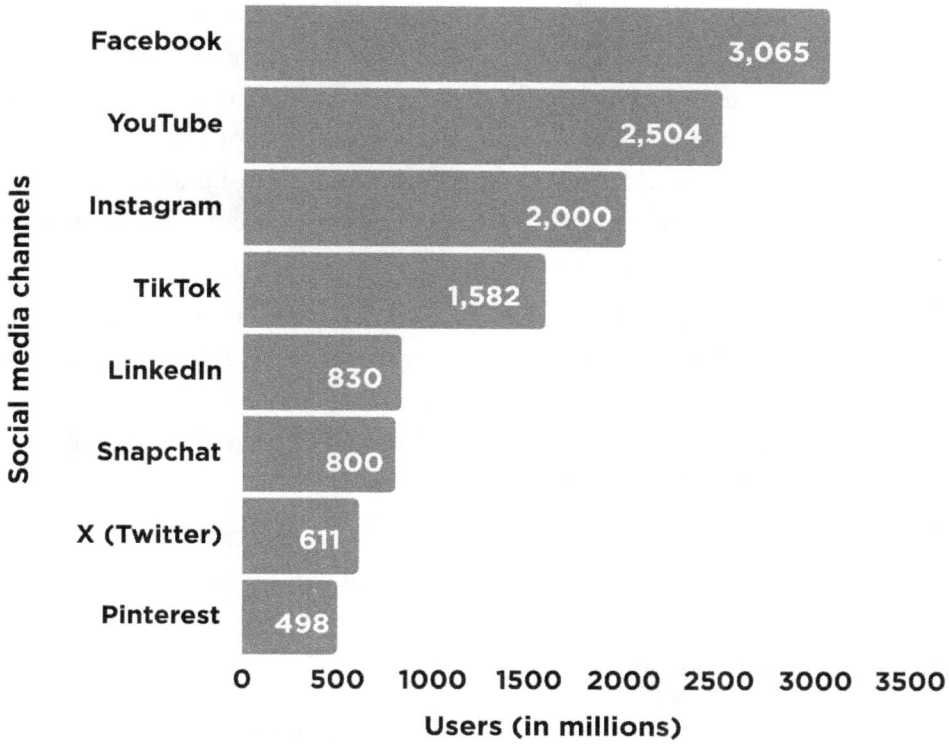

Social media channels	Users (in millions)
Facebook	3,065
YouTube	2,504
Instagram	2,000
TikTok	1,582
LinkedIn	830
Snapchat	800
X (Twitter)	611
Pinterest	498

Source: Statista (April 2024)

Another critical insight about social media users is that most of them read or observe but don't contribute, except for the odd like. In the United States, about 49 percent of Facebook users say they occasionally post content, followed by 42 percent of Instagram users and 33 percent of X (formally Twitter) users.[207] The rest of the platforms have less than 11 percent of users contributing content regularly. Unsurprisingly, more young people (aged eighteen to twenty-nine) are social media users, at 84 percent, and they are more likely to post content regularly.[208] Sweden has the honor of having the highest number of young people engaged in social media, at 96 percent.[209] Confidence in using digital technology helps build confidence in contributing to these dynamic communities.

Building a robust brand presence and reputation on social media requires a strategic approach tailored to your brand's objectives, whether B2C or B2B. Essentially, there are three ways you can build a brand presence:

Brand Profile: Select the best platforms for your brand's presence, build your brand's story, and highlight your brand personality through social posts. Develop a content strategy and calendar. Develop an audience organically through valuable and engaging content and interact regularly with your followers.

Paid Ads: Use paid social ads like Facebook/Instagram/LinkedIn ads and promoted tweets on X (formally Twitter) to reach more extensive and targeted audiences. Tailor ad content specifically for each platform that makes sense. While this tactic is better suited to selling products, you can still tailor a brand campaign to support your values and culture through employee team-building programs, awards, significant announcements, corporate social engagement (CSE) initiatives, ESG programs, and other general social topics.

Influencer Marketing: Collaborate with social media influencers who are relevant to your social values concerning your employees (DE&I strategy), customers (transparency and CSE strategy), and society (ESG strategy). This helps leverage their follower base and builds further credibility. For more on this, check out "Influencers" in chapter 28, Sponsorships.

SOCIAL MEDIA BRAND PROFILE CHECKLIST

Choose the Right Platform

- Research where your target audience spends their time.
- Consider the platform's alignment with your brand's image and content style.
- Evaluate the platform's features and advertising options.

Create a Compelling Profile

- Use your brand's official name as the username/handle if it's available.
- Create a professional and memorable profile picture, typically your brand logo.
- Design an attractive and brand-aligned cover/header image.
- Write a clear and concise bio or description that includes:
    - Who you are
    - What you do or offer
    - Your brand's unique value proposition
    - A call to action (CTA), such as "Shop now" or "Learn more"

Contact Information and Links

- Include a link to your website.

- Add contact information (email, phone number, address) if appropriate.
- Link to other social media profiles your brand owns.

Content Strategy

- Plan the types of content you will post (images, videos, stories, live streams).
- Create a content calendar to maintain a consistent posting schedule.
- Establish a consistent visual theme or style for your content.
- Determine the voice and tone of your posts (professional, casual, humorous).

Engagement Plan

- Decide how you will engage with followers (comments, messages, mentions).
- Plan for how you will handle customer service inquiries through social media.
- Set guidelines for response times and communication style.

Growth Strategy

- Identify key influencers or partners in your industry for potential collaborations.
- Consider paid advertising options to increase reach.
- Use hashtags effectively to gain visibility in relevant conversations.

Analytics and Measurement

- Set up any tracking tools or integrate analytics features offered by the platform.
- Determine key performance indicators (KPIs) to measure success (followers, engagement rates, website traffic).

Security Measures

- Secure your account with a strong password and two-factor authentication.
- Assign roles and permissions carefully if multiple team members have access.

Legal Compliance

- Ensure that your content adheres to the platform's terms of service.
- Verify that you have the rights to all images, videos, and music used in your posts.

Continuous Improvement

- Regularly review analytics to understand what works and what doesn't.
- Stay updated with new features and trends on the platform to keep your strategy fresh.
- Be prepared to adapt and refine your approach based on feedback and performance data.

Final Note

- Remember that each social media platform has its distinctions, so it's vital to tailor certain aspects of your efforts to the platform you're focusing on.

MEMES

Memes have carved out a unique niche in branding strategies, functioning as a digital lingua franca that can catapult a brand into the spotlight on social media channels. The essence of a meme's integration into branding lies in its viral nature; a well-crafted meme can traverse the expanse of the internet at an astonishing pace, often reaching far beyond a brand's existing audience. This virality is a double-edged sword, though, as it requires a keen understanding of the meme's context to avoid potential pitfalls.

The success of a meme in branding hinges on its relatability. By tapping into universally shared emotions or experiences, brands can foster a sense of kinship with their audience. Netflix, for instance, has adeptly used memes to create buzz around their shows. Its use of screen captures from "Stranger Things" with witty captions resonated with viewers, encouraging shares and discussions that extended the show's reach organically.

Another critical aspect of memes is engagement. Memes invite interaction—likes, shares, and comments—which can significantly amplify a brand's presence on social media. Denny's has exemplified this through its surreal and humorous meme campaigns that often go viral, prompting users to engage with the brand in unconventional ways. One specific successful example was its "zoom in" campaign, which asked users to zoom in on an image, such as a stack of pancakes, to discover hidden messages within the image, such as "has this distracted you from overwhelming existential dread?" and "don't look at the next tweet." The next tweet in the thread contained a similar image with more hidden messages, creating a chain of engaging, humorous content.

Memes can also reflect a brand's identity and values if chosen wisely. They can convey a brand's personality, humor, and relevance, especially when they tie into current trends or internet culture. Gucci's #TFWGucci campaign is a prime example, where the company collaborated with artists to create high-fashion memes that both engaged its audience and underscored its luxury status.

However, brands must navigate meme culture carefully. Memes are temporary by nature and can quickly become dated. Additionally, a meme that misfires or comes off as tone-deaf can harm a brand's reputation. To reach a younger demographic, McDonald's created a meme for the Double Cheeseburger with the phrase "I'd hit it," which was intended to mean "I'd like to get that burger." However, the slang term "hit it" can also be interpreted as a sexual reference, and this double entendre did not sit well with the public. There was immediate backlash as many consumers found it inappropriate, especially for a family-oriented brand like McDonald's. The company quickly pulled the campaign. The key is maintaining authenticity and ensuring that any meme you use aligns with your brand's overall messaging and values.

Memes can be a potent tool in a branding strategy when used with savvy and sensitivity. They offer a cost-effective means to increase brand visibility, create shareable content, and engage with audiences on a level that feels personal and immediate. When executed correctly, memes can yield impressive results, endearing brands to consumers who value humor and digital savviness.

BRAND PLACEMENT

According to a *Forbes* study, 99 percent of US households subscribe to at least one or more streaming services.[210] How do brands get in on the action? The traditional fifteen, thirty, or sixty-second commercial doesn't always fit the new entertainment models. The answer is placing your product right in the movie or show.

Brand placement offers significant benefits for building a brand within the competitive landscape of advertising. As consumers increasingly evade traditional commercials, product placement emerges as a compelling strategy, seamlessly integrating into program content and thus becoming more difficult for viewers to ignore. This method enhances brand recall and attitude and primes viewers for subsequent advertisements, increasing their attention to the brand.[211]

From Sheldon on CBS's hit *The Big Bang Theory* using Purell hand sanitizer after handling a live snake, to the large red Coke cups spotted on the judges' table on Fox's *American Idol*, these memorable moments drive brand awareness—paid or not. Purell's wasn't a paid placement, but Coca-Cola's was a thirteen-year paid commitment.

At a time when Coke was losing ground to Pepsi, particularly in connecting with the youth market, the $10 million sponsorship deal with *American Idol* presented an unprecedented opportunity.[212] The show's massive viewership, which averaged 12.7 million viewers in its first season and soared in subsequent seasons, provided Coke with a highly engaged audience. The strategic placement of Coke's iconic red cups in front of top pop icons and judges created a robust and recurring brand presence that was difficult to replicate through traditional advertising channels.

This partnership allowed Coca-Cola to tap into a cultural phenomenon that transcended age and demographics, making the brand synonymous with the popular music reality show. The integration went beyond mere product placement; it was a comprehensive promotional platform that included retail promotions, national tours, and music sales, akin to a major sports sponsorship.[213] Coca-Cola leveraged *American Idol* to launch new advertising campaigns and to foster a connection with rising musical talent, further embedding the brand into the entertainment landscape.

Online Audio

PODCASTS

There are over 460 million podcast listeners globally, and over one-third of Americans are regular listeners.[214] The appeal of podcasts lies mainly in their on-demand nature, allowing listeners to choose what they want to hear and when—unparalleled flexibility provided through audio providers like Apple and Spotify. This is further enhanced by the wide variety of topics, offering something for every interest, be it true crime, entrepreneurship, comedy, or niche hobbies. The accessibility of podcasts on various devices like smartphones, tablets, and computers enables people to incorporate listening into different parts of their daily routines, like traditional radio. Unlike many other media forms, podcasts can delve deep into topics in a one-to-two-hour format or in short, digestible sound bites. The personal connection fostered by many podcast hosts often leads to a strong sense of loyalty among regular listeners. Developing a professional podcast requires only a decent microphone, a headset, a quiet room, and a high-speed internet connection. If you include a video, you might need a ring light. So, anyone can start a podcast with only a few hundred-dollar investments. Of course, like for social influencers, building a following takes time, creativity, and hard work, and it can take many episodes before anyone wants to associate their brand with a show. However, increased investments and monetization in the podcasting industry have led to high-quality content, attracting more listeners and growing this channel. In certain respects, podcasts harken back to the beginning of radio broadcasts, like the fact that the hosts typically read the advertisements. This approach brings authenticity to the ad while necessitating a harmonious fit with the show's content.

AUDIO BRANDING

There are over 75 million smart speakers in homes worldwide, a number that's growing exponentially. Amazon has sold more than half a billion Alexa-enabled devices since Echo debuted in late 2014.[215] The company is currently collaborating with auto industry partners (including Audi, BMW, Ford, Lincoln, Lexus, and Toyota) to make Alexa available on the go. Voice-powered applications are expected to continue to explode.

Patrick Gauthier, VP at Amazon Pay, says, "We are at the cusp of a major transformation. Voice interfaces will give birth to new complementary experiences." Gauthier envisions smart speakers playing a pivotal role in providing product details and facilitating brand building.

To capitalize on this technology, brands must ensure their virtual assistant presence is as recognizable as their visual branding. Imagine Alexa enthusiastically describing your brand or Siri seamlessly processing your brand's voice commands. The key is to develop a distinct and consistent voice persona that aligns with your brand identity. Consider establishing a Wikipedia brand presence, as several virtual assistants pull information from this source. Other possible tactics include voice branding and voice search optimization through natural language queries.

CHATBOTS

Integrating a chatbot into your customer service strategy can supercharge your brand's capabilities. Chatbots can provide valuable information to potential buyers while simultaneously gathering insights to help you improve your offerings. They consistently deliver your brand's messaging and can access all available data, ensuring customers receive a personalized and optimal experience.

The chatbot market is experiencing rapid growth, with Grand View Research estimating an annual average growth rate of 23 percent from 2023 to 2030.[216] This surge is unsurprising, as over 45 percent of customers now prefer interacting with chatbots over human representatives. Consequently, many brands are turning to chatbots to enhance their customer experience.

When developing a chatbot, it's crucial to ensure its voice accurately reflects your brand's identity and target demographic. Carefully consider factors such as gender, personality, and accents to create a literal brand voice that resonates with your audience. By leveraging artificial intelligence, your brand can anticipate customers' needs and provide better solutions around the clock.

Chatbots offer a powerful opportunity to elevate your customer service, gather valuable insights, and consistently reinforce your brand's messaging. By crafting a chatbot voice that aligns with your brand's persona and resonates with your target audience, you can deliver a seamless and personalized experience, ultimately driving customer satisfaction and loyalty.

26 | TRADITIONAL ADVERTISING

Traditional advertising, in media such as print (newspapers, magazines), broadcast (TV, radio), direct mail, and outdoor advertising (billboards, posters), has been used for many years, even centuries. These methods were the primary ways businesses advertised before the advent of the internet.

Traditional advertising generally focuses on broad demographic data and mass media channels to reach a wide audience. It's often used for brand building and creating awareness. However, it can be harder to measure the effectiveness of traditional advertising compared to digital advertising, which offers more precise targeting and analytics. While conventional advertising may decline as advertisers shift their budgets toward digital advertising, you might consider the benefits of traditional advertising, such as great trust and credibility, non-intrusiveness, local solid market impact, and greater engagement with your branding message.

Global Traditional Advertising Spend by Channel

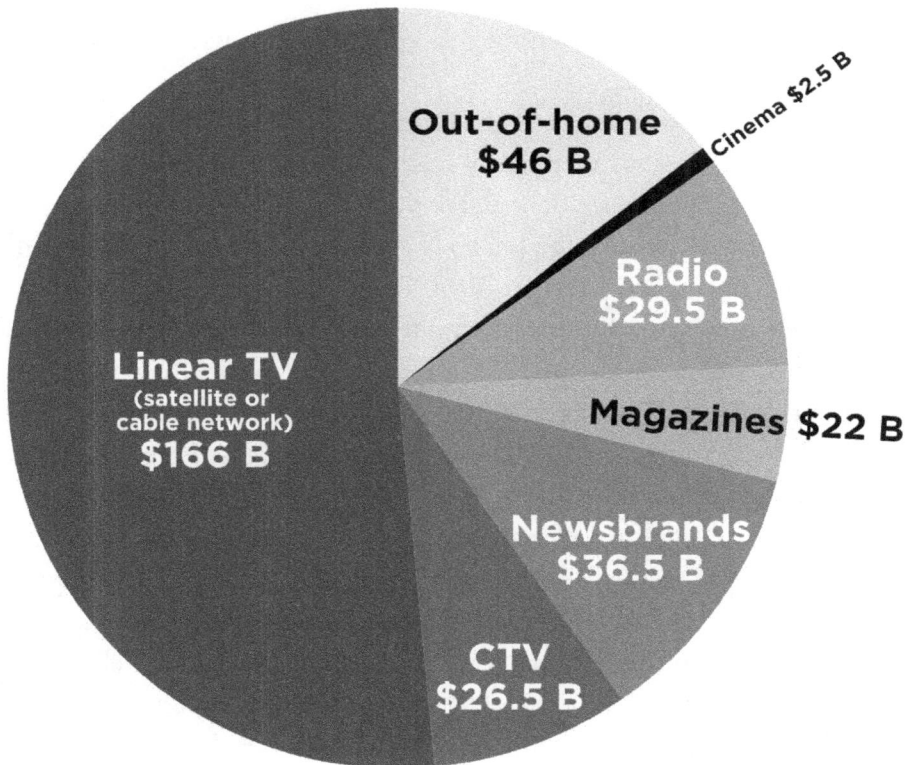

Source: WARC Media (2022)

Television

After World War II, television sets became affordable, and the programming made them worth the investment, even if they were black and white. Not until the early 1980s did color television exist in every home.

Back in the beginning, one of the greatest and most influential sitcoms in television history was *I Love Lucy*. The comedic series centered around the goofy antics of Lucy Ricardo, played by Lucille Ball, and her husband Ricky Ricardo, played by her real husband Desi Arnaz, creator and producer of the show. In 1953, the episode featuring the birth of their son, little Ricky, attracted over 44 million views or 72 percent of American households. For the first four seasons, the solo advertiser was the tobacco company Philip Morris, which paid approximately $100,000 per episode for five minutes of commercial time, or just over one million in today's dollars.[217] They even had Lucy and Ricky endorsing the product. Philip Morris shared the stage with Procter & Gamble for the remaining two seasons.

Compare this to 2023's Super Bowl record viewership of 115 million Americans, reaching only 40 percent of households for a whopping $7 million for one thirty-second commercial during the 3.5-hour broadcast with over 80 competing commercials.[218]

Today's television advertising scene is like guerrilla warfare, where there are opportunities to reach enormous numbers of potential customers quickly and efficiently *if* you have the right message on suitable programming. With the right inspiring creative, your brand can become a legend in sixty seconds, as in Apple's "1984" commercial, shown during 1984's Super Bowl XVIII. The athlete in red shorts running with a sledgehammer to demolish a computer screen aired only once over fifty years ago, and we are still talking about it. However, except for watching Super Bowl ads, most viewers today try to avoid watching ads on TV, instead taking the break time to double down on other activities like eating, emailing, texting, reading posts, and going to the bathroom.

Currently, US television penetration is over 96.5 percent. In 2018, it was equivalent to 304 million viewers and was still growing at about 0.5 percent per year.[219] In that same year, US Facebook users were estimated to be 222 million, and this number is currently increasing by about 1 percent per year.[220] So, television advertising isn't going away, it's just changing. In 2022, global advertising spending on linear TV (i.e., TV that's programmed and watched as scheduled through a satellite or cable network) was $166 billion, which had dropped by 5.4 percent from the previous year, and it is projected to continue this downward trajectory.[221] Meanwhile, advertising spending on connected TV (CTV; i.e., TV that's delivered digitally and on-demand through the internet) is growing exponentially. In 2023 US CTV ad spend hit $24.6 billion and is projected to surpass $42 billion by 2027.[222] Despite this growth rate, CTV is a quarter of the advertising spend of linear TV. While the CTV landscape is fragmented, advertisers there can benefit from enhanced targeting and measurement options, live interactivity, and e-commerce potential.

Linear TV is where the big mega brands play with multimillion-dollar marketing budgets. There is a sense of prestige associated with television (unless you are a local advertiser with a small budget, which is typically obvious from the production quality). Big brands use television to maintain brand awareness and as a barrier to keep out young, aggressive brands without cash.

We watch TV to be educated, informed, or entertained. In a Canadian study, 47 percent of TV viewers said they watch TV to be informed and educated, while 31 percent said they watch it to be entertained, and the rest said they relax after a busy day.[223] On average, 55 percent of Americans spend one to four hours daily watching TV, with 22 percent watching longer, almost 80 percent taking place in the evening.[224]

People haven't stopped watching TV. It's how they consume TV that is different. The idea of curling up on the couch with a bowl of popcorn to watch a show or movie may sound foreign to younger people who consume video content all day long as they commute to work, ride the elevator, or stand in line at the coffee shop waiting for their order.

The smartphone has a personalized experience and lets users control what they want to consume and when. Over half of adults watch video daily on their smartphones; no surprise, over 80 percent of generation Z is committed to daily watching.[225] Data from Netflix indicates that 60 percent of viewing is watched through a television; when it comes to smartphone viewing, there are two distinct subgroups: one group is watching teen-focused content, and the other group is watching adult sexual content.[226] As various streaming platforms consider ad-based models, advertisers must deeply understand these differences and usage patterns.

Before the smartphone invasion, we relied on Nielsen ratings to measure advertising success. Advertisers would buy gross rating points (GRPs), calculated based on the percentage of the target audience exposed to the message and the number of times the message was aired during the campaign. The other important component in any advertising plan is the campaign's duration. Did you want to reach maximum GRPs in a few weeks or months? This depended on your strategy and the buying patterns of your customers. Of course, the big problem with this formula was its inability to measure the creative impact of the message. If the commercial stank, you'd wasted much money for nothing. If it was memorable, emotional, and tactically impactful, you might only have needed to show it once. But we know this isn't always the case.

Beyond Nielsen ratings, today there is a wealth of real-time metrics to assess the reach and success of an advertising campaign, such as Google Trends, website traffic, social media listening, and product sales or inquiries. Suppose you bypass the traditional linear TV and focus on the internet CTV that offers on-demand video, live TV channels, and original programming on platforms like YouTube, Netflix, Hulu, Amazon Prime Video, Disney+, and HBO Max. In that case, you can access almost real-time viewership metrics for any call to action (CTA) links or offers you put out. CTV allows you the ability to react to the data by reducing your spend or increasing it to get the desired results.

The challenge with advertising on TV is its major barrier to entry: cost. While you might get your brand on a local TV station for pennies, with the station doing the creative production complete with big starbursts and a screaming salesperson, a professional commercial aired at primetime costs money—big money. Add a famous actor like Matthew McConaughey, who Salesforce hired as a spokesperson in 2023, and your production budget can exceed $10 million, which doesn't include the airtime![227]

Will TV advertising disappear? Eventually, linear TV will vanish, but CTV will continue to evolve with cutting-edge technologies, higher-definition visuals, crystal-clear audio, and better storytelling. TV advertising will continue to be a powerful channel to evoke emotions, create desire, and build brand narratives that will remind customers what your brand feels like. Augmented and virtual reality will also create immersive brand experiences that only our imaginations can see today. Integrating generative AI and machine learning will only enhance the experiences and allow advertisers to deliver custom personalization to create brand affinity and loyalty, and generate higher investment returns. As these changes occur, so will the seamless integration of other physical and digital advertising channels to create a brand metaverse.

Radio

In today's complex media landscape and busy lives, radio can still be a powerful and effective channel for building a brand. Despite the rise of digital platforms, radio reaches a broad audience, with Nielsen reporting that 91 percent of US adults tune in each week.[228] The medium's unique combination of broad reach, affordability, frequency of message delivery, and targeted demographic appeal makes it a potent tool for brand building. Additionally, radio advertising is cost-effective, fosters a sense of trust and credibility, and offers ample room for creative storytelling. These factors make radio a significant component of a comprehensive marketing strategy, capable of driving brand awareness, reinforcing brand values, and ultimately influencing consumer behavior.

Over a century ago, radio advertising was introduced in New York City. By 1930, almost 90 percent of radio stations in the United States broadcasted advertising.[229] Before radio advertising, print (newspapers, posters, flyers, etc.) and word-of-mouth were the primary advertising sources. In the 1920s, about 23 percent of Black people and 4 percent of the rest of Americans couldn't read.[230] Radio quickly became the primary source of up-to-the-minute news, live theater, fiction reading, sports and religious broadcasting, and music.

In chapter 13, Brand Sound, I discuss the importance of audio branding, especially music, as a robust connector to our memory. Advertising jingles were invented for the radio, like "Snap, Crackle, Pop" for Kellogg's Rice Krispies. A memorable, catchy jingle—or a distinctive voice like Matthew McConaughey's—can make an advertisement stand out, enhancing brand recognition and recall.

Radio advertising remains a relevant and powerful medium today. Despite the rise of digital channels, radio's accessibility, portability, and seamless integration into daily routines make it a valuable advertising platform. Radio is the most accessible channel globally, available for free without an internet connection or subscription. Its portability allows listeners to tune in while driving, working, or multitasking at home. Remarkably, radio commercials are part of the listening experience and daily routine, with listeners rarely muting or avoiding them.

The enduring popularity of radio is evident, with over 90 percent of Americans over 18 listening to one of the 15,000+ radio stations every month. [231] Globally, there was over 45,000 radio stations identified in 2016.[232] Radio has proven resilient, adapting to changing technologies and listener habits, remaining an important channel for news, music, entertainment, and advertising in the twenty-first century. Akin to television, radio is a trusted source of information, with nearly 70 percent of listeners tuning in while on the go or multitasking. [233]

Moreover, radio's accessibility has further increased with the rise of smart speakers like Amazon Echo, Google Home, Apple HomePod, and Sonos One, making it even more convenient for listeners. Radio's ability to seamlessly integrate into daily routines, coupled with its accessibility and portability, makes it a powerful advertising medium that continues to thrive in the modern era.

Compared to TV advertising, radio ads are cheap. Many factors determine the cost of an average thirty-second ad, such as time of day, placement, radio station demographics and market size, competition, seasonality, etc. For example, a thirty-second radio ad in New York City, with a potential reach of 7.8 million people based on thirty-eight radio stations, would cost approximately $1,400 per ad. Compared to Topeka, Kansas, with a reach of 123,000 people and twelve radio stations, would set you back only $25 per ad.[234] Of course, these costs don't include creative production, which can be anywhere from $500 to $50,000, depending on creative development, talent, and music copyright. Add in Matthew McConaughey's voiceover, and you can throw out any reasonable budget.

If you have an urgent message, you can produce it in the morning and have it on the radio that afternoon to millions of listeners. The radio creative can complement and easily repurpose other channel assets like voiceovers, music, and theme. While there are hundreds of radio stations to choose from, listeners have only a few go-to stations based on their preferred music and program formats (news, talk show, entertainment, comedy, etc.), allowing brands to reach niche markets that align with their brand target audience.

Digitization and AI are still in the early stages of transforming the radio listening experience. But think about the endless possibilities of dynamic creativity as AI customizes your message in real-time based on music genres, becoming a proxy for consumers' moods, understanding their actions (working, driving, walking) and frame of mind. Customized messaging is truly possible one day with the help of generative AI geotargeting from your smartphone.

Fast food restaurants like McDonald's and Subway are major radio advertisers because they literally drive customers into their locations with product promotions. Many companies build a brand personality through humor on the radio. A funny example is Bud Light's "Real American Heroes," later renamed "Real Men of Genius," a campaign developed by DDB Chicago that began with a series of twelve sixty-second radio spots in 1998. Each commercial focused on a mock tribute to men in overlooked professions or eccentric traits and habits, like the figure skater, the grocery store cart wrangler, and the really, really, really bad dancer. The campaign was so successful that it aired over two hundred "Real Men of Genius" spots over several years. In 2019, Bud Light produced a series of "Internet Heroes of Genius" audio spots on various streaming audio platforms.

Print

Print advertising has seen the most significant shift in its role and significance in brand building in the last ten years. While it's no longer the dominant force it once was, print advertising still holds value in certain contexts and for specific target demographics, such as baby boomers and affluent professionals.

Because boomers grew up with print media, they put more trust and credibility in print ads and spend more time reading through content than younger generations without the distractions of digital media. Yet as print becomes more cost-prohibitive and less environmentally friendly, fewer people will be interested in buying newspapers and magazines, and these will continue to disappear.

However, with a physical mailbox, direct mail can be a unique place to stand out against the digital noise. Today, getting physical mail is a novelty. According to the US Postal Service, over 80 percent of direct mail is read or opened, compared to only 30 percent of emails. The response rate for direct mail is 4.4 percent, while the response rate for email is only 0.12 percent.[235]

Glossy magazines are an art form with a cachet, showcasing beautiful images in fashion, travel, architecture, and collectibles, which resonates well with luxury consumers. High-end image-based magazines have seen a resurgence, supported robustly by luxury brands that value these publications' prestige and targeted reach. Luxury brands, focusing on exclusivity and high-quality presentation, find a natural ally in glossy magazines that exude sophistication and cater to an affluent readership. The tangible nature of these magazines complements the tactile allure of luxury goods, allowing for a sensory branding experience that aligns with the consumer's expectations for premium products.

Moreover, the editorial environment of high-end magazines provides a curated context that can enhance the perceived value of luxury advertisements. The readers of such publications often lead an aspirational lifestyle, and ads placed alongside relevant content can benefit from the halo effect of the surrounding editorial prestige. This audience is also more likely to appreciate the craftsmanship and design that goes into creating luxury goods and the high-quality print of the magazines. For example, Vogue, a fashion bible for over a century, continues to be a premier advertising destination for luxury fashion brands like Chanel, Louis Vuitton, and Dior. These brands craft visually stunning advertisements that speak to Vogue's fashion-forward audience. The magazine's reputation for showcasing the latest in high fashion through lush photography and exclusive content makes it an ideal platform for luxury brands aiming to reach consumers who appreciate the finer things in life.

Despite the growth of digital advertising, a segment of the consumer population still enjoys the leisurely pace and immersive experience of reading a physical magazine. Luxury brands have capitalized on this by investing in creative, visually striking ad campaigns that stand out on the pages of these publications. By doing so, they maintain their traditional customer base and reinforce their brand identity as purveyors of elegance and exclusivity. This strategic partnership between luxury brands and high-end magazines demonstrates a mutual recognition of the value of print media in maintaining a robust and sophisticated brand presence.

Out-of-Home

Out-of-home (OOH) advertising is a powerful medium for brand building, offering unique advantages in the increasingly fragmented media landscape. OOH advertising encompasses a variety of formats, including billboards, transit ads, street furniture, and digital signage, all strategically placed to reach consumers on the go.

One of the critical strengths of OOH advertising is its high-impact visibility. Billboards, for example, offer large-scale canvases that can capture the attention of drivers and pedestrians alike. These ads are often located in high-traffic areas, ensuring maximum exposure to a broad audience. This repeated exposure can increase brand recognition and help to keep the brand top-of-mind among potential customers.

OOH advertising also benefits from being part of the consumer's environment, seamlessly integrating into their daily routines. Unlike online ads that can be blocked or skipped, OOH ads cannot be turned off, making them a constant in the public space. This unavoidable presence means that brands can consistently reach their audience, including those who may be less accessible through digital channels due to ad fatigue or avoidance.

Moreover, OOH advertising allows for creative and engaging campaigns that can generate buzz and become landmarks or talking points in their own right. Innovative use of technology in digital OOH can lead to interactive experiences, further engaging the audience and creating memorable brand encounters. For instance, a digital billboard that changes content based on the time of day or weather conditions can demonstrate a brand's dynamism and relevance. In an innovative advertising campaign, McDonald's used digital billboards that would change their display depending on the weather. On a sunny morning, the billboard would show a bright image of an Egg McMuffin, enticing morning commuters to think of McDonald's for their breakfast needs. Alternatively, if it started raining, the billboard could switch to an image of a warm cup of coffee or a comforting meal, suggesting a cozy stop at McDonald's to escape the bad weather. A billboard scene of bathers frolicking on a sunny beach with a brilliant blue sky makes a strong juxtaposition against the reality of a bitterly cold January day.

The physicality of OOH advertising also lends itself to location-based targeting. Brands can place their messages in specific neighborhoods or near retail locations to drive foot traffic and immediate action. This strategic placement ensures that advertising efforts align closely with the brand's target demographics and market segments. Spotify has leveraged its vast data on user preferences to create personalized, localized billboard campaigns. Using humorous and relatable user data, like playlist names or listening habits, they've crafted messages that resonate with passersby, highlighting the brand's personal, user-centric approach.

Coca-Cola has been dominant in New York's Times Square for years. Its bright, iconic red-and-white billboards are not just advertisements; they've become landmarks. Dynamic digital screens allow Coca-Cola to display engaging content that captures the attention of passersby, reinforcing the brand's image as a classic yet modern staple in people's lives.

Out-of-home advertising supports brand building by offering high-visibility, non-intrusive placements that integrate into consumers' everyday lives, fostering recognition and engagement through creative, contextually relevant campaigns. It's an enduring medium that complements digital strategies and helps brands stand out in a crowded marketplace.

27 | EVENTS AND PROMOTIONS

Events and promotions can be powerful tools for building brand awareness and loyalty. When done correctly, they can help you connect with potential customers, generate buzz about your brand, and create a positive experience. There are several reasons to implement an event or promotion to attract attention, such as launching a product, increasing brand visibility, engaging customers and the community, announcing partnerships and collaborations, promoting social media content, and soliciting direct feedback. Not all events and promotions are created equal. It's important to make sure the event or promotion aligns with your brand commitment and appeals to your target audience in a meaningful way.

Events

Events offer a unique and immersive experience that goes beyond traditional marketing channels. They provide an opportunity for brands to create intimate connections with their audience through multisensory engagement. Unlike passive advertising, events allow for deeper interactions and potential for meaningful engagement. Attendees can see, touch, hear, and even taste the brand experience, fostering a stronger emotional connection. When you attend an event, you are surrounded by other people who are interested in the same thing as you. This creates a sense of community and belonging. Harley-Davidson motorcycles understood this, and it set up Harley Owners Group (H.O.G.) events across North America. Chapters popped up everywhere, and the company started sponsoring rallies to showcase new motorcycles. It was a win-win. The cult-like group attracted over half a million participants and the Harley nation was born. "I'm very into the Harley myth," says Alvin LaSalle, a sixty-three-year-old electrical contractor from California.[236] To prove it, he proudly displays Harley's trademark wings tattooed on his arm. The Hells Angels are loyal fans who supposedly use the Harley owner's manual as a bible at wedding ceremonies. Harley-Davidson's biggest challenge today is making the H.O.G. cooler for millennials, whose parents are still driving them.

Connecting with your audience personally creates a deeper connection and can be more memorable than any other marketing activity. At events, you can physically see how customers interact with your products and learn about their interests—vital information for improving your products and services.

Brand promotion can significantly benefit from events, mainly when targeting the media. Take the Chrysler Corporation, for instance, which was on the brink of bankruptcy in 1980, having lost the public's trust in its capability to produce quality vehicles. When Lee Iacocca assumed leadership of the company, he leveraged US President Carter's loan guarantees worth $833 million to launch two compact cars: the Plymouth Reliant and Dodge Aries, also known as K-cars. The company's goal was not only to regain customer confidence but also, of course, to make a profit.

Facing financial constraints, Chrysler needed to generate enthusiasm about its new products. It did this by hosting extravagant private media events throughout North America. These events were so lavish that they could have been mistaken for those hosted by luxury brands like Mercedes Benz. Automotive journalists were treated to fine dining and premium beverages, making them feel valued and important.

The strategy worked. The journalists were impressed, and the news about K-cars spread. In the first year alone, Chrysler sold 410,000 K-cars. By 1983, Iacocca had repaid the government loans ahead of schedule. According to auto historian David Lewis, no other company had ever rebounded from such a precarious position with essentially a single product.[237]

This case demonstrates how events, when attended by the right influencers, can generate buzz for a brand. They catalyze the spread of word, videos, and images and boost brand awareness.

Here are some specific tips for creating a successful event that generates buzz:

Choose the Right Target Audience: Who do you want to reach with your event? Once you know your target audience, you can tailor your event to their interests and needs.

Create a Strong Theme: Your event should have a clear theme that will resonate with your target audience. The theme should be reflected in everything from the event's décor to the activities and entertainment. Make the event photo and video worthy. Wow and surprise your audience.

Invite the Right Influencers: Who are the key people in your market who can help spread the word about your brand? Invite them to be speakers, panelists, or attendees.

Create a Buzzworthy Agenda: Your event should include activities and entertainment to engage your guests. Be sure to include something for everyone, such as recognizable keynote speakers, newsworthy panel discussion topics, or potential networking activities.

Promote the Event Effectively: Promote your event through all your communication channels, including social media, email, and print. The more people that know about your event, the more successful it will be.

Follow Up After the Event: Follow up with your guests and thank them for attending. Use this opportunity to collect feedback and provide a platform for an ongoing conversation.

Promotions

A promotion is a set of activities to increase the visibility, sales, and effectiveness of a product, service, or brand. It can take various forms, including advertising, public relations, sales promotions, and direct marketing.

Promotions can involve special offers such as discounts, rebates, freebies, buy one get one free (BOGO) offers, contests, or giveaways communicated through various channels such as TV and radio ads, online advertising, social media, email marketing, and in-store displays.

Promotions' primary goals are attracting new customers, retaining existing ones, increasing product awareness, and stimulating demand. They can also help differentiate a product or brand from competitors, reinforce the brand image, and encourage customer loyalty.

Promotions can become a detractor for branding if not executed carefully. An overreliance on frequent discounts and promotions may dilute the perceived value of a brand, causing consumers to associate the brand solely with low prices rather than its unique value proposition, quality, or identity. Additionally, promotions that are inconsistent with the brand's positioning or target audience can create confusion and undermine the brand's credibility. For example, deep discounts offered by a luxury brand may contradict its premium positioning and exclusivity. In highly competitive markets, promotions can become a race to the bottom, with brands constantly trying to outdo each other with deeper discounts or more aggressive offers, leading to a commoditization of the brand.

28 | SPONSORSHIPS

Sponsorship is not just about logos on jerseys, name mentions, or event banners; it's about creating meaningful partnerships that resonate with consumers and enhance the brand's overall perception. When executed thoughtfully, sponsorship can significantly build a solid and enduring brand identity. Sponsorship is a strategic marketing approach where a company pays to be associated with a particular event, team, individual, or organization in order to promote its brand and products. This concept has become a cornerstone of modern marketing strategies for companies looking to enhance their brand visibility, foster positive brand associations, and reach specific target audiences. Several types of sponsorships exist, such as events, teams, media, and venue naming.

Event Sponsorship

The most common form of sponsorships are events where a brand is associated with an event's theme or cause, such as music festivals, sports tournaments, art exhibits, conferences, and charity fundraisers. These are often treated as industry or community contributions made by a company as a good corporate citizen. But if used correctly, these are brand-building events. Here are a couple of simple examples.

WIN-WIN-WIN

My company had an opportunity to be the sponsor of the keynote speaker at an industry conference. The speaker was Clara Hughes, a dual-season Olympian. She is the only athlete in history to win multiple medals at the Summer and Winter Olympic Games—a total of six. Her journey to the podium wasn't easy, as she shared her mental health struggles in her book *Open Heart, Open Mind*—the foundation for her talk. Some companies might pass on this opportunity, thinking it too controversial. We saw this as a hero story of overcoming adversity—a perfect fit for many brands. Most sponsors would be happy if their CEO introduced Clara to a whole house of industry leaders. But this was only the beginning. Once committed to the sponsorship, we asked for more of Clara's time. The morning of the talk, she joined a private informal breakfast where she mingled with specially invited customers. Each received a signed copy of her book. After her fantastic speech, we announced that Clara would be available to sign copies of her book. We would provide the book for free but requested a donation to Clara's charity promoting mental health initiatives. While we acquired the book at a discount, the total amount of donations collected surpassed the retail price by two times. We also had people available to take pictures with participants' smartphones with Clara in front of a logo backdrop. The attendees shared these images on social media. These tactics substantially increased the value we got from our sponsorship and positioned our brand's values with those of an incredible Olympian.

For a national agriculture conference, a company I worked for was late to the sponsorship game, and all that was left was sponsoring the reception before the gala awards dinner. The reception took place in the hotel's lobby outside the ballroom. How do you promote your brand in that situation? Flash your logo on the walls? Display little tent cards on the cocktail tables? Offer a special branded drink? All of these ideas had merit, but we knew they would do little to promote our brand values. We had bolder ideas. We hired an actual bull and wrangler to show up in the lobby with our logo painted on his massive belly—creating a photo opportunity. How often does anyone get a chance to get a picture of themselves all dressed up and standing beside a giant bull? But that wasn't all. We wanted to promote one of our major products, a new canola seed. If you have ever seen a canola field, you may recall the brilliant yellow color of the plants when they bloom. We had the cocktail tables decorated with flower arrangements, except the flowers were canola flowers. Finally, to pull it all together, we asked for five minutes at the gala dinner to have our CEO welcome everyone to the gala. Remember, we weren't the gala sponsor. Another competitor was. Our CEO welcomed the guests, and as he finished his thoughtful message, he said, "We are bullish on agriculture." The audience went wild. Even the evening's entertainment commented on the bull and our brand.

As both of these stories illustrate, the sponsorship commitment is only the start. You need to invest more resources and creativity to leverage each opportunity and connect the event to your brand's values; otherwise, you're just another logo in a sea of logos. Remember, a brand isn't what it does but how it makes a customer feel. If you can tie your sponsorship to a feeling, that will always be more significant than logo recognition.

Trailblazer energy drink brand Red Bull is renowned for its sponsorships in extreme sports. To the tune of over $1 billion, they sponsor athlete events and even have their own teams in sports like Formula 1. Red Bull focuses on the emotions and aspirations associated with its brand's ethos by aligning with adrenaline-fueled mountain bikers, snowboarders, skydivers, and other high-performance athletes. The sponsorship events are just the beginning, as the company repackages the live content for other channels featured by its media company Red Bull Media House and its magazine, *The Red Bulletin*. The best part is the enormous amount of user-generated content that participants and fans share. The incredible power of authentic, thrilling non-advertising content contributes to Red Bull's brand credibility. Its most publicized event was the 2012 Red Bull Stratos project, which featured skydiver Felix Baumgartner freefalling 128 kilometers or almost 80 miles from the edge of space. Over 8 million people watched the live YouTube stream event. Beyond the live event, social media and new media channels echoed this story worldwide. If you count the YouTube views of the various posts on this one event, there are almost 300 million. That would give any brand wings!

Brands like Audi have made their mark by sponsoring prestigious events such as film festivals, including the Sundance Film Festival, where they receive on-site branding and mentions in promotional materials and sometimes provide additional services like VIP transportation. Even grand-scale events like the Oscars or Grammys attract corporate sponsorships, offering brands the chance to be associated with the glamour and prestige of these high-profile ceremonies and the cherished gift bags given to the nominees. These sponsorships can be highly effective branding tools, offering companies a platform to reach new audiences and reinforce their brand image in association with a popular event. Big or small, these types of sponsorships can advance your branding strategy beyond branding recognition and into the realm of coolness.

Team Sponsorship

Sponsoring a sports team is a more secure investment in sports marketing than individual athlete sponsorship, where a single athlete's missteps can have significant repercussions. Companies like Nike, Adidas, and Puma sponsor sports teams and have their logos prominently displayed on team jerseys, which millions of fans see. The financial entry point for team sponsorship can be pretty accessible, with costs varying based on the level of play, location, sport, and media exposure. Sometimes the sponsorship doesn't need to be financial, but can be an in-kind sponsorship. An "in-kind" product or service agreement is a type of sponsorship where goods, services, or expertise are provided instead of money. In these arrangements, the value is exchanged not in cash but by offering products or services with a specific value. You might hear these brands called the official suppliers of equipment, supplies, accommodations, transportation, etc. Fanatics, a sports e-commerce and retail operation, recently replaced Adidas as the official uniform supplier for the NHL from 2024 to 2034, for example.

A sponsorship can begin modestly at the local amateur or junior levels and scale up to the professional sphere through semi-professional ranks, often adjusted to local market conditions and audience size. There are also opportunities to incorporate your brand into the team's name over a long-term commitment. Avoid the knee-jerk reaction of a CEO sponsoring their child's sports team. Have a specific process for evaluating and leveraging every opportunity to ensure each one fits and builds on the brand strategy. If necessary, you can always consider just making a philanthropic donation to the child's team with no expectation of using the opportunity to build your brand, and then move on to more valuable brand-building opportunities.

Media Sponsorships

A media sponsorship is when a company supports a media entity, such as a television or radio program, a podcast, or even a live event operated by a particular media outlet. In exchange, the sponsoring company gains advertising, brand visibility, and other opportunities. For instance, Coca-Cola and AT&T have been high-profile sponsors of the popular television show *American Idol*, where their brands are seamlessly integrated into the show's content. Similarly, local businesses, like car dealerships, often sponsor segments on radio stations, such as traffic updates or weather reports, which typically include mentions of their business. Podcasts have also become popular spots for sponsorships, with hosts often reading out ads or discussing products within their episodes; for example, the well-known podcast *Serial* has featured sponsorships from Squarespace and Mailchimp.

Financial institutions might sponsor a particular business section of a newspaper, magazine, radio, or podcast to gain consumer exposure. In some cases, these are advertorials, which are more than just ads but are long-form editorial or journalistic articles. While these articles are marked as "advertisements," if they're written well with valuable in-depth information, audience engagement can be high compared to direct advertising. The advantage of these types of sponsorships is more than just advertising; it can create greater audience engagement and value with special offers and content. The digital world has opened even more possibilities, with companies sponsoring online video series on platforms like YouTube or articles on news websites. Social media campaigns are also fertile ground for sponsorships, where companies back social media challenges or campaigns that require participants to create content aligned with the sponsor's brand.

Name Rights Sponsorship

Naming rights sponsorship can be part of a branding strategy where a company purchases the exclusive rights to name a public venue such as a stadium, arena, or theater. This type of sponsorship is particularly prevalent in sports, where stadiums and arenas serve as homes for professional teams, and in the arts, where theaters and concert halls host various events. The company that acquires these rights benefits from significant brand exposure due to the venue's prominence in media coverage and public discourse, and its role as a landmark. The Staples Center in Los Angeles was a well-known instance where an office supply company secured the naming rights, in 1998, for the downtown LA venue for a bargain price of

$100 million for ten years.[238] After it became home to the Lakers squads that Kobe Bryant and Shaquille O'Neal led to three consecutive championships in the early 2000s, Staples signed another naming rights deal in perpetuity, until the owners bought the rights back in 2019 for an undisclosed amount. In 2021, the iconic sports and entertainment venue signed a new twenty-year naming rights agreement with Crypto.com for $700 million.[239]

Similarly, MetLife Stadium is home to the New York Giants and New York Jets. The public get a constant reminder of the insurance company when the stadium is mentioned during broadcasts and by fans. These sponsorships often extend for many years and involve a substantial financial investment, but they offer the sponsoring brand a permanent advertisement that reaches residents, visitors, and television audiences worldwide.

The Ideal Sponsorship

To help evaluate if a sponsorship is a fit with your brand values and branding strategy, here are some questions to consider:

Brand Objectives and Alignment

- How well does the sponsorship align with the company's overall branding objectives?
- Does the sponsorship maintain consistency with the brand's values and image?
- Will the sponsorship effectively reach the target audience?
- Are there opportunities for brand differentiation through sponsorship?
- Could the sponsorship lead to long-term partnerships or customer relationships?

Audience and Reach

- What is the size and demographic profile of the event's or initiative's audience?
- Are the event's audience and the brand's target customer base aligned?
- What engagement levels does the audience have with the event or initiative?
- How does the audience view current and past sponsors?

Exposure and Visibility

- What visibility will the brand receive before, during, and after the event/initiative?
- Is exclusive sponsorship an option, or will there be multiple sponsors?
- What are the types and sizes of branding placements available?
- Are there opportunities to use or amplify the team/event logo and name?
- What media coverage is anticipated, and what is its expected scope?
- How will the sponsorship enhance the brand's online and offline presence?

Engagement and Activation

- What opportunities are available for audience engagement?
- What are the available marketing opportunities through this sponsorship?
- How can activity content, social media, and digital platforms be used for further engagement?

Financial Considerations

- What is the total cost associated with the sponsorship opportunity?
- Are in-kind product or service contributions possible?
- What additional costs might be incurred for activation, promotion, staffing, etc.?
- Is there evidence to suggest a potential return on investment from the sponsorship?
- Are co-sponsorship opportunities available to share costs?
- What are the specified payment terms and conditions?
- Does financial reporting indicate that the sponsored organization is financially sound?

Legal and Compliance

- Have all contractual obligations and rights been thoroughly reviewed?
- Are there any potential legal or compliance issues with this sponsorship?
- How are intellectual property rights addressed within the agreement?
- What are the stipulated terms regarding cancellation, indemnity, and liability?
- Have all potential risks been identified and assessed?

Evaluation Metrics

- What metrics will be used to evaluate the success of the sponsorship?
- How will data be collected to measure these metrics?
- What constitutes a successful outcome for the sponsorship from a branding perspective?
- How will audience engagement and brand exposure effectiveness be assessed after the event?

Competitor Analysis

- Are there any competitors that also sponsor this event or initiative?
- What benefits have competitors historically realized from similar sponsorships?
- Is there potential to gain a competitive edge through participation in this sponsorship?

Miscellaneous

- Does the sponsorship agreement include an opportunity for product exclusivity?
- Are additional benefits included in the sponsorship, such as VIP experiences for clients or employees, ticket allocations, or special side events?
- Does the sponsorship facilitate community engagement or complement corporate social responsibility (CSR) initiatives?

By thoroughly evaluating these questions, you can decide whether a particular sponsorship opportunity will likely meet your strategic branding goals and provide a satisfactory return on investment (ROI).

Partnership

Brand partnerships, where companies collaborate to leverage each other's strengths and expand their branding reach, have become a strategic trend in the branding world. These alliances allow brands to tap into new markets, share resources, and leverage each other's brand equity and customer bases. A classic example is the collaboration between Nike and Apple, which resulted in the Nike+ product line combining Nike's athletic wear expertise with Apple's technology prowess. This partnership allowed both brands to reach a wider audience and enhance their offerings with the added value of integrated technology in sports apparel.

Another example is the collaboration between GoPro and Red Bull. GoPro's action cameras capture extreme sports content that Red Bull promotes, including the highly successful Red Bull Stratos project mentioned earlier. This partnership benefits both by aligning GoPro with high-adrenaline sports and reinforcing Red Bull's image as an energy drink for the adventurous.

These partnerships can be highly beneficial, providing cross-promotion opportunities and access to each brand's loyal customer base. However, there are risks involved. Brand mismatches can lead to confusion or dilution of brand identity if the partnering companies' values or market positions are not well-aligned. Moreover, any negative publicity or issues associated with one brand can spill over and impact the perception of its partner brand. Therefore, while the potential rewards are significant, brand partnerships must be approached with careful consideration and strategic alignment to ensure mutual benefit and success.

Influencers

Using influencers in marketing strategies has become increasingly popular, particularly for reaching younger audiences who spend significant time on social media platforms. Influencers, who are often seen as peers or aspirational figures by their followers, can lend authenticity and relatability to a brand. In 2023, the global influencer market value exceeded $21 billion, and it continues to grow.[240] A study conducted by e-commerce influencer marketing platform Sideqik indicates that trust in influencers continues to increase, and that influencers often drive 66 percent of purchase decisions. Sixty-four percent of those surveyed said influencers help them discover new brands.[241] Another exciting trend the survey found about the various social media platforms is that they are used less to connect with friends than with celebrities and influencers (except for Facebook, where 88 percent of users log on to keep up with real-life friends). This means that Instagram and TikTok are the best places for influencers to build their audiences, increase authenticity, and promote brands. So, brands should be focusing on influencers who are most active on these platforms.

The power of an influencer comes from their ability to reach a large and loyal audience and curate content in an engaging, personalized, and authentic way while providing value to their audience. At the same time, working with an influencer gives brands consumer insights, motivations, and preferences. Influencers cover all different types of interests, follower sizes, expertise, and abilities. Unlike in traditional media, influencers' genres or categories are still classified based on their interests, knowledge, and talent. The more famous they are, the less an influencer's expertise matters, as long as their trust level is high. Social media channels generally categorize their influences by number of followers, using terms like nano influencer (<15,000 followers), micro-influencer (15,000–50,000), midi influencer (50,000–500,000), macro influencer (500,000–1 million), and mega influencer (>1 million).

Currently, there doesn't seem to be a consensus on what makes a good engagement rate (measured by number of passive likes, comments, reshares, and total views) and there are no standard industry metrics to compare against for the various social media platforms or from one influencer to another. Therefore, it's essential to establish clear goals and key performance indicators (KPIs) for your brand before the campaign, and to consistently monitor and analyze the data throughout and after the campaign. Gathering feedback from each influencer and their audience can also provide valuable insights for future influencer marketing strategies.

The Brand Loyalty Formula is still applicable here. It's still paramount to provide relevant creative content, fit with the audience, and post with appropriate frequency and timing. What is different and vital in the world of social media is using relevant, popular, and niche-specific hashtags, understanding the platform's algorithms, and determining the best creative content format (stories, live stream, reels, etc.) for the message. One significant advantage of social media over traditional advertising is that performance results are available almost instantly. You can access metrics like likes, comments, shares, and saves by the hour or day to understand what content resonates with the audience. This will allow you to adapt quickly based on these insights.

TYPES OF INFLUENCERS

The types of influencers change all the time, as more people become influencers by accident or by design, by creating a unique experience for their followers. Influencer categories can be segmented by:

Subject Matter: Cooking, learning, lifestyle, health and wellness, fitness, sports, fashion, childcare, beauty

Interests/Hobbies: Traveling, food, parenting, gaming, photography, writing, art, pets

Subject Matter Expertise: Doctors, entertainers, athletes, educators, trainers, authors, podcasters, IT experts

Corporate Brand: Employees, CEOs, academics, thought leaders, ESG initiatives, customers

Political/Activism: Cause-related, not-for-profit, politicians, candidates, thought leaders, environmental experts, news reporters

Celebrity: Musicians, athletes, movie stars, singers, actors, comedians, leaders, CEOs, wealthy people

Business: Entrepreneurs, consultants, start-up leaders, speakers, authors

When Adidas partnered with influencer and reality TV star Kylie Jenner, the brand capitalized on her massive social media following to promote their products to a younger demographic that values trendsetters. Similarly, Dunkin' Donuts collaborated with TikTok star Charli D'Amelio, resulting in a new Dunkin's cold brew menu item named "The Charli," which helped the brand engage with gen-Z consumers who follow her content.

The benefits of using influencers include increased brand visibility, higher engagement rates, and the potential for rapid growth in brand awareness. Influencers can create content that resonates with and is shared among their followers, leading to organic marketing reach that traditional advertising might struggle to achieve.

However, there are risks associated with this strategy. Influencers may behave unpredictably, and any controversy they become involved in can negatively affect the brand's image. Moreover, if the influencer's audience perceives the partnership as inauthentic or purely transactional, it can lead to a backlash against the influencer and the brand. Additionally, there is the risk of over-saturation; as more brands employ influencer marketing, distinguishing these efforts and maintaining consumer interest can become increasingly challenging.

Influencer branding aims to tap into the influencer's engaged audience to increase brand awareness, establish authenticity, and ultimately build brand credibility and trust. This dynamic and personalized approach to brand building leverages the power of social proof and word-of-mouth at scale. It can significantly amplify a brand's presence and contribute to its growth and success.

Integrating sponsorships, partnerships, and influencers into a branding strategy can increase brand awareness and strengthen brand identity and consumer loyalty. For example, Glossier, a beauty and skincare brand, grew primarily through influencer marketing by leveraging high-profile and micro-influencers to create authentic content around its products. The brand focuses on real people using their products in real-life scenarios, which has helped them build a loyal customer base.

29 | SPOKESPERSON

To love a brand, you need to trust a brand. Trust is one of the primal instincts humans have relied on to form bonds and work together for centuries. That's why people connect with people. In a Nielsen trust survey, 88 percent of respondents said they most trust recommendations from people they know.[242] A brand can build a trusted connection with customers by putting a face (real or fake) to the company. Providing a face for the brand immediately helps differentiate it from the competition and makes it more human, approachable, and authentic.

Some brands are virtually synonymous with their founder and CEO, especially in eponymous brands named after them, like Henry Ford, Coco Chanel, Michael Dell, Walt Disney, Martha Stewart, Oprah Winfrey, Mary Kay, and Louis Vuitton. These people shared not only their names with their brand, but also their unique stories and values. Product quality was paramount, and it came with a personal commitment that consumers could trust. Who better than the founder of a brand to tell their customers their story? Especially a story that is the driving force behind why they do what they do.

Then there are the brands that have founders and CEOs that are just as famous as the brand, such as Amazon's Jeff Bezos, Virgin Group's Sir Richard Branson, Tesla and X's Elon Musk, Meta's Mark Zuckerberg, Microsoft's Bill Gates, and Spanx's Sarah Blakely.

Many founders and CEOs don't have the desire or skillset to be the face of their brand, nor do they have the time to invest in building their own cachet. The best alternative is to hire a celebrity to become a brand spokesperson and endorser. Celebrities bring instant awareness and trust to a brand as they convert their fan base into brand consumers, Nike being a prime example with its long-standing Michael Jordan partnership.

Of course, any human spokesperson comes with risks, as a person can always do something to break the trust of their followers. Depending on the severity of their actions, they can directly impact a brand they are associated with.

Let's examine each of these options and explore their merits, advantages, and disadvantages.

Founder and CEO

Who better to represent a brand than the person who created it in the first place? Their brand story, passion, and commitment are intrinsically tied to their brand and products. How better to articulate the brand's "why" than the person who conceived it? However, most brands don't start with a purpose or mission but with a crazy idea that turns into a product or service. It may take a few years of blood, sweat, and tears before the brand's "why" becomes evident.

Start-ups, small businesses, and entrepreneurs can benefit from fostering a personal connection with their communities via their CEO or leader. Professionals like coaches, consultants, influencers, and authors are all brands. However, they must be careful not to let the brand be more significant than themselves. They need to have an exit strategy in case they ever decide to sell the brand or retire.

High-end or luxury brands can also benefit from putting a face to the exclusivity and premium experience. For example, having the chef of an eponymous restaurant come out of the kitchen to greet customers and ask about the meal can significantly affect the final tip.

Brands that sell a lifestyle or an ideology (like caring, fitness, health, eco-friendly, etc.) have a better chance of generating recognition and media attention if they have a charismatic and passionate brand ambassador who lives and breathes the brand's values. Dame Anita Roddick, the founder of the highly successful "anti-cosmetic" brand The Body Shop, promoted a more ethical way to sell health and wellness. She helped change business language, incorporating social change in human rights, animal welfare, the environment, and community trade. As an activist, she demonstrated that a business could be profitable and ethical without spending a cent on advertising.

In the business-to-business arena, having a brand face can also help make your brand stand out. Even nonprofit organizations can profit from having a recognizable face associated with a cause. Donors, supporters, and volunteers appreciate connecting with a brand leader who is emotionally invested in a worthy mission.

While any brand can use a brand ambassador strategy effectively, it's important to make sure the person representing the brand aligns with its values, resonates with the target audience, and authentically promotes the brand's products or services. Also, remember a brand ambassador's goal is not to sell products or services but to build a community around the brand's values and mission.

Here are some actions that a brand owner can take to fulfill this role effectively:

Live the Brand: Embody the values and mission of your brand. Consistently demonstrate these values in your actions and decisions every day.

Communicate Clearly: Perfect the brand elevator pitch that resonates with your audience, and don't be afraid to repeat it multiple times. Again, be consistent in your words, tone, and style.

Be the Face: Actively participate and engage with your audience through social media, public appearances, events, and media engagements. Passionately share your story and the brand's "why" to create a personal connection with your audience.

Show Empathy: Listen to your brand community's needs and concerns and respond in a way that demonstrates that you care and value their input.

Build a Network: Expand your influence and relationships with other industry leaders, influencers, and potential customers. The more people know your brand and what it stands for, the more opportunities there will be to grow.

Embrace a Better World: Be the voice supporting diversity, equity, and inclusion in the workplace and your communities, and align your brand with social and environmental causes that resonate with your values.

Stay Informed and Educated: Don't assume you have all the answers. Keep current on industry trends, market dynamics, technology, and customer preferences to continue improving. Seek to learn more about the world and how changes affect your industry, business, and customers.

Celebrity

The quickest way to get your brand noticed and to increase sales is to have a famous singer, musician, actor, or athlete endorse your brand. An economic study by the Harvard Business School found that signing a big-name celebrity resulted in a sales increase of approximately 4 percent relative to competitors and a quarter of a percentage increase in stock returns.[243]

Using celebrities to influence consumer behavior has been around since Roman times when gladiators recommended oils and wines to their fans. One of the first recorded celebrity endorsements was for Waltham Watches, high-quality pocket watches that used Reverend Henry Ward Beecher in an advertisement in *Harper's Weekly* in 1870. The prominent and charismatic Beecher served at the Plymouth Church in Brooklyn, New York, where his captivating preaching style and progressive views on social issues made him immensely popular—until 1875, when he was accused of adultery in a highly publicized trial that had a lasting impact on his reputation and endorsement opportunities. But that didn't stop other brands from employing entertainers and movie stars. In the early 1900s, the highly competitive and growing cigarette industry used comedians Fatty Arbuckle and Harry Bulger and movie stars such as Fred Astaire, Ethel Barrymore, Jack Benny, and Henry Fonda. In 1934, baseball hitter Lou Gehrig of the New York Yankees was the first athlete to appear on a Wheaties cereal box with the slogan "The Breakfast of Champions." Since then, hundreds of athletes from different sports have been on the front of the Wheaties box, including Jesse Owens, Babe Ruth, Shaquille O'Neal, Michael Jordan, Tiger Woods, and Serena Williams.

Throughout her career, Oprah Winfrey repeatedly proved that an authentic celebrity with dedicated followers can influence them to buy almost anything—this became known as the Oprah Effect. When Oprah endorsed a product because she truly loved it, it would immediately experience a significant boost in sales and brand recognition. Her book club is estimated to have sold over 55 million books of its seventy selected titles. Then there were her annual "Oprah's Favorite Things" lists, from which selected products sold out overnight. Spanx's sales skyrocketed when Oprah enthusiastically promoted the brand as one of her "Favorite Things" in 2000. In 2015, Oprah bought a 10 percent stake in WeightWatchers and became its spokesperson when the company struggled. After her involvement and endorsements, the company's stock more than doubled, gaining five million new subscribers.[244]

The more famous the celebrity, the greater the cost, of course. But there is also value in less-well-known celebrity endorsements with niche appeal. Ultimately, the decision should be based on alignment with your brand's values, target audience, and marketing objectives with a thorough cost-benefit analysis and a clear understanding of the potential risks and rewards.

Mascot

A mascot can be a person, a fictional character, an animal, or an inanimate object. Mascots often possess anthropomorphic qualities, embodying human characteristics like talking, walking, and dancing. They can originate from cartoons, illustrations, and animations, such as those commonly found on cereal boxes.

Mascot branding plays a vital role in visually and emotionally connecting with fans and consumers, creating iconic symbols that encapsulate the associated brand or team's values, spirit, and identity. In addition, the mascot's presence fosters a strong bond between the audience and the represented entity.

The term "mascot" finds its origins in the French word *mascotte*, which translates to "good-luck charm." The first documented sighting of a sports mascot was at Yale's football and baseball games in 1892, well before Harvard considered adopting a mascot. Before each Yale game, a purebred English bulldog named Handsome Dan would proudly parade across the field. Since then, eighteen different bulldogs have held the esteemed title of Yale's mascot.[245] If you visit Yale's Payne Whitney

Gymnasium, you can see the original Handsome Dan, stuffed and standing guard in a protective glass case.

Any creature or object can be anthropomorphized today thanks to advancements in digital technology, computer-generated imagery, and 3D animation. These allow us to bring mascots to life in various settings, such as sports games or special events. And of course live mascots in oversized costumes can interact with customers at such events, creating an engaging and immersive experience.

One of the notable advantages of using a mascot is the ability to have complete control over its physical characteristics and personality. Operators can dictate their actions and words, ensuring a consistent representation. However, it is worth mentioning that there have been some instances, such as in Japan, of unauthorized mascot look-alikes used to disrupt events by attempting to damage the brand's reputation.[246]

As the owner of a mascot, you can modify or adjust every aspect of the character, particularly when your target audience's demographics and sociographic preferences change. Unlike humans, mascots are carefully orchestrated and do not age, like the Wendy's mascot with her recognizable red pigtails and freckles. Even after fifty-three years, she remains forever nine years old. There was only one occasion when her appearance differed: she was temporarily transformed from a redhead to a greyhead in Canada to support the fight against age discrimination, a conversation that had been sparked when renowned news anchor Lisa LaFlamme embraced her natural gray hair and was terminated after thirty-five years of service.

The primary purpose of mascot branding is to infuse the brand with human qualities by associating them with a symbolic character that reinforces the brand's image and delivers promises customers can resonate with. When executed effectively, a mascot can establish a memorable and distinct identity that separates your brand. In addition, a mascot can be the most straightforward and swiftest way to differentiate your product and service in a world inundated with countless brand messages and images.

According to a 2021 whitepaper by the Moving Picture Company (MPC), incorporating a character-driven approach in long-term campaigns can lead to an 11-percent-greater chance to increase market share gain compared to campaigns that do not feature a character.[247] Additionally, brand campaigns with mascots yield an 8 percent boost in profit gains and attract nearly 9 percent more new customers. A 2018 study also revealed that mascot branding advertising campaigns generated an 8-percent-higher voice share than campaigns without mascots.[248]

Interestingly, despite these compelling advantages, the use of mascots in branding has witnessed a decline of 30 percent over the past three decades.[249] Currently, only 4 percent of brand ads in the US employ mascots.[250] This presents a significant opportunity for brands to capitalize on if they aim to enhance profitability, increase their share of voice, and foster deeper emotional connections with customers.

Mascots hold a special place in our hearts for multiple reasons beyond serving as the face and personality of a brand. They possess an inherent charm, like babies or pets, eliciting feelings of protectiveness, playfulness, and simplicity. Their primary objective is to capture your attention and, ideally, win your affection. They can also be designed to be attractive, funny, charming, and endearing, bringing joy, laughter, and excitement to audiences. Their playful and lively nature can be captivating and enjoyable to watch or interact with. Finally, their personalities and actions evoke emotional resonance, creating feelings of affection and fondness.

Due to their human-like characteristics, people are naturally drawn to mascots, developing stronger emotional connections compared to brands without mascots.

Unlike celebrities who demand fees for every appearance, mascots are managed by a team of brand stewards who meticulously oversee every word, expression, and action. Mascots undergo extensive scrutiny and consumer testing to ensure their presence evokes the desired emotional response. Every aspect is carefully orchestrated, leaving nothing to chance.

By harnessing the power of mascot branding, brands can forge a distinctive and engaging identity that resonates with consumers on a deeper level, driving growth and profitability.

HUMAN MASCOT

One of the first human mascots debuted in 1877 on a Quaker Oats cereal package. The US Patent Office registered the trademark as "a figure of a man in 'Quaker garb.'" In the seventeenth century, George Fox initiated the Quaker Movement, also known as the Religious Society of Friends. This movement was not solely centered around religious beliefs but was a way of life rooted in simplicity, respect, honesty, and integrity. Interestingly, the co-owners of Quaker Oats, Henry Seymour and William Heston, were not Quakers themselves. Nonetheless, they chose the name and mascot image for its positive connotations, symbolizing good quality and ethical values—traits they wanted the Quaker Oats brand to embody.[251] Even after nearly 150 years, this brand mascot has remained essentially unchanged.

One of the most controversial brand mascots was Aunt Jemima, associated with the Aunt Jemima pancake mix brand, which debuted in 1889. Aunt Jemima, a portrayal of a Black southern woman dressed as a "mammy," represented a character who worked in the kitchen of a white family. The mascot drew inspiration from a minstrel show featuring a song called "Old Aunt Jemima." Nancy Green, a formerly enslaved person from Kentucky, portrayed the Aunt Jemima character from 1890 until 1923. Throughout history, the depiction of Aunt Jemima has faced criticism and protest from civil rights activists and the Black community as a racist caricature of an enslaved Black woman. After multiple alterations to the mascot's image, the brand and mascot were ultimately retired in 2021, making way for the Pearl Milling Company.

Another iconic humanoid mascot emerged in 1898 with the creation of the Michelin Man by cartoonist Marius Rossillon for the Michelin tire company. This mascot was made up of a collection of white tires, making him resemble a formidable snowman. André and Edouard Michelin had founded the company in 1891 and revolutionized the tire industry by inventing removable pneumatic tires. Although the founders and subsequent CEOs have come and gone, the Michelin Man has endured and remains relevant today, spinning his way across the globe.

Leo Burnett, a titan of advertising, left an indelible mark on the industry with his innovative use of mascots to build brand identity. Launching his agency during the Great Depression, Burnett was instrumental in reviving struggling brands by tapping into the "inherent drama" of products.[252] He transformed the Green Giant mascot from a menacing figure into a friendly giant, aligning the brand with symbols of strength and vitality, which elevated the Green Giant Company to national fame.[253]

Burnett's genius was further demonstrated in the rebranding of Marlboro cigarettes. Originally marketed to women, the brand found success after Burnett reimagined it for a male audience, epitomized by the rugged Marlboro Man. This icon connected smoking with masculinity and individuality, until advertising regulations changed in 1999.[254]

Burnett's philosophy centered on the belief that every product has an inherent story that resonates deeply with consumers when linked with universal archetypes or symbols. His approach made mascots a cornerstone of brand building, proving they could forge powerful, symbolic connections with audiences.

The story of Ronald McDonald demonstrates how a human mascot can become an iconic branding symbol by evolving beyond a marketing gimmick into a multidimensional character that makes personal connections. Though initially conceived to sell burgers, Ronald was transformed through market research and strategic redesign into a trusted, relatable friend to children. His journey shows that the most effective human mascots are not mere spokespeople but beloved personalities with richness, depth, and heart who build enduring bonds with their audiences. McDonald's precision in shaping Ronald's personality and experiences enabled him to provide unique one-on-one interactions that traditional ads couldn't replicate. Ultimately, the qualities making Ronald seem real empowered him to become a valuable icon.

Ronald McDonald's success as a mascot can be attributed to several key elements:

Relatable Human Persona: Ronald's human qualities made him a relatable and approachable figure for children and families, fostering a personal connection with the brand.

Strategic Brand Alignment: The mascot was carefully aligned with McDonald's core values and messaging, symbolizing fun and family-friendly dining experiences.

Consistent Characterization: Across different actors and media, Ronald maintained a consistent personality and appearance, which helped in building a strong, recognizable brand identity.

Targeted Audience Engagement: Ronald effectively influenced family dining decisions by focusing on children, positioning McDonald's as a "fun eating" destination for the younger demographic.

Multi-channel Presence: Ronald's presence on television, in parades, at events, and through licensed products created multiple touchpoints for consumer engagement.

Evolution Over Time: The character evolved from a simple mascot to a representative of philanthropic efforts, deepening the brand's emotional connection with its audience.

Cultural Resonance: Ronald became a cultural icon, achieving near-universal recognition among American children, comparable to Santa Claus.

Like many human mascots, Ronald McDonald is not just a mascot but an integral part of the McDonald's brand, contributing significantly to its global success and enduring legacy.

ANIMAL MASCOT

The profound connection between humans and animals, deeply rooted in our evolutionary history, has been leveraged by brands to create influential mascots that resonate with consumers on an emotional level.[255]

Brands like Disney have capitalized on this connection, creating timeless characters such as Mickey Mouse, which have won audiences' hearts and driven the brand to a multibillion-dollar success. Similarly, R.J. Reynolds's Camel cigarettes used the exotic appeal of a camel to dominate the US tobacco market despite subsequent declines due to health awareness.

Animal mascots have also been pivotal in the breakfast cereal industry, with characters like Tony the Tiger and Toucan Sam becoming synonymous with their respective brands. The global breakfast cereal market is projected to skyrocket to a staggering $108 billion by 2030, with Kellogg's and General Mills commanding nearly 60 percent of the market share.[256] The strategic use of animal mascots offers control, adaptability, and a cost-effective alternative to human endorsements, tapping into the inherent cultural meanings that animals convey. Studies reveal that dogs are the most popular animals in advertising due to their association with happiness, family, and loyalty.[257] The most famous dog mascot could arguably be Snoopy, the beagle from the *Peanuts* comic strip created by Charles M. Schulz. Known for his imaginative adventures, independence, and charm, Snoopy has been used in branding by MetLife Insurance and as a mascot for NASA.

Let's not forget the cat lovers and Morris the Cat, who helped build the 9Lives cat food franchise of over fifty years. Morris made his debut in 1968 after he was discovered at the Humane Society in Hinsdale, IL. The orange tabby cat had the right attitude and starred in over fifty 9Lives commercials, including several Super Bowl appearances. In 1983, *Time* magazine declared Morris "the feline Burt Reynolds." *US* magazine called Morris the "animal star of the year" for three years from 1982 to 1984). He is also credited with "writing" three books on cat care. Over the years, this finicky cat food connoisseur has downplayed his negative attitude to reach the new millennial customer with a more "charmingly choosy" attitude. Not surprisingly, this cat is on all the social media channels. Morris has been played by at least three different tabby cats, maybe more.

Animal mascots are a potent branding tool that can evoke deep emotional connections, embody brand attributes, and drive significant market success.

OBJECT MASCOTS

Object mascot branding has the incredible ability to bring life and personality to various products. By adding eyes, a nose, and a mouth, you can make an object captivate consumers. This approach is a fantastic way to highlight a product's uniqueness or category, as demonstrated by iconic mascots like the Pillsbury Doughboy, the Kool-Aid Man, and even Microsoft's infamous Clippy.

The Pillsbury Doughboy, made of the same dough found in the company's baking products, is a prime example of a lovable mascot that embodies freshness, warmth, and homemade goodness. The Doughboy has become synonymous with Pillsbury's brand image with his iconic chef's hat and scarf, giggly voice, and playful personality. The memorable commercials featuring a finger poking his belly and his infectious giggle have significantly contributed to Pillsbury's remarkable tenfold growth in sales in thirty years—from $81 million to $840 million.[258]

In 1975, the Kool-Aid Man burst onto the scene, instantly captivating kids with his energetic and irreverent antics. Breaking through walls like a wrecking ball and exclaiming his famous "Oh, yeah!" catchphrase, the Kool-Aid Man became a beloved mascot and helped propel Kool-Aid to a top spot in the soft drink category. His popularity extended to comic books and video games, solidifying his cultural impact.

However, not all mascots enjoy the same success. Clippy, the paper clip assistant introduced by Microsoft in 1996, is an example of a mascot that failed to resonate with its audience. While initially intended to assist users in navigating the complexities of word processing, Clippy quickly became an annoyance and an invasion of privacy. The character's lack of likability, compounded by its intrusive behavior, led to its eventual decline and removal from Microsoft Office products.[259]

These examples highlight the importance of defining a mascot's personality, values, attributes, and essence in alignment with the brand. A mascot should be likable and serve as a positive representation of the brand's character and message. The Pillsbury Doughboy and the Kool-Aid Man successfully personified their respective brands' qualities and resonated with consumers, increasing sales and brand recognition.

In summary, object mascots have the power to enhance branding efforts by infusing products with personality. Companies can create memorable and impactful connections with consumers by carefully crafting mascots that embody the brand's values and resonate with the target audience.

MASCOT FUTURE

In today's brand-saturated environment, mascots have a bright future. They don't come with all the hassles of humans, who can be unpredictable and inconsistent, deviating from brand scripts and expectations. Mascots don't age or change in appearance and are not subject to human frailties and mortality. Mascots offer timeless consistency and can evolve as needed to stay relevant to trends. They can also become stars in the virtual world.

History has proven that mascots have outlasted their human counterparts, offering a reliable and unchanging face to a brand. They carry no political or social baggage, making them a safe choice to avoid controversy. With society's push toward inclusivity, brands must scrutinize their mascots to avoid perpetuating stereotypes, particularly regarding gender, race, and ethnicity.

Research has shown that while animal mascots are prevalent, there is an imbalance in representation concerning gender and race portrait by these animals.[260] As brands work to correct these disparities, there's a trend toward creating non-human mascots that are neutral and inclusive.

However, mascots should not be the sole focus of a brand strategy. They must complement an overarching brand narrative with solid positioning, a unique value proposition, and consistent communication. Professional designers and branding experts can ensure that a mascot aligns with a brand's broader goals.

Mascots resonate with people for various reasons, including entertainment value, emotional connection, nostalgia, and social appeal. They should be thoughtfully integrated into a brand's strategy to enhance differentiation and create memorable customer experiences.

Ultimately, mascots should evoke affection that extends to the brand itself. Successful mascots often possess qualities of cuteness, innocence, and relatability. Pixar's desk lamp mascot is a great example that demonstrates how a non-human character can become endearing through human-like behaviors without appearing too human-like, which could cause audience discomfort.[261] Striking the right balance is essential to ensure that the mascot's appeal remains captivating and relatable.

Although mascots may not be an ideal fit for luxury, high-end, mature, modern, or serious brands like those in the healthcare, finance, security, or professional services sectors (such as law, accounting, or consulting firms), for others they can serve as powerful branding tools when implemented as part of a comprehensive strategy that aligns with a company's identity and values. Mascots have the potential to build deep emotional connections with audiences and act as enduring symbols for brands operating in competitive markets. When carefully designed and integrated into a brand's overall positioning and target audience, mascots can effectively represent a company's personality and foster lasting relationships with consumers.

30 | DIGITAL CONTENT

Digital content is the new king; content creation and distribution have become central to a brand strategy. In the digital age, brands are no longer just providers of products or services; they are storytellers, educators, and entertainers. The democratization of media through digital channels means that any brand can adopt the role of a content creator, akin to traditional media outlets like newspapers, magazines, radio, and TV stations. Agile brands that can anticipate the future and take advantage of digital opportunities will win.

Brands are increasingly taking on the mantle of content creators, a shift that underscores the importance of engagement in the modern marketplace. With consumer attention being a highly prized commodity, the ability to craft and disseminate compelling content is crucial for capturing and maintaining interest. This evolution from mere product or service providers to content producers allows brands to engage with audiences more deeply, transcending traditional advertising methods that may no longer resonate as effectively with a media-savvy public.

Moreover, by offering valuable and relevant content, brands position themselves as authorities within their respective fields. This authoritative stance cultivates trust among consumers, who turn to these brands for reliable information and solutions. Red Bull, for instance, which I've mentioned a few times, exemplifies this approach by aligning its brand with high-energy sports and adventure content, reinforcing its image as an energizing beverage.

Content creation also plays a pivotal role in community building. When a brand consistently delivers content that resonates with its audience, it fosters a sense of belonging among its consumers. This community is not just a customer base but a group of brand advocates who share common interests and values reflected in the brand's content. A loyal community is instrumental in driving word-of-mouth promotion and sustaining long-term brand loyalty.

From an operational perspective, being a content creator enhances a brand's visibility online. Search engines reward quality content with higher rankings, which translates to increased visibility for the brand, making it more accessible to potential customers searching for related topics. The strategic use of keywords and the provision of valuable content are key to a brand's search engine optimization (SEO), to ensure it remains prominent in search results.

Furthermore, assuming the role of a media publisher grants brands unparalleled control over their messaging. This level of control allows brands to craft their narrative directly without reliance on external media outlets that may dilute or misrepresent their messaging. By creating their own content, brands like Red Bull can ensure their stories are authentic and align with their brand values.

Lastly, published content yields a wealth of data and insights into consumer behavior. Brands can track engagement metrics, such as shares, comments, and time spent on a page, to understand what resonates with their audience. This information is invaluable for refining future marketing strategies and can guide product development to better meet consumer needs.

The ability to engage audiences, establish trust, build communities, enhance online visibility, control messaging, and gather consumer insights places brands that excel in content creation at a distinct advantage in the competitive digital landscape. Here are some tips to get started:

Define Your Voice and Niche: Determine what unique perspective your brand brings. Patagonia, for example, focuses on outdoor adventures and environmental sustainability, aligning with its brand image as a company that produces high-quality outdoor gear while promoting environmental activism.

Invest in Quality Production: Whether it's articles, videos, or podcasts, the content must be professionally produced to stand out. Apple sets a high standard with well-produced videos and visuals that showcase the sleek design and innovative features of their products, often with a minimalist and artistic approach.

Build a Content Team: Assemble a team of writers, editors, videographers, and social media managers who can consistently produce and distribute content.

Diversify Content Formats: Create a mix of written articles, videos, podcasts, infographics, and live streams to cater to different preferences and platforms. Ensure your content aligns with and complements your brand's vision and mission.

Create a Content Calendar: Plan your content to ensure a steady stream of timely and relevant material.

Engage with Your Audience: Use content as a two-way conversation. Encourage comments, shares, and feedback to create an interactive experience.

Measure and Analyze: Use analytics tools to track engagement and understand what works. Use these insights to continuously refine your content strategy.

Leverage Partnerships: Collaborate with influencers, other brands, or content creators to expand your reach and add credibility to your content.

Promote Your Content: Use social media, email newsletters, SEO, and even paid advertising to ensure your content reaches your target audience.

Remember, the goal is not merely to produce content for its own sake or to mimic a media outlet; instead, it is to use the content as a means to an end, that end being the strengthening and proliferation of the brand's presence in the market. Content should act as a beacon, drawing in consumers with its relevance and resonance and guiding them toward a deeper connection with the brand. In doing so, you can cultivate a lasting relationship with your audience, turning consumers into loyal advocates.

31 | REVIEWS

Customer reviews and ratings are pivotal, serving as the digital equivalent of word-of-mouth endorsements for brands. They are the linchpins of credibility and trustworthiness in an online world where every consumer has a platform to share their experiences. While aspiring to the coveted five-star rating, brands often find their true mettle tested not by their praise but by how they handle criticism. The digital landscape is fraught with potential pitfalls, as customers have myriad outlets such as review sites, social media, and blogs to express dissatisfaction. The accurate measure of a brand's strength is found in its response to less-than-perfect reviews—how promptly and effectively it addresses concerns and whether its customer service can turn a negative into a positive.

Therefore, the importance of monitoring and managing your reviews cannot be overstated. Active review monitoring lets brands stay informed about customer sentiment and swiftly address concerns. When a brand encounters less-than-flattering reviews, responding with both explanation and empathy is crucial. A well-crafted response to a negative review should acknowledge the customer's experience, explain if necessary, and show genuine compassion for any inconvenience caused. This transparent communication can transform a negative perception into a positive one by demonstrating the brand's commitment to customer satisfaction.

Moreover, brands must maintain professionalism online, especially when engaging with dissatisfied customers. Engaging in public disputes can further harm a brand's image; instead, brands should aim to de-escalate the situation. A constructive approach is to invite the customer to continue the conversation through more direct communication channels. By asking the disgruntled customer to contact a call center or customer service team, brands move the conversation from a public forum to a private one, where issues can be addressed in detail without exposing them to the scrutiny of other potential customers.

This strategy prevents the escalation of conflict and shows other customers and prospects that the brand is proactive and serious about resolving issues. Moreover, it provides an opportunity for personalized service recovery efforts that can lead to the customer revising their initial negative review or spreading positive word-of-mouth after a satisfactory resolution. In essence, the careful handling of online reviews is a critical component of reputation management. It plays a significant role in building and maintaining a trustworthy and customer-centric brand image.

An untarnished record of exclusively positive reviews can paradoxically arouse suspicion, as authenticity in customer feedback is expected. A mix of positive and negative reviews, on the other hand, can lend credibility to a brand's image. The brand's empathetic and constructive engagement with its customers can transform challenges into opportunities for building stronger relationships. The innovative concept of two-way reviews, where businesses can also provide customer feedback, introduces a new dynamic to the review process, fostering a sense of mutual respect and understanding.

Ultimately, the most impactful endorsements arise spontaneously from satisfied customers. Unsolicited user-generated content—photos, videos, or glowing testimonials—represents the zenith of brand loyalty. Such content is a testament to a brand's success in meeting and exceeding customer expectations, embodying the essence of an authentic and credible brand presence in the digital age.

FISKER'S COLLISION WITH VIRAL REVIEW

A single review of the Fisker Ocean vehicle, posted by Marques Brownlee, a popular YouTuber known as MKBHD who has over 18 million subscribers, cast the electric vehicle start-up Fisker in a negative light. Brownlee's video, which garnered over 4.4 million views in less than a month, harshly criticized the Ocean SUV for its various issues ranging from unlabeled buttons and unmonitored solar panels to software glitches. The situation worsened when a senior Fisker engineer's attempt at damage control backfired, as a recorded call admitting to ongoing software issues was made public, attracting an additional 3.6 million views.

This event underlines the power and influence of social media personalities in shaping public opinion about products. With more subscribers than some of the leading traditional media outlets combined, Brownlee's negative review had significant repercussions. However, despite the adverse coverage, Fisker did inadvertently gain substantial brand awareness, introducing the company to consumers who might have been previously unaware of it.

Furthermore, the financial challenges faced by Fisker are highlighted, with the company's market capitalization experiencing a significant decline, raising concerns about its ability to continue operations and long-term viability. Despite a successful initial valuation and a promising start for Henrik Fisker's new venture after the failure of his first company, Fisker's Ocean SUV became known for its subpar quality compared to competitors.

While Fisker gained untold media attention, not all of it was positive. The company must now navigate this challenging period by addressing the product issues raised and rebuilding consumer trust. The situation serves as a cautionary tale for start-ups about the importance of product quality and the impact of influential reviews in today's digital landscape.

Good and Bad Reviews

Online reviews play a crucial role in shaping a brand's reputation and influencing potential customers' purchasing decisions. Positive reviews can attract new clients, while negative reviews can deter them. As such, it's essential for brands to have a well-rounded strategy for both garnering good reviews and responding to bad ones. Here are some actionable tips to ensure a strong online presence and a positive brand experience:

PROACTIVE

Media Training: Conduct thorough media training for company representatives, including engineers, to help them handle communications effectively.

Crisis Management Plan: Develop a comprehensive crisis management plan that includes potential negative review scenarios.

Monitoring Systems: Set up social media and online monitoring systems to quickly identify when reviews or comments go viral.

Influencer Engagement: Build relationships with key influencers in your industry to facilitate better communication and feedback.

Feedback Loop: Create a system for collecting and analyzing customer feedback for continuous product improvement.

Legal Preparedness: Have legal counsel ready to advise on potential repercussions and actions in case of false or damaging claims.

Leverage Testimonials: Obtain permission to use positive reviews as testimonials on your website and in marketing materials.

Engage with Reviewers: Build relationships with reviewers by thanking them and engaging with their content.

Amplify through PR: Use public relations strategies to broadcast positive reviews to a broader audience.

Celebrate Internally: Share positive feedback with your team to boost morale and encourage continued good work.

REACTIVE

Respond Swiftly and Publicly: Publicly acknowledge and thank reviewers for their positive feedback to show appreciation and engagement. Act quickly to address any issues raised in a review, recognizing the input and outlining steps for resolution.

Direct Engagement: Reach out to reviewers directly to discuss their concerns and offer solutions or further clarification.

Cross-Promote: Collaborate with a positive reviewer for cross-promotional opportunities that benefit both parties.

Public Statement: If necessary, issue a public statement or press release to address significant issues raised by a review and clarify any misinformation.

Feature Reviews: Highlight positive reviews on your website, newsletters, and social media channels.

Customer Outreach: Inform customers about your actions to address issues raised, possibly through an FAQ or community forum update.

Positive reviews are valuable assets for a brand. By taking these proactive and reactive actions, a company can maximize the benefits of the excellent press and reinforce its brand. While negative reviews are uncomfortable, they can add value if a brand listens and learns to rise to the occasion. By taking proactive and responsive steps, a brand can better prepare for, manage, and recover from the impact of viral reviews that may not be favorable.

BRAND CONTENT SUMMARY

In the intricate dance of brand engagement, the "where" is as crucial as the "what." The brand can forge a lasting and profound relationship with customers by meticulously selecting touchpoints that resonate most effectively with their daily lives. These touchpoints, ranging from the vibrant visuals of advertising to the personal recommendations of word-of-mouth, are not just fleeting moments but are integral parts of a continuous narrative that weaves into the customer's journey. The story of planning a vacation to Cancun illustrates this beautifully, showing how a brand can become a trusted companion from the first flicker of desire for a getaway to the eager anticipation of morning beach yoga.

The brand's presence must be strategic and pervasive, leveraging many channels—be it through social media hashtags that catch the eye during a commute or the credible endorsement of a colleague across the boardroom table. Whether a podcast mention sparks interest or an app promises an enriching stay, each interaction is a thread in the tapestry of brand loyalty. By remembering the Brand Loyalty Formula, you can dissect these interactions to ensure that each touchpoint—advertising, social media, direct communication, and beyond—aligns perfectly with your target audience's desires and lifestyle, thus creating an emotional attachment beyond the product or service itself.

In conclusion, a brand can create a lasting, deep relationship with customers by being present at every stage of their journey, delivering content that meets and exceeds expectations, and continuously engaging with them through the most impactful channels. Through this omnipresence and understanding of the consumer's needs and habits, a brand transforms from being just a choice to becoming a beloved and integral part of a customer's narrative.

Consider these questions to start the conversation about the best path to follow for your brand:

- Where do your brand's target customers typically spend their time, and how can you establish a presence in those spaces?
- Which touchpoints have historically had the most significant impact on your customers' decision-making processes?
- What types of content have you found to be most engaging for your audience, and on which platforms does this content perform best?
- How can you integrate the brand into the daily routines of your customers to become a natural part of their conversation?

- What opportunities can you create to foster organic interactions with the brand's customers?
- How can you use the data you have on customers to tailor conversations at each touchpoint for a more personalized experience?
- When are the brand's customers most open to communication, and how can you engage them during these optimal times?
- How do you ensure message consistency across all channels to maintain a unified voice when initiating conversations?
- What creative approaches can you take to stand out to its customers and initiate dialogue in a competitive marketplace?
- What metrics can you use to assess the success of different touchpoints in sparking conversations with your customers?
- How can customer feedback inform how you start conversations at various touchpoints?
- How are the brand's conversation-starting strategies aligned with its customers' overall journey and experiences with the brand?
- What role do influencers, partners, and brand advocates play in starting conversations on behalf of the brand with potential new customers?
- How can you use storytelling at different touchpoints to begin engaging and meaningful conversations on behalf of the brand?
- What strategies can you implement to ensure that conversations initiated at one touchpoint can be continued or escalated smoothly through others?

Part Five

BRAND CONSISTENCY
THE HOW

"It is not only enough to state what your brand
stands for, what is important is to do that consistently
and repeatedly so that your brand endures."
—Vani Kola, venture capitalist and founder of Kalaari Capital

In the realm of brand alchemy, "how" a brand delivers is akin to the practiced magician's sleight of hand—subtle, refined, and perfected over countless performances. The secret elixir, much like the consistency of a well-rehearsed spell, keeps the audience—customers, in this case—spellbound and coming back for more. The pivotal C of *consistency* transcends mere creativity and vision; it embodies meticulous processes, steadfast policies, precise procedures, and peak performance. Here, the science of operations illuminates the path, while rigorous controls conjure a reliable and enchanting experience at every encounter.

Imagine if you could apparate between Starbucks locations in Sydney, Berlin, Shanghai, and Seattle, all within the same tick of a clock. Would the non-fat latte you ordered whisper the same comforting incantation to your taste buds? Unquestionably, yes. The sorcery lies in the standardization of Starbucks's core offerings—meticulously defined quality specifications for ingredients, uniformity in design aesthetics, consistent branding elements, and harmoniously calibrated equipment. Like diligent apprentices, the baristas are uniformly trained and garbed, ensuring the spell is cast identically worldwide. This meticulous orchestration of quality control is not merely implemented but measured and refined through customer engagement and feedback, and the predictive desires of its clientele.

Yet a brand's essence isn't solely captured by its rulebook or the watchful eyes of brand guardians. The genuine enchantment stems from a brand's unwavering commitment to its core "why"—the purpose that fuels its every action and decision. A brand must not just exist but live its ethos daily, ensuring that with each sunrise, it steadfastly upholds the values it professes to stand for. This is the magic that brands must master—the art of consistency that, like the most captivating of spells, keeps its audience returning time and time again. This is also where the brand attains its power.

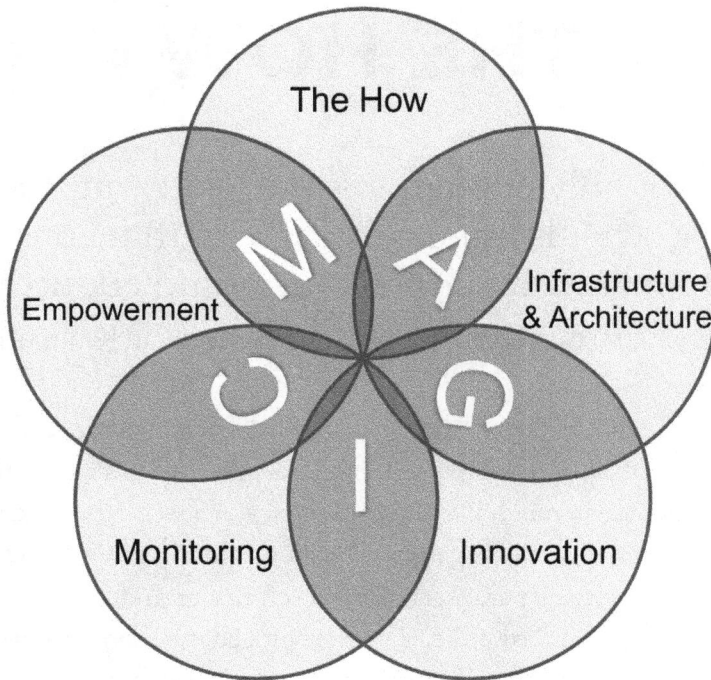

The How

Infrastructure & Architecture

Empowerment

Monitoring

Innovation

32 | THE MAGIC BEHIND THE BRAND

DISNEY'S MAGIC

On a business trip to Florida, my colleagues and I took the "Keys to the Kingdom Tour," a behind-the-scenes look at Disney World's Magic Kingdom. As Disney World patrons, we stand in awe of the colors, imagery, sounds, smells, and endless activities and actions. It's an emotional roller-coaster. It's indeed a happy place. What I learned on the "Keys to the Kingdom Tour" is that this happy place is on the second floor of a massive infrastructure.

Hidden below all the wonderment is another floor where the 77,000 employees run in and out of costumes, staff whizz around in electric golf carts, and merchandise and products move from location to location. Corridors go in all directions, with multiple staff rooms, rest areas, cafeterias, and staff lockers. You could easily think you were in a spotless white factory with all the pipes of various sizes running everywhere.

The park's meticulous design ensures that everything above ground seems flawless. No character is ever out of place, thanks to the "utilidor" tunnel system below. Characters like Cinderella, Mary Poppins, Aladdin, and Jasmine meet guests at their designated spots without any visible signs of having emerged from the bustling activity below. This seamless operation caters to more than 57,000 daily visitors, keeping the illusion intact while the real work remains out of sight.

The tour guide shared anecdotes highlighting Walt Disney's obsession with maintaining a pristine environment in his parks. One notable story involved an experiment to determine the optimal placement of trash bins. Disney distributed wrapped candies to guests and observed how long they would hold onto the wrappers before discarding them. This observation determined the spacing of trash receptacles throughout the park to ensure cleanliness.

When someone asked about recycling practices, we learned that all waste is funneled to a central sorting facility below the park. Disney had been sorting waste long before recycling became mainstream. However, recognizing that guests are accustomed to looking for designated recycling bins, these have been strategically placed throughout the park to align with visitor expectations. It is clear that Walt Disney was a perfectionist, and his attention to detail is evident in every aspect of the park.

A brand can achieve and sustain this level of excellence by ensuring that every team member understands the importance of ownership over the minutiae. This involves establishing stringent guidelines and systems for consistency—evident in how Disney parks manage waste with precision, training employees to prioritize detail and embody the brand's core values, meticulously overseeing every customer touchpoint to craft an effortlessly "magical" experience, and perpetually pushing the boundaries to exceed customer expectations.

To build a consistent brand experience that resonates with customers and stands the test of time, you need to focus on empowering team members, establishing robust rules and infrastructure, providing thorough education, monitoring diligently, and relentlessly innovating. These pillars not only define the operational excellence of a brand but also shape the emotional connection it fosters with its audience. Let's look at each of these in greater depth.

Empowerment

When you immediately think of consistency, what likely comes to mind are specifications, templates, and guidelines, not empowerment. However, empowerment is pivotal in cultivating brand consistency, as it resonates through every layer of a brand's strategy. By fostering an internal culture where employees are empowered, brands create passionate advocates who deliver uniform, positive customer experiences. Your employees, equipped with autonomy, become instrumental in executing decisions that mirror the brand's core values, thus ensuring consistent representation. A brand can only be sustained over time not by rules on paper but through passionate, attentive employees who understand the value of a consistent brand experience.

Having a work environment that allows employees to bring their authentic selves to work brings a richness of diverse ideas to the table. This, in turn, encourages consistent engagement and innovation, as employees are more likely to draw on their full potential when they feel genuinely seen and appreciated. When employees feel empowered, they are likelier to become enthusiastic advocates for the brand. They'll understand their role in the company's mission and be motivated to deliver consistent, positive customer experiences.

One well-known example of a company that empowers its employees to fix customer problems on the spot is the Ritz-Carlton Hotel Company. The Ritz-Carlton has a policy that allows employees to spend up to $2,000 per incident, without manager approval, to solve a guest's problem or enhance their stay. This policy ensures that customer issues are resolved promptly and satisfactorily, demonstrating high trust in the employees' judgment and a solid commitment to customer service.

This empowerment leads to happier customers and instills a sense of ownership and pride among the staff, as they are directly involved in creating memorable experiences for guests. It's a prime example of how allowing employees to bring their authentic selves to work and make on-the-spot decisions can benefit everyone involved.

Simultaneously, empowering customers by valuing their feedback, offering personalized experiences, and ensuring they feel heard and appreciated nurtures brand loyalty. This loyalty is further cemented when customers perceive the brand as attentive and capable of providing consistent, tailored solutions. Brands that offer personalized experiences empower customers by giving them control over specific product or service aspects, creating a consistent perception of the brand as attentive and responsive to individual needs.

Uber revolutionized the taxi industry by empowering customers with unprecedented control over their transportation experience. Using the Uber app, customers can select the type of vehicle that best suits their needs and budget, from a simple economy ride to a more luxurious option. After their journey, they can rate their driver, holding the driver accountable for the service provided and influencing their standing on the platform. The app's real-time tracking feature allows customers to see the exact location of their ride and its estimated arrival time, providing the convenience of planning their schedule with precision. Furthermore, the app facilitates direct communication between customers and drivers, preserving privacy and enhancing coordination. The seamless electronic payment process eliminates the need for cash, streamlining transactions for a safer and more efficient user experience. By integrating these features, Uber delivers personalization and empowerment that dramatically enhances customer satisfaction and transforms the dynamics of hailing a cab.

Lastly, a brand's engagement in social responsibility initiatives and community programs underscores its commitment to societal empowerment. This solidifies the brand's reputation as a positive contributor to the community and ensures a consistent perception of the brand as an entity invested in driving meaningful change.

Empowerment is a strategic thread that strengthens brand consistency and fortifies the overall brand identity when woven through the various aspects of a brand—from its culture and customer interaction to its employees and community involvement.

Infrastructure and Rules

Creating an overall branding infrastructure that includes strategy, policies, standard operating procedures (SOPs), guidelines, trademarks, and templates is crucial for maintaining a consistent brand image globally and locally. Here's why each component is vital:

Brand Strategy: This is the foundation of branding infrastructure. A clear brand strategy outlines the company's value proposition, promise, positioning, and key messaging. It guides how the brand should be perceived in the market and ensures that all branding efforts align with the company's long-term goals. A well-defined strategy helps maintain consistency across different markets by providing a common direction for brand activities. In essence, it becomes the measuring stick for evaluating all brand initiatives.

Brand Policies: Brand policies are the rules that govern how the brand is applied. They ensure that everyone in the organization, partners, and vendors understand what is permissible when representing the brand. Policies might include rules around logo usage, partnerships, sponsorships, and employee conduct. These policies help protect the brand's integrity and legal rights, especially in a crisis.

Standard Operating Procedures (SOPs): SOPs are detailed, written instructions to achieve uniformity in the performance of specific functions within the company, as well as suppliers and partners. For branding, SOPs might dictate how to respond to customer inquiries, deploy advertising campaigns, or onboard new employees into the brand culture. SOPs ensure that no matter where an operation occurs, it's done in a way that upholds the brand's standards.

Brand Guidelines: Brand guidelines often include visual identity guidelines (covering things like logo usage and size, color palette, typography) and tone of voice for communications. These guidelines are essential for maintaining a coherent visual and communicative presence across various platforms and regions. These instructions can cover all aspects of multiple treatments and environments (such as signage, gifts, digital, print, B&W, and various backgrounds) so that partners or employees can understand the physical mechanics of displaying the company brand consistently and practically. Guidelines help ensure that the brand is instantly recognizable and that all materials reflect the brand's core attributes.

Brand Trademarks: Trademarks are essential for establishing a unique identity for your brand, distinguishing it from competitors, and signaling consistent quality to consumers. The legal protection afforded by trademark registration is a powerful tool that allows businesses to take action against the unauthorized use of their brand elements. As a brand grows, its trademark becomes an asset, potentially increasing in value and becoming a vital part of the company's intellectual property portfolio. Make every effort to protect a unique name for any product, service, system, or program; even catchy slogans should be trademarked if possible. Successfully registering your trademark gives you exclusive rights and is an effective way to prevent others from using similar marks that could confuse customers. For example, Oprah Winfrey has over 80 trademarks on various words, phrases, and logos.

However, simply registering a trademark isn't enough; it's essential to actively monitor its use in the marketplace to prevent unauthorized usage, which could dilute your brand or confuse consumers. To demonstrate your trademarks, you must actively use the ™ symbol for unregistered trademarks, and the ® symbol for registered ones. If you find instances of infringement, it's essential to enforce your rights promptly—like sending cease-and-desist letters and pursuing legal action if necessary. Remember that the value of a trademark lies in its consistent use and the consumer trust it builds, so maintaining the trademark by using it regularly and in the same manner as it was registered is critical to preserving its integrity and the consistency of your brand.

A brand that failed to protect its trademark and quickly lost its trademark status is Thermos. Originally, "Thermos" was a brand name for a line of vacuum flasks produced by a company of the same name in Germany. The term was trademarked in the early twentieth century, and the Thermos brand dominated the market. Over time, however, consumers and even competitors began to use the word "thermos" to refer generically to any vacuum flask, regardless of manufacturer. The company failed to protect its trademark aggressively, allowing the term to become so common in everyday language that it was no longer associated exclusively with the Thermos brand.

In 1962, a US court ruled that the name "Thermos" had become generic and was no longer entitled to trademark protection.[262] As a result, any company could use the lowercase "thermos" to describe their vacuum flasks, which significantly impacted the original Thermos company's brand recognition. Despite this setback, Thermos remains one of the most popular brands in the world. The better solution is to protect your trademark, like Kleenex did with its facial tissues, long before it becomes synonymous with the generic term.

Brand Templates: Templates for documents, presentations, business cards, email signatures, social media posts, and marketing materials help maintain visual and messaging consistency. They save time and resources by eliminating the need to create new designs from scratch for every new piece of communication or collateral and prevent deviations from the established brand guidelines. While employees are the first to get bored with design structures, layouts, and colors, customers love consistency as they can quickly identify the brand. Brand familiarity also signals brand reassurance.

When a company operates worldwide, these elements become even more critical due to the complexity of managing cross-cultural differences, multiple languages, and diverse legal environments. A robust branding infrastructure ensures that no matter where a customer interacts with the brand—whether in New York or New Delhi—they have a consistent experience that reinforces their brand perception. This consistency builds trust, loyalty, and recognition, which is essential for a solid global presence.

Education

Education and training are pivotal in achieving brand consistency because they ensure that every employee understands the brand's core values, voice, and visual identity. This alignment is crucial as consistent representation of the brand reinforces recognition and trust among consumers. When employees are well-trained, they become brand ambassadors, whether designing communication materials, interacting with customers, or representing the company online or at events. Every new employee should be indoctrinated into understanding the brand story and all aspects of brand consistency.

For example, Starbucks invests more than 20 percent of its profits into employee training and development. Starbucks says, "These investments have led to a more consistent partner experience..." and "improvement in our customer connection scores..."[263] Baristas are trained to make coffee and provide a consistent and inviting experience for customers. This includes everything from the preparation of drinks to the ambiance in the store, which is designed to be uniform across the globe, reinforcing the Starbucks brand as a third place between home and work.

Beyond employees, the brand encompasses various stakeholders interacting with and representing the brand in multiple capacities. Customers are at the heart of brand understanding—they consume the brand and serve as its advocates, making their grasp of what the brand stands for essential for organic growth through word-of-mouth. Partners and suppliers are integral to the supply chain, and aligning with the brand's values ensures that the final product or service is consistent with its image. Distributors and retailers act as the brand's touchpoints in the market; their insight into the brand strategy is critical for maintaining uniformity in marketing and sales approaches. Therefore, never forget to promote your brand story. It is a powerful message for connecting with audiences on an emotional level, and it should be integrated subtly into various aspects of communication. This important brand narrative can be immersed into communication materials, product packaging, social media interactions, and customer service practices. By consistently reflecting the brand's origin, journey, and values across these platforms, the story becomes an omnipresent backdrop to the consumer's experience.

For example, a brand might include elements of its origin story on its website's "About Us" page, using language and imagery that evoke its history and ethos. Social media posts could highlight milestones or throwbacks that remind followers of the brand's journey. Even product design can tell a part of the brand's story, such as incorporating heritage colors or motifs that have historical significance.

Other key stakeholders who should be versed in the brand's infrastructure are agencies and creative partners. Their deep understanding of the brand's core message is vital for producing authentic and resonant content. In the case of franchising, franchisees become the local face of the brand, necessitating rigorous training to uphold and deliver on the brand's standards. Each of these groups plays a significant role in maintaining a cohesive brand image critical to building recognition and fostering loyalty.

A brand's commitment to education and training can create a robust and consistent brand image that customers recognize and trust worldwide. This consistency is a crucial driver of customer loyalty and business success.

Monitoring

Brand health is a barometer for your brand's market position and sustainability, and it's critical that you monitor it. A healthy brand typically enjoys strong customer loyalty, a positive reputation, and the ability to command premium pricing, all of which contribute to long-term consistent business success. By keeping a pulse on brand health, companies can proactively manage their brand equity, identify growth opportunities, address issues, and mitigate risks associated with market changes or competitive threats.

Here are key metrics to monitor for brand health, customer perceptions, market changes, and potential threats.

BRAND AWARENESS

Unaided Recall: The ability of a consumer to remember your brand without any prompts. Conduct surveys that ask respondents to name brands within your category without any prompting. Benchmark this against your competitors.

Aided Recall: The ability of a consumer to recognize a brand when prompted with a name or visual identifier. Use the same surveys, this time with prompts such as logos or brand names, and measure recognition rates. Benchmark this against your competitors and monitor trends.

BRAND REPUTATION AND EQUITY

Net Promoter Score (NPS): Measures customer loyalty and likelihood that they will recommend your brand.

Brand Sentiment Analysis: Evaluates positive, negative, or neutral sentiments expressed in social media, reviews, and other channels.

Share of Voice (SOV): The amount of conversation about your brand compared to competitors.

CUSTOMER PERCEPTIONS

Customer Satisfaction Scores (CSAT): Provides immediate feedback on customer experiences with a product or service. Ask customers to rate their satisfaction with your product or service on a scale, typically after an interaction.

Customer Reviews and Ratings: Online reviews and ratings, from platforms like Google, Yelp, Trustpilot, or industry-specific review sites can reflect customer satisfaction and areas for improvement.

MARKET POSITION AND SHARE

Market Share: The percentage of total sales or revenue that a particular brand captures within a specific market. It is a measure of a brand's relative size and dominance compared to its competitors in that market.

Brand Penetration: The percentage of households or individuals within a given market or population that have purchased or used your brand. It is a measure of how widely a brand has penetrated or reached its target market.

FINANCIAL METRICS

Revenue Attributed to Branding Efforts: The amount of sales growth that's connected to marketing campaigns. You can use marketing attribution models to connect specific marketing initiatives to revenue increases.

Price Premium: The additional amount customers are willing to pay for your brand over a generic or store-brand product. Compare your pricing with competitors' for similar products and measure the difference.

CUSTOMER BEHAVIOR AND ENGAGEMENT

Repeat Purchase Rate: The frequency at which customers return to buy your brand. You can track it through customer relationship management (CRM) systems that monitor purchase frequency over time.

Engagement Rate on Social Media: Interactions relative to your number of followers or reach. Use social media analytics tools to measure likes, shares, comments, etc., relative to your followers or reach.

MARKET CHANGES AND THREATS

Trend Analysis: Monitoring industry trends to anticipate shifts in consumer behavior or emerging technologies. Use tools like Google Trends to monitor search interest in topics relevant to your industry.

Competitive Analysis: Keeping an eye on competitors' moves to gain insights into market dynamics and potential threats. Regularly review competitor activities through public communications, financial reports, and third-party analysis.

SOCIAL MEDIA LISTENING

With the proliferation of social media platforms and the increasing influence they hold over consumer behavior and perceptions, it is crucial for brands to actively monitor and engage with online conversations about their products, services, and industry. The importance of social media listening for a brand cannot be overstated, as it offers numerous benefits:

Real-Time Feedback and Insights: Social listening provides immediate real-time access to what customers say about your brand. This can help you quickly gauge public reaction to your products, campaigns, or company news, allowing for timely responses and adjustments.

Understanding of Customer Sentiment: By analyzing the tone and context of social conversations, you can appreciate the sentiment behind the mentions—whether positive, negative, or neutral. This helps assess the overall health of your brand and identify any potential issues before they escalate.

Competitive Analysis: Social listening isn't just about monitoring your brand but also about keeping an eye on competitors. By understanding the conversations around competing brands, you can identify their strengths and weaknesses and find opportunities to differentiate your brand.

Crisis Management: Spotting a negative trend in sentiment or an increasing volume of complaints can be an early warning sign of a potential crisis. Quick action informed by social listening can help mitigate damage to your brand's reputation.

Product Development and Innovation: Customer feedback on social media can be a goldmine for product development. Consumers often share their unfiltered opinions, needs, and desires, which can inspire new product ideas or improvements to existing offerings.

Customer Service and Engagement: Social media is increasingly a customer service channel. Social listening enables brands to swiftly identify and respond to customer inquiries or complaints, often leading to improved customer satisfaction and loyalty.

Identification of Brand Advocates: Those who speak positively about your brand on social media can become valuable brand advocates. Social listening helps you identify these individuals so that you can engage with them and potentially leverage their influence.

Trend Spotting: By tracking broader conversations within your industry, you can spot emerging trends and adapt your marketing strategy accordingly. This can help you stay ahead of the curve and maintain relevance with your audience.

Content Strategy Optimization: Understanding popular topics and the type of content that resonates with your audience can guide your content strategy. This ensures that you create material that engages your target demographic effectively.

Campaign Effectiveness Measurement: Monitoring social conversations can help measure the impact of specific branding campaigns, providing insights into what works well and what doesn't for future planning.

By meticulously tracking and monitoring metrics through internal data analysis, customer feedback, social media monitoring, and market research, brands can understand their market performance and perception, which is vital for shaping branding and marketing strategies, product development, customer experience enhancements, and overarching business tactics. Integrating these data sources ensures reliable, current, and actionable information. Furthermore, social media listening serves as a crucial tool for upholding brand consistency—which is essential for building trust and recognition—by enabling real-time alignment of messaging with core values and audience expectations, acting as a quality control mechanism to ensure all communications are cohesive, and reinforcing the brand's identity and commitments.

Innovation

Staying relevant as a thriving brand requires embracing evolution through a future-focused mindset and continually elevating the customer experience. Rather than rigid rules that enforce consistency, brands must establish adaptive guiding principles and governance that allow for progress. The expectations that delighted customers two years or even two weeks ago may now be simply table stakes. What seems new and innovative today can become ordinary and expected surprisingly quickly in our rapidly advancing world.

Enduring, iconic brands often have an expansive vision beyond their current products to tap into customers' highest hopes, aspirations, and ideals. Apple captured imaginations with its "Think Different" slogan during the early days of the home computer, rallying innovators and creators. That galvanizing, almost rebellious rallying cry remained relevant as Apple evolved from pioneering desktops to unleashing the power of internet-connected handheld devices through iPods and iPhones. The brand promise of unleashing human creativity through ingeniously simple technology persisted even as the delivery mechanism evolved dramatically.

Innovative is the most overused word in business. Search "innovative" on Google and you'll get over 1.5 billion results. However, it is also the most important business concept. Without innovation, a business cannot survive.

In today's world of disruptors, digitalization, generative AI, and the Internet of Everything, every brand is seeking the ultimate innovation to keep them relevant and profitable. Every CEO understands that innovation is crucial to their brand's future. Yet it is often elusive. Every day, formerly popular brands become obsolete.

A brand can ignore reality or look for new opportunities outside its comfort zone. In a commencement address to the University of Washington, Thomas Friedman, author of *The World Is Flat: A Brief History of the Twenty-First Century*, said, "The most important attributes you can have are adaptability and a creative imagination, the ability to be the first on your block to figure out how all these enabling tools, which are now available to so many more people, can be put together in new and exciting profits and, hopefully, also, peace."[264]

Shawn Hunter, the author of *Out Think: How Innovative Leaders Drive Exceptional Outcomes*, defines innovation as the implementation or creation of something new that has immense value to others. "Creativity isn't necessarily innovation," Hunter told *Business News Daily*. "If you have a brainstorm meeting and dream up dozens of new ideas, then you have displayed creativity, [but] there is no innovation until something gets implemented."[265]

START WITH CREATIVITY

Creativity is not just an abstract virtue; it is the driving force behind the success of every trailblazing brand in today's fast-paced digital world. This force propels brands into the vast "blue ocean" expanse, where untapped markets and innovative business models await those daring enough to explore them. The key to unlocking this creative potential lies in cultivating a culture that values creativity and actively nurtures it.

The journey begins with leadership that understands the critical role of creativity and instills this value throughout the organization. Leaders must empower their teams with the knowledge and freedom to innovate, which is easier said than done. If it were simple, every brand would be at the forefront of their industry, effortlessly anticipating and fulfilling every customer need.

In his book *Creativity, Inc.,* Pixar president Ed Catmull emphasizes fostering an environment where risk is managed through resilience, truth-telling is safe, and the relentless pursuit of excellence is the ultimate quest. With a string of blockbuster hits, Pixar's approach to creativity can serve as a beacon for others. Their ethos rests on the belief that while talent is exceptional, what's more important is creating a supportive environment where taking risks is encouraged. At its heart is a commitment to truth, challenging assumptions, and a relentless pursuit of excellence.

Contrary to popular belief, creativity is not a rare quality available only to a select few. Research suggests that most of what we consider creative genius is a learned skill. Knowing this can help demystify the creative process and open the door for more inclusive, diverse thinking within organizations. Filmmaker Jim Jarmusch encapsulates this sentiment by encouraging creative minds to "steal with pride" from various influences, while still ensuring authenticity in their work. Similarly, writer Maria Popova and Sir Richard Branson advocate for synthesizing disparate ideas, an approach Steve Jobs famously described as "just connecting things."

Fostering creativity also means encouraging curiosity and diversity within an organization. Curiosity drives us to explore new possibilities, while diversity brings together varied perspectives that can lead to breakthrough ideas. Companies like Google have leveraged these principles by creating spaces where employees from different backgrounds can interact and share ideas freely.

Moreover, creativity should be playful and fun—it's about experimentation and looking at challenges as opportunities for growth. The story of Apple's iPhone is a testament to this process—an iterative journey marked by risks and failures that eventually revolutionized an industry.

In conclusion, sustaining a brand in today's dynamic landscape requires a steadfast commitment to creativity. It demands an environment that celebrates new ideas and approaches problems with a solutions-oriented mindset. As Steve Jobs aptly put it, it's about "burning with an idea, or a problem, or a wrong that you want to right." In such an environment, creativity flourishes, paving the way for innovation and success.

CREATE ACTION

Creativity is the cornerstone of enduring brand success, with the digital age amplifying its significance. Leadership that understands and fosters a creative culture, as seen in Pixar's belief in a supportive environment for taking risks and striving for excellence, is crucial. As research suggests, creativity is a learned skill that can be cultivated within any organization.

Innovation stems from connecting diverse ideas and experiences, a concept Steve Jobs famously advocated. Curiosity and diversity fuel this creative synthesis, while a playful approach to experimentation allows for transformative ideas to emerge, as evidenced by Apple's iterative journey with the iPhone.

Listening to customers is paramount for sustained innovation. The best ideas often come from customer feedback, while engaging customers throughout the innovation process is also beneficial. Tech giants like Amazon, Apple, Netflix, Facebook, and Google all emphasize empowerment and questioning norms, and they foster a culture where innovation is routine.

Quality control and adaptability are also essential as customer touchpoints evolve. Brands must continually listen, adapt, and elevate experiences to surprise and delight consumers. This balance between a consistent purpose and dynamic delivery is the essence of brand consistency in a rapidly changing world.

Brands prioritizing creativity and innovation keep their customers eagerly anticipating the next breakthrough. By leveraging customer insights, embracing cross-functional collaboration, and fostering a culture of continuous innovation, brands can stay ahead. As Jeff Bezos notes, transformative inventions empower others in their creative pursuits. Companies like Apple and Google exemplify this by encouraging a perpetual "what if" mindset. To remain relevant and captivating, brands must integrate customer-centric innovation into their DNA, ensuring that with each new product or service, they not only meet but exceed the evolving desires of their loyal customers.

33 | BRAND TYPE

Defining your brand's category in the competitive marketplace is akin to choosing your swimming lane; it provides direction, focus, and clarity. By categorizing your brand—be it as luxury, innovative, style, experience, value, performance, service, or conscious—you articulate what your brand stands for and how it is different from the competition. This categorization helps consumers quickly understand your brand's unique value proposition and align their expectations accordingly. It also streamlines marketing efforts, guiding the development of tailored strategies that resonate with your target audience. In essence, knowing your brand's category is the first stroke in the race to capture consumer loyalty and establish a lasting place in the market. Here are the eight brand types:

Luxury Brands: These brands epitomize the height of craftsmanship, quality, and desirability. They cater to an elite clientele seeking exclusivity and prestige, often featuring high prices and a heritage of premium offerings. An example is Rolex, which is renowned for its high-quality timepieces that serve as a symbol of status and achievement.

Innovative Brands: Innovative brands are at the forefront of technology and design. They constantly push the boundaries of what's possible, offering cutting-edge products and services that redefine markets and consumer expectations. Apple stands out as an innovative brand, consistently leading with its high-tech products like the iPhone and MacBook, which combine cutting-edge technology with sleek design.

Style Brands: Style brands focus on aesthetics and trendsetting designs. They appeal to consumers through visual appeal, fashionability, and a keen sense of the contemporary zeitgeist, often leading in their industry with a distinct visual language. Known for its iconic, minimalist designs, Calvin Klein has established a strong style brand identity that emphasizes clean lines, modernity, and affordable sophistication fashion.

Experience Brands: These brands prioritize the customer journey and the overall experience. They create memorable interactions and immersive environments beyond mere transactions to foster deep emotional connections with their audience. Disney is a quintessential experience brand, providing unparalleled entertainment experiences through its theme parks, movies, and merchandise.

Value Brands: Value brands offer reliability at an affordable price. They are known for their practicality, cost-effectiveness, and accessibility, providing good-quality options for budget-conscious consumers. IKEA is a leader among value brands, offering stylish and functional furniture at prices that make good design accessible to the masses.

Performance Brands: Performance brands are synonymous with high-quality functionality and superior capability. They cater to consumers looking for products or services that deliver exceptional results and often lead in their category through innovation in efficiency and effectiveness. Nike is synonymous with performance, providing high-quality athletic wear and footwear designed to enhance athletic performance.

Service Brands: Service-oriented brands focus on customer care and quality of service experience. They excel in meeting customer needs and providing support, often building loyalty through high levels of personal attention and customer satisfaction. Nordstrom is recognized for its exceptional customer service, ensuring every customer receives a personalized and responsive shopping experience.

Conscious Brands: Conscious brands are defined by their ethical, sustainable, and socially responsible practices. They appeal to consumers through their commitment to positively impacting society and the environment, often emphasizing transparency and sustainable business practices. Patagonia is a conscious brand that provides outdoor apparel and actively engages in environmental conservation and sustainability efforts.

These brand categories aim to help businesses strategically position themselves in the marketplace, align with consumer expectations and behavior, and capitalize on their unique strengths to build a loyal customer base.

34 | CYBERSECURITY AND PRIVACY

A robust data system is essential for better service to loyal customers, and it comes with the great responsibility of keeping your customers' personal information from harm and misuse. In a world where data is critical, brand security and privacy stand at the forefront of maintaining customer trust and safeguarding the company's reputation. A breach in these areas can significantly erode customer confidence, causing legal consequences and substantial financial losses.

IBM's 2022 *Cost of a Data Breach Report* said that over 83 percent of organizations had experienced more than one data breach. The severity of a data breach for American brands is not only measured in ransom payments, lost revenues, remediation, and legal fees, averaging over $9 million. It also includes reputation damage, average stock loss of over 7.5 percent, and a mean market cap loss of $5.4 billion for publicly traded companies.[266]

To safeguard your brand effectively, you need a comprehensive cybersecurity strategy that protects both digital and physical assets. This strategy should include advanced data storage and transmission encryption, robust firewalls, and up-to-date antivirus solutions. Regular security audits are crucial to identify and address vulnerabilities promptly.

Educating employees about the importance of data privacy and security is equally important. Employees should be well-versed in best practices for handling sensitive information and be aware of the various methods cybercriminals and malware use to gain unauthorized access to data.

Access to sensitive information should be strictly controlled, ensuring that only authorized personnel have access to it, thereby reducing the risk of internal breaches and limiting the potential damage should a breach occur.

A transparent and compliant privacy policy is essential, aligning with legal requirements such as the General Data Protection Regulation (GDPR) and transparently informing customers about how their data will be used and protected.

Make sure you have an incident response plan for swift action in the event of a breach, detailing procedures for internal response, customer communication, and adherence to regulatory requirements.

Brand security and privacy are imperative for preserving customer loyalty and maintaining a solid brand image. Brands must be one step ahead of threats to keep consumers' data safe and secure.

35 | BRAND ARCHITECTURE

Brand architecture refers to the structured and organized way in which a company manages and presents its various brands, products, and services. It encompasses the hierarchical relationships, naming conventions, visual identities, and positioning strategies that govern how a brand portfolio is organized and communicated to the target audience.

In the construction industry, architecture is foundational, outlining design, materials, and structure. Similarly, a brand architecture is crucial for companies looking to expand beyond a single product, yet it's often overlooked until growth or acquisitions necessitate it. As your business grows, brand architecture becomes critical to avoid creating a complex, fragmented brand portfolio with various product lines and sub-brands that lack a cohesive identity and clear hierarchical structure.

For instance, Microsoft had numerous product names such as Microsoft Office, Microsoft Windows, Microsoft Internet Explorer, Microsoft Outlook, and Microsoft Exchange, among others. However, despite sharing the Microsoft brand name, each product line featured distinct color schemes, icons, and design elements. This lack of visual cohesion created a disjointed and inconsistent brand experience for consumers. While Microsoft has taken steps to address these brand architecture issues, these struggles highlight the importance of establishing a well-defined brand architecture strategy from the outset. A clear brand architecture strategy, encompassing consistent naming conventions, visual identities, brand hierarchies, and positioning, can help your brand avoid confusion and fragmentation.

Brand architecture might seem like a dull topic, but it's vital for scaling a business. Without foresight, companies can struggle with brand coherence, as Apple did during its expansion.

Marketing guru David Aaker identified three brand architecture strategies: branded house, house of brands, and endorsed brands.[267] You may have heard other various terms like umbrella or hybrid brands, but the core concepts remain consistent. Many companies fail to strategize their brand architecture early, leading to customer confusion and misaligned business opportunities.

Branded House

Virgin and BMW exemplify the branded house model, where a single brand ethos extends across all offerings. This approach has pros and cons; it ensures a unified brand image, but it may dilute individual sub-brand experiences. It's important for each sub-brand to have a distinct consumer brand relationships.[268]

House of Brands

Procter & Gamble represents a house of brands, managing over 180 independent brands. This structure allows for brand autonomy, but it can be complex and resource-intensive. A.G. Lafley, past CEO of P&G, said the company's future would be "a much simpler, much less complex company of leading brands that's easier to manage and operate."[269]

Endorsed Brands

The endorsed brand strategy involves a parent brand endorsing its sub-brands, like Courtyard by Marriott or Polo by Ralph Lauren. This model allows for an evolving parent brand vision and adaptation to new trends.

Hybrid Brand Architecture

In reality, many companies operate with a mix of these models. Coca-Cola has various brands under its umbrella, like Sprite and Fanta, while Gap Inc. uses multiple brands to cater to diverse customer segments such as Gap, Banana Republic, Old Navy, Athleta, Intermix, and Hill City. This strategy aims to keep customers within the brand family rather than losing them to competitors.

Brand Architecture Models and Examples

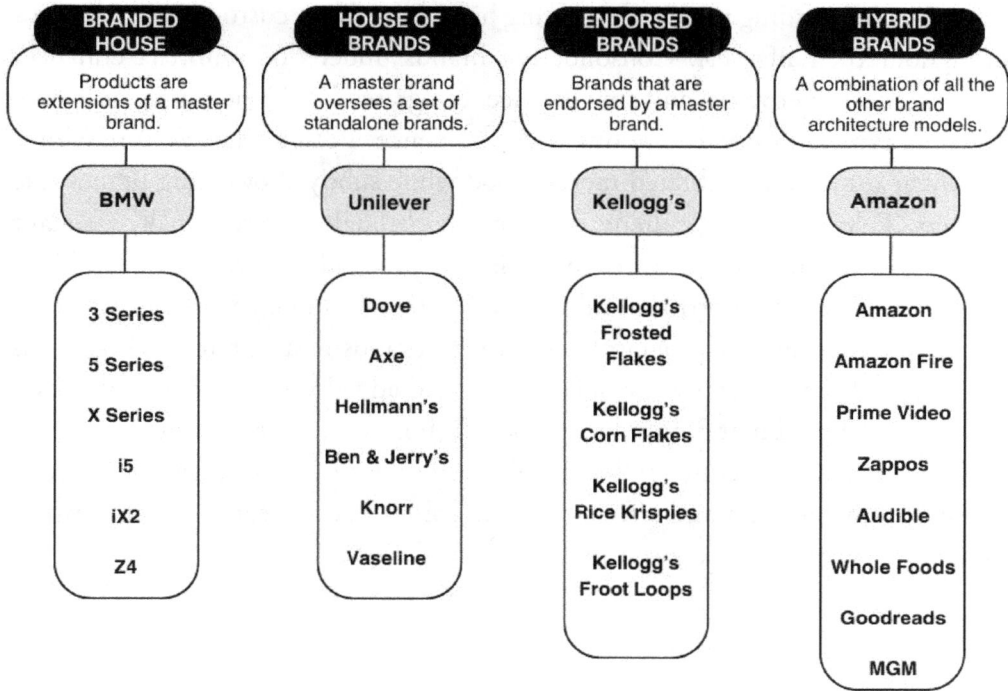

BRANDED HOUSE	HOUSE OF BRANDS	ENDORSED BRANDS	HYBRID BRANDS
Products are extensions of a master brand.	A master brand oversees a set of standalone brands.	Brands that are endorsed by a master brand.	A combination of all the other brand architecture models.
BMW	**Unilever**	**Kellogg's**	**Amazon**
3 Series	Dove	Kellogg's Frosted Flakes	Amazon
5 Series	Axe		Amazon Fire
X Series	Hellmann's	Kellogg's Corn Flakes	Prime Video
i5	Ben & Jerry's		Zappos
iX2	Knorr	Kellogg's Rice Krispies	Audible
Z4	Vaseline	Kellogg's Froot Loops	Whole Foods
			Goodreads
			MGM

Architecture Dynamics

Brand architecture is dynamic and influenced by past decisions and market changes. Master brands must continually reassess their portfolios and adapt to maintain strength and innovation across their brands. A rigid structure can hinder growth and limit new opportunities.

The goal of a master brand is to grow the customer base and profits, often with an inward focus. Ideally, brand architecture should start with a customer-oriented vision, recognizing that a one-size-fits-all approach is ineffective.

In today's diverse market with many different types of consumers with varying needs, preferences, and buying behaviors relying on a one-size-fits-all approach with a single brand might not be the best business model. Companies need to adopt a multi-brand strategy with more flexibility and diversification to remain competitive and relevant in an ever-changing market. However, brands must adjust their architecture to meaningfully engage with various customer segments without causing confusion or diluting their message.

The Future of Brand Architecture

The future of branding involves leveraging big data to foster customer relationships throughout their lifecycle. Consolidating brands under one umbrella enhances efficiency, customer value, and convenience. Integrated brand messaging or loyalty programs expand customer options and confidence. P&G's "Thank You, Mom" multi-year campaign celebrated motherhood while subtly showcasing brands like Pampers, Tide, Duracell, Pantene, and Bounty through an emotionally resonant narrative about mothers' sacrifices for their athletic children. This approach highlighted P&G's diverse portfolio and its family-oriented values. Similarly, Marriott Bonvoy's unified loyalty program across thirty brands and 7,000 hotels rewards members with unique experiences, flexibility, and added value for frequent travelers. Such integrated branding strategies benefit both customers and brands.

While brand architecture can be complex and driven by business needs, focusing on the customer journey and offering relevant solutions can create a strong network of master and sub-brands.

36 | BRAND MORTALITY

Today, breakthrough technology renders products obsolete overnight, and innovative business models often topple established ones. No brand is guaranteed perpetual relevance. Jim Mullen, founder of MullenLowe Advertising, emphasizes that brands are a company's most crucial yet vulnerable asset.[270] While tangible resources may depreciate or be destroyed, enduring brand loyalty is the bedrock for sustainable, profitable growth—a fact often neglected by business leaders who take actions that deplete their brand equity without recognizing impending risks, leading to the downfall of many brands.

The lessons from brands that have disappeared or are struggling to survive are clear and numerous. Rebranding is complex, costly, and fraught with fear and risk, which is why so few manage to do it successfully. The brand graveyard offers stark lessons about how indecision, denial, arrogance, and fear can be fatal.

To keep your brand vital and avoid becoming another cautionary tale, consider these six essential lessons:

Brand Experience: Loyalty isn't inherited; it's earned and re-earned. In an era where consumers are switching from Ford to Tesla, companies like Apple and Samsung retain customers by consistently meeting their evolving expectations. In 2018, NewVoiceMedia reported that brands lost over $75 billion due to poor customer service in a year.[271] Brands risk obsolescence without personalization and seamless integration of online and offline experiences.

Innovation: Stagnation is a death sentence for brands. With rapid advancements like 5G and GenAI reshaping industries, continuous innovation is non-negotiable. Brands that fail to innovate become irrelevant—ask Nokia or any newspaper.

Shifting Audience: Brands must resonate with millennials and gen Z, who prioritize values like sustainability and innovation. Failure to adapt to new customer needs can be fatal, as we saw with the decline of once-popular products like the Walkman.

Trend vs. Fad: Discerning lasting trends from fleeting fads is critical. Products that don't adapt to enduring market shifts become historical footnotes.

Courage to Change: Brands need the boldness to evolve with changing markets. Kodak's and BlackBerry's reluctance to embrace digital innovations led to their downfalls.

Viable Business Models: A sustainable business model is crucial for longevity. The airline industry's history is littered with failures due to unsustainable practices.

In summary, brands must be agile, innovative, and attuned to their audiences to navigate a marketplace where change is the only constant. Disregarding these principles can lead to rapid decline and eventual extinction.

Brand Health Checklist

Conducting regular brand health checks is vital to maintaining a strong, consistent, and relevant brand. Use the following comprehensive checklist to evaluate key aspects of your brand, including strategy, positioning, emotional connections, intellectual property protection, and adaptability. By assessing these areas, you can identify strengths and weaknesses, and implement necessary improvements to keep your brand thriving and resonating with your loyal customers.

- Have you clearly defined your brand strategy and positioning?
- Are your branding elements consistently applied across all touchpoints?
- How frequently do you review and update your branding materials?
- Are you effectively communicating your brand message to your target audience?
- How well are you differentiating your brand from competitors?
- Are you consistently delivering on your brand promise?
- Are you building an emotional connection with your customers?
- How quickly and effectively do you adapt your branding to changing market conditions and customer needs?
- Are you actively protecting your brand assets and intellectual property?
- Are you investing enough resources and time into building and nurturing your brand?
- Does your brand accurately reflect the company's values and mission?
- Is your brand consistently presented across all channels and materials?
- How are you protecting the brand's intellectual property through trademarks and copyrights?
- What measures are you taking to monitor and manage the brand's online reputation?
- How are you engaging with customers and stakeholders to understand their needs and preferences?

- Are you staying current with industry trends and adapting the brand as needed?
- Is your brand alignment in sync with the company's overall business strategy?
- Are you maintaining authenticity and transparency in all your branding efforts?
- Do you have a consistent tone of voice and personality for the brand?
- How often do you review and update the brand to ensure it remains relevant and practical?

BRAND CONSISTENCY SUMMARY

By ensuring that every team member understands the value of ownership over details, establishing stringent guidelines and systems for uniformity—as in how Disney parks manage cleanliness with precision, training employees to prioritize meticulousness and embody the brand's core values, diligently overseeing each customer touchpoint to craft a seamless "magical" experience, and continually pushing boundaries to surpass expectations, a brand can achieve and sustain excellence.

The pivotal pillars of empowering staff, implementing robust infrastructure and rules, providing thorough training, vigilant monitoring, and relentless innovation are instrumental in constructing a uniform and memorable brand experience that enthralls and retains loyal customers. These pillars characterize a brand's operational excellence and shape the emotional connection it develops with its customers.

Disney's flawless facade and the stories that unfold within its walls are not just magic; they are the fruits of an unwavering commitment to consistency—a commitment that every successful brand must emulate.

Answer these questions to begin developing strategies for ensuring a consistent brand experience:

- How can your brand empower employees at all levels to take ownership of the customer experience and make real-time decisions that align with its values?
- What stringent guidelines and systems can you implement across all locations and channels to ensure uniformity in representing the brand?
- How can employees be continually educated and trained to deeply understand and embody the brand's core values and messaging in every interaction?
- What key metrics should you track at customer touchpoints to monitor consistency and quickly address any issues?
- How can your employees be encouraged to think creatively about improving processes while remaining aligned with the brand pillars?
- What emotional connections can you create with customers through a reliable, recognizable brand experience?
- How can you maintain brand consistency across online and offline channels as the brand grows?
- What systems can you implement to ensure new products or communications align seamlessly with the brand identity?
- How can you monitor shifting consumer expectations and preferences and adapt the brand experience accordingly?

- What brand assets and intellectual property should you actively protect through trademarks and copyrights?
- How can you maintain a consistent brand personality and tone of voice across all customer communications?
- What training programs will most effectively equip your staff to deliver exceptional, on-brand customer service?
- How can you monitor competitor moves and differentiating factors to lead with your brand strengths?
- What metrics can you use to measure the ROI of your brand's consistency efforts?
- How can you innovate while ensuring new offerings or initiatives align with the core brand identity?

Part Six

BRAND LOYALTY
CONCLUSION

"Satisfaction is a rating. Loyalty is a brand."
—Shep Hyken, renowned customer service expert

Brands can outlive humans, often thriving for many years by effectively representing their products or services and by skillfully implementing the five key principles of branding: Commitment, Construction, Community, Content, and Consistency. The five C's of branding serve as a guiding framework for brands to navigate the complex branding world and forge meaningful and memorable connections with consumers.

Commitment is the foundation, reflecting a brand's dedication to its purpose, vision, and values. It's about a brand's promise and unwavering resolve to deliver on it, earning customer trust and loyalty.

Construct refers to the structured identity and image a brand builds. It encompasses the brand's unique selling propositions, voice, personality, and systematic approach to carve out a distinct position in a noisy marketplace—creating a recognizable brand image that is aesthetic, timeless, and distinctive.

Community is the cultivation of an ecosystem where customers, employees, and stakeholders actively engage and advocate for the brand as a unified group. It's about fostering relationships and creating a sense of belonging that resonates with the brand's core values—a theoretical place that a community calls home.

Content is the currency of branding, encompassing all forms of communication that a brand uses to inform, entertain, educate, and share stories with its audience. Quality content that aligns with the brand's voice and values can elevate its awareness and memorability. It must have a robust, unique, and clear voice that speaks to its stakeholders in a way they relate to.

Consistency is the thread that weaves all the other elements together, ensuring that every interaction with the brand reinforces its identity and promises. Consistency of execution across all aspects is how a brand builds its power. To retain this social power, it is crucial to maintain a coherent perception in the consumer's mind and across all touchpoints.

The reality is that change is the only constant in the marketplace. Brands must be agile and ready to evolve with shifting consumer expectations and behaviors, market conditions, and technological advancements. Those unable to pivot swiftly or effectively may be outpaced by disruptive newcomers or blindsided by groundbreaking innovations. In today's rapidly transforming environment, even a brand with a superior product is not immune to obsolescence.

The challenge for brands is to remain relevant by embracing transformation without losing sight of their core identity. They must continuously listen, learn, and innovate to maintain a competitive edge. A brand's ability to integrate change into its DNA can make the difference between becoming a cherished legacy and fading into history as a cautionary tale of resistance to change. Regardless of its market dominance or product excellence, no brand can afford complacency in an age marked by radical shifts and relentless innovation.

Even with these five C's firmly in place, brands must recognize that they operate in a landscape of perpetual change. The branding process is continual, requiring constant attention to technological shifts, societal norms, consumer attitudes, trends, and social consciousness. The brand is the red thread that weaves throughout your organization, from the suppliers you work with, to who you hire, to how you treat your employees and customers, to how you sell your products and services, to how you communicate with all your stakeholders. The thread ties everything together and defines what you stand for and how it makes your employees, influencers, and customers feel. And if they love it, they will become loyal ambassadors for life.

Start your Brand Loyalty Strategy

This book is filled with many ideas, tactics, and ways to build a brand. To determine the right approach for your brand, start with establishing a strategy, by answering the following questions.

COMMITMENT (WHY)

Brand Purpose

- What is your brand's reason for being, beyond making a profit?
- How does your brand make a difference in the world or your customers' lives?

Core Values

- What are the non-negotiable values that define your brand's character and actions?
- How do these values influence your business decisions and customer interactions?

Vision Statement

- What future do you want to help create for your customers through your brand?
- How does your vision set you apart from competitors?

Mission Statement

- What are you here to do?
- How does your mission align with your vision and values?

Brand Promise

- What is the commitment you are making to your customers?
- How will you ensure that you deliver on this promise consistently?

CONSTRUCT (WHAT)

Unique Selling Proposition (USP)

- What makes your brand unique in the marketplace?

- How do you communicate this uniqueness to your audience?

Brand Identity

- What are the critical elements of your visual identity (logo, color scheme, typography)?
- What is your brand voice, and how will it be reflected in your communications?
- What unique experience do you want your brand to be known for?

Brand Feeling

- What feeling do you want to leave whenever your customer interacts with your product or service?

Coolness

- Are you continuously innovating and reinventing your brand to stay relevant and ahead of the curve?
- Does your brand foster a sense of community and belonging around your brand while maintaining an aura of exclusivity?
- Are you skillfully managing and balancing the eleven cool factors to create a cohesive and appealing brand image?
- How do you embrace risk-taking and unconventional approaches while staying true to your brand's purpose?

COMMUNITY (WHO)

Target Audience

- Who are your ideal customers?
- What are their demographics, psychographics, and behaviors?

Stakeholder Engagement

- Who are your key stakeholders (employees, partners, influencers)?
- How will you involve them in the brand-building process?

Brand Advocacy

- How will you encourage and empower customers to become brand advocates?
- What programs or platforms will you use to facilitate this advocacy?

CONTENT (WHERE)

Content Strategy

- What types of content will you produce (blog posts, videos, audio, info-graphics, etc.)?
- What are the key messages and stories you want to tell through your content?

Content Distribution Channels

- Which platforms will you use to distribute your content (social media, advertising, website, email, etc.)?
- How will you tailor content to fit the context of each channel?

CONSISTENCY (HOW)

Customer Experience

- How will you ensure a consistent brand experience across all touchpoints?
- What systems or standards will you put in place to maintain this consistency?

Brand Messaging

- How will you keep your messaging aligned across different platforms and campaigns?
- What processes will you use to review and update your messaging as needed?

Visual and Verbal Identity Reinforcement

- How will you reinforce your visual and verbal identity in every piece of communication?
- What guidelines will you establish for the consistent use of your brand assets?

Market Adaptability

- How will you stay informed about market trends and consumer behaviors?
- What is your process for adapting your strategy in response to market changes?

Innovation

- How will you foster a culture of innovation within your brand?
- What mechanisms will you put in place to encourage and implement new ideas?

AFTERWORD

As I put down my pen after finishing this book, I can't help but think about the long road that's led me here. I've been in the branding and marketing game for over thirty years, launching countless campaigns and writing more blog posts than I can count. Even so, I'm constantly reminded that what I know is just the tip of the iceberg. As things change so fast, today's insights might be outdated tomorrow.

But there's something comforting in knowing that despite all this change, the way our brains work—the deep-down stuff that drives our choices and desires—hasn't changed. No matter how many new gadgets we use, we're still the same people underneath.

Our brains can't race to keep up with the latest tech; they change slowly, sticking to their timeless rhythm. The fundamental acts of human thought—thinking, reading, writing—echo through time unchanged, as if in defiance of the tumultuous world they inhabit.

History repeats itself, and the lessons we learn often get forgotten and then rediscovered. In this sense, brands are like lighthouses; they stay put through all the chaos of progress and setbacks. The most intelligent people in the room know that we must build brands on values like diversity and equality, yet somehow we're still wrestling with old biases while chasing after money and success.

Our emotions are pretty much hardwired into us and have been for generations. While science and technology have reshaped our basic needs in developed societies, our primal instincts have been redirected toward power and affluence—we are now witnessing a time where a tiny fraction of us holds a near-mythical portion of our overall wealth: $222 trillion in the hands of just 63 million individuals, or 0.07 percent of the world's population.[272]

But underneath all this change is a solid foundation: the real purpose of brands. They're the thread that connects with our wants and needs. And as long as humans are humans—with all our feelings and thoughts—brands will have a place in our world.

Content will transform. The printed word may fade into memory as we navigate new realms of entertainment and information. But the essence—the heart of branding that endears a product to its audience—will not change. Emerging technologies like machine learning and generative AI promise a future in which brands and consumers engage in unprecedented dialogue.

In the future, some brands will falter; others will flourish. New visionaries will emerge to redefine markets with brands that must embrace the five C's to weave their narrative through every touchpoint like a red thread to the consumer's heart. While ever-evolving in its delivery, the brand story will continue to resonate with those timeless chords of loyalty and feeling.

So, let's turn the page with anticipation, for the branding story is far from over. It is a narrative perpetually rewritten, its core tenets steadfast as it adapts to an ever-changing stage. The essence of what connects us to brands—their ability to fulfill our needs and wants—will endure as long as human hearts beat and minds wander.

NOTES

1   Fortune Media, "Walmart Tops the Fortune Global 500 List for 10th Consecutive Year," Cision, August 2, 2023, https://www.newswire.ca/news-releases/walmart-tops-the-fortune-global-500-list-for-10th-consecutive-year-840567470.html.

2   Preslav Mladenov, "A New Study Reveals Which Company Collects Most of Your Data and Which - the Least," Phone Arena, August 30, 2022, https://www.phonearena.com/news/a-new-study-reveals-which-company-collects-your-data-the-most-and-which-the-least_id142112.

3   Fraser Institute, "As the World Shifted to Free Markets, Poverty Rates Plummeted," November 13, 2018, https://www.fraserinstitute.org/blogs/as-the-world-shifted-to-free-markets-poverty-rates-plummeted.

4   Julia Blackwelder, *Now Hiring: The Feminization of Work in the United States, 1900–1995* (Texas A&M University Press, 1997).

5   Thom Braun, *The Philosophy of Branding: Great Philosophers Think Brands* (Kogan Page Business Books, 2004).

6   Klaus Fog, Christian Budtz, Philip Munch, and Stephen Blanchette, *Storytelling: Branding in Practice* (Springer Berlin Heidelberg, 2016).

7   Stephanie Chevalier, "Biggest Online Retailers in the U.S, 2023, by Market Share," Statista, November 6, 2023, https://www.statista.com/statistics/274255/market-share-of-the-leading-retailers-in-us-e-commerce/; *Walmart Annual Report 2023,* Walmart, January 31, https://corporate.walmart.com/content/dam/corporate/documents/esgreport/reporting-data/tcfd/walmart-inc-2023-annual-report.pdf.

8   Sam Anderson, "How Many Ads Do We Really See in a Day? Spoiler: It's Not 10,000," The Drum, May 3, 2023, https://www.thedrum.com/news/2023/05/03/how-many-ads-do-we-really-see-day-spoiler-it-s-not-10000.

9 "Advertising – Worldwide," Statista, April 2024, https://www.statista.com/outlook/amo/advertising/worldwide.

10 Barry Schwartz, *The Paradox of Choice: Why More Is Less* (Echo, 2004).

11 Joseph Carroll, "Americans Satisfied with Number of Friends, Closeness of Friendships," Gallup, March 5, 2004, https://news.gallup.com/poll/10891/americans-satisfied-number-friends-closeness-friendships.aspx.

12 Yonhap News, "Japan's Oldest Companies," May 14, 2008.

13 Jim Collins and Jerry I. Porras, *Built to Last: Successful Habits of Visionary Companies* (HarperBusiness, 2002).

14 Brendan Cooney, "Most Memorable New Product Launch 2016," Sentient Decision Science, March 4, 2016, https://www.sentientdecisionscience.com/most-memorable-new-product-launch-2016/.

15 Bob Nease, *The Power of Fifty Bits: The New Science of Turning Good Intentions into Positive Results* (Harper Business, 2016).

16 Steve Jobs, "Marketing Is About Values," YouTube, 1997, https://www.youtube.com/watch?v=22jfMkMXl68.

17 Aldo Cundari, *Customer-Centric Marketing: Build Relationships, Create Advocates, and Influence Your Customers* (Wiley, 2015).

18 Mark Sinnock, "Havas' Meaningful Brands Report 2021 Finds We Are Entering the Age of Cynicism [press release]," Havas, May 25, 2021, https://www.havas.com/press_release/havas-meaningful-brands-report-2021-finds-we-are-entering-the-age-of-cynicism/.

19 Siladitya Ray, "Threads Now Fastest-Growing App in History—With 100 Million Users in Just Five Days," *Forbes*, July 10, 2023, https://www.forbes.com/sites/siladityaray/2023/07/10/with-100-million-users-in-five-days-threads-is-the-fastest-growing-app-in-history/?sh=466ba37149ab.

20 Emma Roth, "Threads Is Struggling to Retain Users—But It Could Still Catch Up to X," The Verge, September 26, 2023, https://www.theverge.com/2023/9/26/23890592/threads-meta-monthly-users-data-x-twitter.

21 Larry Light, "The Economics of Brand Value," *Forbes*, March 6, 2019, https://www.forbes.com/sites/larrylight/2019/03/06/the-economics-of-brand-value-creation/.

22 Bruce Berman, "Latest Data Show that Intangible Assets Comprise 90% of the Value of the S&P 500 Companies," IP CloseUp, January 19, 2021, https://ipcloseup.com/2021/01/19/latest-data-show-that-intangible-assets-comprise-90-of-the-value-of-the-sp-500-companies/.

23 Annie Brown, Jack Gregory, and Sacha Wunsch-Vincent, "Intangible Assets Grew to USD 74 Trillion. Which Are the Most Intangible-Asset Intensive Firms?" WIPO, November 11, 2022, https://www.wipo.int/global_innovation_index/en/gii-insights-blog/2022/intangible-assets.html.

24 Vikas Shah, "The Economics of Branding," Thought Economics, October 19, 2023, https://thoughteconomics.com/the-economics-of-branding/.

25 Michelle Bitran, "The State of Customer Loyalty in 2018" Yotpo, September 17, 2018, https://www.yotpo.com/blog/customer-loyalty-survey-data/.

26   Bitran, "The State of Customer Loyalty in 2018."

27   Victoria Bough et al., "Experience-Led Growth: A New Way to Create
      Value," McKinsey & Company, March 23, 2023, https://www.mck-
      insey.com/capabilities/growth-marketing-and-sales/our-insights/
      experience-led-growth-a-new-way-to-create-value.

28   Market.US, "Bottled Water Market Projected to Soar to USD 551.2 Billion by
      2033 | Remarkable CAGR of 5.3% [press release]," Globe Newswire, December 12,
      2023, https://www.globenewswire.com/news-release/2023/12/12/2794578/0/en/
      Bottled-Water-Market-Projected-to-Soar-to-USD-551-2-Billion-by-2033-Remarkable-
      CAGR-of-5-3.html.

29   M. Ridder, "Volume of Bottled Water Worldwide 2014-2027," Statista,
      December 14, 2023, https://www.statista.com/forecasts/1301145/
      worldwide-volume-of-bottled-water-market.

30   *Kantar BrandZ Most Valuable Global Brands,* Kantar, June 14, 2023, https://www.kantar.
      com/campaigns/brandz/global.

31   Jim Stengel, Cait Lamberton, and Ken Favaro, "How Brand Building and Performance
      Marketing Can Work Together," *Harvard Business Review*, May-June, 2023, https://hbr.
      org/2023/05/how-brand-building-and-performance-marketing-can-work-together.

32   Ekshika Raj, "Unhinged or Genius? Deconstructing Liquid Death's Marketing Strategy,"
      Pepper Content, July 17, 2023, https://www.peppercontent.io/blog/unhinged-or-ge-
      nius-deconstructing-liquid-deaths-marketing-strategy/; *Monster Beverage Corporation
      (MNST),* Stock Analysis, January 26, 2024, https://stockanalysis.com/stocks/mnst/
      revenue/.

33   Neil Patel, "How to Tell Your Brand Story to The World," *Forbes*,
      December 3, 2014, https://www.forbes.com/sites/neilpatel/2014/12/03/
      how-to-tell-your-brand-story-to-the-world/?sh=2711b5f712e0.

34   Jonah Sachs, *Winning the Story Wars: Why Those Who Tell—and Live—the Best Stories
      Will Rule the Future* (Harvard Business Review Press, 2012).

35   Talon Homer, "How Many Books Are There in the World?" HowStuffWorks, October
      12, 2022, https://entertainment.howstuffworks.com/arts/literature/how-many-books.
      htm.

36   Jon Hamm, "Why Agencies and Brands Need to Embrace True Storytelling,"
      Adweek, September 23, 2013, https://www.adweek.com/brand-marketing/
      why-agencies-and-brands-need-embrace-true-storytelling-152534/.

37   Susan Gunelius, "How to Write Brand Stories that Build
      Emotional Connections," *Forbes*, September 24, 2013, https://
      www.forbes.com/sites/work-in-progress/2013/09/24/
      how-to-write-brand-stories-that-build-emotional-connections/?sh=124b5be979a2.

38   Seth Godin, interview by Nick Warren, "Seth Godin on Storytelling," Stories
      Mean Business, 2013, https://storiesmeanbusiness.com/seth-godin-on-story/
      seth-godin-on-storytelling/.

39   Apple Inc., "Think Different [advertisement]," directed by TBWA\Chiat\Day, 1997.

40   John Mariani, "The Only Ketchup You Ever Need," *Esquire*, October 27, 2011, https://www.esquire.com/food-drink/food/a11437/new-heinz-kethcup-6531429/.

41   Allen Adamson, "Define Your Brand's Purpose, Not Just Its Promise," *Forbes*, November 11, 2009, https://www.forbes.com/2009/11/11/brand-defining-marketing-cmo-network-allen-adamson.html?sh=4a56a9825109.

42   Jim Stengel, *Grow: How Ideals Power Growth and Profit at the World's Greatest Companies,* (Crown Business, 2011).

43   Richard Laermer and Mark Simmons, *Punk Marketing: Get Off Your Ass and Join the Revolution* (HarperCollins, 2009).

44   Disney Institute, "Customer Service 101: Happiness Is a Purple Balloon," Disney Institute Blog, July 13, 2021, https://www.disneyinstitute.com/blog/customer-service-101-happiness-is-a-purple-balloon/.

45   Gary Gebhardt, Gregory Carpenter, and John Sherry Jr., "Creating a Market Orientation: A Longitudinal, Multifirm, Grounded Analysis of Cultural Transformation," *Journal of Marketing* 70, no. 4 (2006): 37–55, https://doi.org/10.1509/jmkg.70.4.037.

46   Scott M. Davis, "The Power of the Brand," *Strategy & Leadership* 28, no. 4 (2000): 4–9, https://doi.org/10.1108/10878570010378636.

47   "Sheer Driving Pleasure," BMW, August 27, 2020, https://www.bmw.com/en/automotive-life/the-history-of-the-bmw-slogan.html.

48   Julian Barnes, "The Making (or Possible Breaking) of a Megabrand," *New York Times*, July 22, 2001, https://www.nytimes.com/2001/07/22/business/the-making-or-possible-breaking-of-a-megabrand.html.

49   Jack Neff, "Ten Years In, Dove's 'Real Beauty' Seems to Be Aging Well," *AdAge*, January 22, 2014, https://adage.com/article/news/ten-years-dove-s-real-beauty-aging/291216.

50   Christopher Stringer and Clive Gamble, *In Search of the Neanderthals: Solving the Puzzle of Human Origins* (Thames & Hudson, 1993).

51   Christopher Cherniak, "The Bounded Brain: Toward Quantiative Neuroanatomy," *Journal of Cognitive Neuroscience* 2, no. 1 (1990): 58–68, https://doi.org/10.1162/jocn.1990.2.1.58; Michel A. Hofman, "Design Principles of the Human Brain: An Evolutionary Perspective," *Progress in Brain Research*, no. 195 (2012): 373–90, https://doi.org/10.1016/B978-0-444-53860-4.00018-0.

52   Robert Sheldon, Erin Sullivan, and Brien Posey, "Terabyte (TB)," TechTarget, October 2021, https://www.techtarget.com/searchstorage/definition/terabyte; Jim Donnelly, "How Much Is a Terabyte?" MASV, June 17, 2022, https://massive.io/file-transfer/how-much-is-one-terabyte/.

53   Tim Lince, "'We're Running Out of Good Trademarks'—Groundbreaking Study Reveals 81% of Common Words Are Registered Marks," World Trademark Review, February 23, 2018, https://www.worldtrademarkreview.com/article/were-running-out-of-good-trademarks-groundbreaking-study-reveals-81-of-common-words-are-registered-marks.

54   World Intellectual Property Organization, *World Intellectual Property Indicators 2023*, https://www.wipo.int/edocs/pubdocs/en/wipo-pub-941-2023-en-world-intellectual-property-indicators-2023.pdf.

55   Riley Stoltenburg, "US Book Reading Statistics (National Survey 2024),"
      Test Prep Insight, January 3, 2024, https://testprepinsight.com/resources/
      us-book-reading-statistics/.

56   Nicholas Rizzo, "Over 50% of Americans Haven't Read a Book in the Past
      Year [2022 Study]," WordsRated, July 13, 2022, https://wordsrated.com/
      american-reading-habits-study/.

57   Robert Passikoff, "10 Brand and Marketing Trends to Watch in 2019," E-Commerce
      Times, December 7, 2018, https://www.ecommercetimes.com/story/10-brand-and-
      marketing-trends-to-watch-in-2019-85727.html.

58   Stacey McLachlan, "23 YouTube Stats That Matter to Marketers in 2023," Hootsuite,
      February 14, 2022, https://blog.hootsuite.com/youtube-stats-marketers/.

59   Muninder Adavelli, "How Many Videos Are Uploaded on YouTube
      Every Day?" Techjury, July 27, 2023, https://techjury.net/blog/
      how-many-videos-are-uploaded-to-youtube-a-day/.

60   Maryam Mohsin, "10 TikTok Statistics That You Need to Know in 2023," Oberlo,
      August 11, 2023, https://www.oberlo.com/blog/tiktok-statistics.

61   Julia Stoll, "Number of Netflix Paid Subscribers Worldwide From 1st Quarter 2013 to
      2nd Quarter 2024," Statista, May 22, 2024, https://www.statista.com/statistics/250934/
      quarterly-number-of-netflix-streaming-subscribers-worldwide/.

62   Nielsen, "Nielsen: The Gauge Reveals Streaming Surpassed Cable for the First
      Time in July, Capturing its Largest Share of TV Viewing to Date [press release],"
      Cision PR Newswire, August 18, 2022, https://www.prnewswire.com/news-releases/
      nielsen-the-gauge-reveals-streaming-surpassed-cable-for-the-first-time-in-july-capturing-
      its-largest-share-of-tv-viewing-to-date-301608224.html.

63   Xerox, *20 Ways to Share Color Knowledge,* fact sheet, 2017, https://www.office.xerox.
      com/latest/COLFS-02UA.PDF.

64   Matt Moran, "Website Color Statistics: What's the Best Color for Websites?" Colorlib,
      April 1, 2024, https://colorlib.com/wp/website-color-statistics/.

65   Xerox, *20 Ways to Share Color Knowledge.*

66   Gregory Ciotti, "Color Psychology in Marketing and Branding Is All About Context,"
      Help Scout, May 16, 2024, https://www.helpscout.com/blog/psychology-of-color/.

67   Andrew J. Elliot and Henk Aarts, "Perception of the Color Red Enhances the Force and
      Velocity of Motor Output," *Emotion* 11, no. 2 (2011): 445–49, https://doi.org/10.1037/
      a0022599.

68   Satyendra Singh, "Impact of Color on Maketing," *Management Decision* 44, no. 6
      (2006): 783–89, https://doi.org/10.1108/00251740610673332.

69   Paul A. Bottomley and John R. Doyle, "The Interactive Effects of Colors and Products
      on Perceptions of Brand Logo Appropriateness," *Marketing Theory* 6, no. 1 (2006):
      63–83, https://doi.org/10.1177/1470593106061263.

70   David J. Linden, *Touch: The Science of the Hand, Heart, and Mind* (Penguin Books,
      2016).

71   Linden, *Touch.*

72   William F. Chaplin et al., "Handshaking, Gender, Personality, and First Impressions," *Journal of Personality and Social Psychology* 79, no. 1 (2000): 110–17, https://doi.org/10.1037/0022-3514.79.1.110.

73   Linden, *Touch*.

74   Dacher Keltner, "Hands On Research: The Science of Touch," *Greater Good Magazine*, September 29, 2010, https://greatergood.berkeley.edu/article/item/hands_on_research.

75   Jeremy Hsu, "Just a Touch Can Influence Thoughts and Decisions,"LiveScience, June 24, 2010, https://www.livescience.com/8360-touch-influence-thoughts-decisions.html.

76   Peter Dizikes, "The Magic Touch," MIT, News, June 25, 2010, https://news.mit.edu/2010/haptic-0625.

77   Martin Lindstrom, *Brand Sense: Sensory Secrets Behind the Stuff We Buy* (Free Press, 2005).

78   Alberto Gallace and Charles Spence, *In Touch with the Future: The Sense of Touch from Cognitive Neurosciences to Virtual Reality* (Oxford University Press, 2014).

79   Paul Page, "Today's Top Supply Chain and Logistics News from WSJ," *Wall Street Journal*, June 18, 2015, https://www.wsj.com/articles/todays-top-supply-chain-and-logistics-news-from-wsj-1434622396.

80   Saabira Chaudhuri, "IKEA Can't Stop Obsessing About Its Packaging," *Wall Street Journal,* June 17, 2015, https://www.wsj.com/articles/ikea-cant-stop-obsessing-about-its-packaging-1434533401.

81   Alexandra Sifferlin, "My Nose Made Me Buy It: How Retailers Use Smell (and Other Tricks) to Get You to Spend, Spend, Spend," *Time*, December 16, 2013, https://healthland.time.com/2013/12/16/my-nose-made-me-buy-it-how-retailers-use-smell-and-other-tricks-to-get-you-to-spend-spend-spend/.

82   "The Home Fragrance Market Size, Share & Industry Analysis, by Product Type, Distribution Channel, and Regional Forecast, 2024–2032," Fortune Business Insights, May 29, 2024, https://www.fortunebusinessinsights.com/home-fragrance-market-102422.

83   Aradhna Krishna, *Customer Sense: How the 5 Senses Influence Buying Behavior* (Palgrave Macmillan, 2013).

84   Marisa Sanfilippo, "The Smells That Make Shoppers Spend More," *Business News Daily*, January 24, 2024, https://www.businessnewsdaily.com/3469-smells-shoppers-spend-more.html.

85   Sifferlin, "My Nose Made Me Buy It."

86   Carly Lewis, "When Scent Crosses the Ethical Line," *Globe and Mail*, September 10, 2014, https://www.theglobeandmail.com/life/fashion-and-beauty/beauty/when-scent-crosses-the-ethical-line/article20517586/.

87   Charmain Kosek, "Researchers Find Scent of Money," UPI, September 7, 1992, https://www.upi.com/Archives/1992/09/07/Researchers-find-scent-of-money/6750715838400/.

88   Malcolm Gladwell, "The Ketchup Conundrum," *New Yorker*, August 29, 2004, https://www.newyorker.com/magazine/2004/09/06/the-ketchup-conundrum; Malcolm

Gladwell, "Choice, Happiness and Spaghetti Sauce," TED Talk, 2004, https://www.ted.com/talks/malcolm_gladwell_choice_happiness_and_spaghetti_sauce?language=en.

89   N. Ramanjaneyalu, "Blind Taste Test of Soft-Drinks—A Comparison Study on Coke and Pepsi," *International Journal of Application or Innovation in Engineering & Management* 2, no. 12 (2013): 244–47, https://www.scribd.com/document/201703028/IJAIEM-2013-12-26-071#.

90   Lauren Y. Atlas and Tor D. Wager, "Expectancies and Beliefs: Insights from Cognitive Neuroscience," in *The Oxford Handbook of Cognitive Neuroscience*, vol. 2, The Cutting Edges, ed. Kevin N. Ochsner and Stephen Kosslyn (University of Oxford Press, 2013), 359–81.

91   Maria Konnikova, "What We Really Taste When We Drink Wine," *New Yorker*, July 11, 2014, https://www.newyorker.com/science/maria-konnikova/what-we-really-taste-when-we-drink-wine.

92   Julia Faria, "Advertising Spending of Selected Beer Manufacturers in the United States in 2021," Statista, January 6, 2023, https://www.statista.com/statistics/264998/ad-spend-of-selected-beer-manufacturers-in-the-us/.

93   Thomas Robinson et al., "Effects of Fast Food Branding on Young Children's Taste Preferences," *Archives of Pediatrics & Adolescent Medicine* 161, no. 8 (2007): 792–97, https://doi.org/10.1001/archpedi.161.8.792.

94   Ken Bruno, "Can't Get It Out of Your Head: Best Ad Jingles," *NBC News*, July 15, 2010, https://www.nbcnews.com/id/wbna38150349.

95   Daniel Jackson, Richard Jankovich, and Eric Sheinkop, *Hit Brands: How Music Builds Value for the World's Smartest Brands* (Palgrave Macmillan, 2013).

96   Kevin Perlmutter, "What Marketers Can Learn from Tinder Behavior," Linkedin, January 26, 2016, https://www.linkedin.com/pulse/brand-love-swipe-left-world-kevin-perlmutter/.

97   Colleen Fahey and Laurence Minsky, *Audio Branding: Using Sound to Build Your Brand* (Kogan Page Publishers, 2017).

98   Kevin Perlmutter and Nora Bradshaw, "Addressing Today's Top Brand," *Journal of Branding Strategy* 5, no. 2 (2016): 1–8.

99   Hokuma Karimova, "The Emotion Wheel: What It Is and How to Use It," Positive Psychology, December 24, 2017, https://positivepsychology.com/emotion-wheel/.

100   Kendra Cherry, *The Everything Psychology Book, 2nd ed.* (Adams Media, 2010).

101   Jessica Stern and J.M. Berger, *ISIS: The State of Terror* (HarperCollins, 2015).

102   Alex Altman, "No President Has Spread Fear Like Donald Trump," *Time*, February 9, 2017, https://time.com/4665755/donald-trump-fear/.

103   Carly Miller, "The Dangerous Power of Emotional Advertising," Contently, April 14, 2016, https://contently.com/2016/04/14/dangerous-power-emotional-advertising/.

104   Dan Pilat and Sekoul Krastev, "Why Do We Buy Insurance," The Decision Lab, May 3, 2024, https://thedecisionlab.com/biases/loss-aversion.

105   Frank Furedi, "What Swine Flu Reveals About the Culture of Fear," Spiked, May 5, 2009, https://www.spiked-online.com/2009/05/05/what-swine-flu-reveals-about-the-culture-of-fear/.

106   Lily Rothman, "Why Americans Are More Afraid Than They Used to Be," *Time*, January 6, 2016, https://time.com/4158007/american-fear-history/.

107   Eric Brymer and Robert Schweitzer, "Extreme Sports Are Good for Your Health: A Phenomenological Understanding of Fear and Anxiety in Extreme Sport," *Journal of Health Psychology* 18, no. 4 (2012), https://doi.org/10.1177/1359105312446770.

108   Laurie Burkitt, "From Trusted to Busted: Brands Have a Credibility Crisis," *Forbes*, February 25, 2010, https://www.forbes.com/2010/02/25/toyota-tiger-consumer-faith-cmo-network-trusted-to-busted-brands.html?sh=6cb8e807383b.

109   Morgen Witzel, "Maple Leaf Food's Response to a Crisis," *Financial Times*, April 29, 2013, https://www.ft.com/content/8c8d3668-adb5-11e2-82b8-00144feabdc0.

110   Peter McGraw and Joel Warner, *The Humor Code: A Global Search for What Makes Things Funny* (Simon & Schuster, 2015).

111   Jack Schafer, "People Will Like You If You Make Them Laugh," *Psychology Today*, August 3, 2016, https://www.psychologytoday.com/ca/blog/let-their-words-do-the-talking/201608/people-will-you-if-you-make-them-laugh.

112   Rohit Bhargava, *Likeonomics: The Unexpected Truth Behind Earning Trust, Influencing Behavior, and Inspiring Action* (Wiley, 2012).

113   Umair Bashir, "Preferred films and shows by genre in the U.S. as of March 2024" Statista, May 17, 2024, https://www.statista.com/forecasts/997166/preferred-films-and-shows-by-genre-in-the-us.

114   "These Are the Entertainment Genres Gen Z Is Watching More Than Millennials," YPulse, April 27, 2022, https://www.ypulse.com/article/2022/04/27/these-are-the-entertainment-genres-gen-z-is-watching-more-than-millennials/.

115   Michael D. Curran, "Is Funny Enough? Analysis of the Impact of Humor in Advertisements," El Segundo: Ace Metrix, 2012, http://www.acemetrix.com/wp-content/uploads/2015/09/Ace_Metrix_Insight_Funny.pdf.

116   Aflac, "Aflac Recognized as a Top 25 Brand [press release]," PR Newswire, March 24, 2015, https://www.prnewswire.com/news-releases/aflac-recognized-as-a-top-25-brand-300054785.html.

117   Gardiner Morse, "Hidden Minds," *Harvard Business Review*, June 2002, https://hbr.org/2002/06/hidden-minds.

118   Rae Ann Fera, "The Rise of Sadvertising Why Brands Are Determined to Make You Cry," Fast Company, April 5, 2014, https://www.fastcompany.com/3029767/the-rise-of-sadvertising-why-brands-are-determined-to-make-you-cry.

119   Harsh Verma, "'Cool' Branding and Marketing," MarketingCrow blog, Apr 17, 2013, https://marketingcrow.wordpress.com/2013/04/17/cool-branding-and-marketing/.

120   Lucinda Southern, "How the UK Defines the 'Cool' Factor of Hot Brands like Sonos and Netflix," Digiday, September 29, 2015, https://digiday.com/marketing/uk-defines-cool-factor-hot-brands-like-sonos-netflix/.

121   Sara Bird and Alan Tapp, "Social Marketing and the Meaning of Cool," *Social Marketing Quarterly* 14, no. 1 (2008): 18–29, https://doi.org/10.1080/15245000801898399.

122   Clive Nancarrow, Pamela Nancarrow, and Julie Page, "An Analysis of the Concept of *Cool* and Its Marketing Implications," *Journal of Consumer Behaviour* 1, no. 4 (2001): 311–22, http://www.sundigital.uk/Journals-ABS-2star/An%20analysis%20of%20 the%20concept%20of%20cool%20and%20its%20marketing%20implications.pdf.

123   Rajendran Sriramachandramurthy, "What's Cool? Examining Brand Coolness and Its Consequences," (PhD diss., Southern Illinois University Carbondale, 2009), OpenSiuc.

124   Sandra Maria Correia Loureiro and Rui Lopes, "Characteristics of Cool Brands: The Development of a Scale," ANZMAC Conference, January 2011, https://www. researchgate.net/publication/233925463_Characteristics_of_Cool_Brands_The_ Development_of_a_Scale; Caleb Warren et al., "Brand Coolness," *Journal of Marketing* 83, no. 5 (2019), https://doi.org/10.1177/0022242919857698.

125   Caleb Warren and Margaret C. Campbell, "What Makes Things Cool? How Autonomy Influences Perceived Coolness," *Journal of Consumer Research* 41, no. 2 (2014): 543–63, https://doi.org/10.1086/676680.

126   Wolfgang Schaefer and J.P. Kuehlwein, *Rethinking Prestige Branding: Secrets of the Ueber-Brands* (Kogan Page, 2015).

127   Jim Harter, "Globally, Employees Are More Engaged—and More Stressed," Gallup, June 13, 2023, https://www.gallup.com/workplace/506798/globally-employees-engaged-stressed.aspx.

128   *Edelman Trust Barometer 2021: The State of Trust in a World After COVID-19,* Edelman, 2021, https://www.edelman.com/sites/g/files/aatuss191/files/2021-01/2021-edelman-trust-barometer.pdf.

129   Lee Frederiksen, Sylvia Montgomery, and Karl Feldman, *Inside the Buyer's Brain: The Buyer Persona Research Report,* Hinge Research Institute, 2018.

130   *Employee Activism in the Age of Purpose: Employees as Brand Ambassadors,* Weber Shandwick, 2016.

131   Jay Baer, *Hug Your Haters: How to Embrace Complaints and Keep Your Customers* (Penguin Random House, 2016).

132   Deloitte, *Purpose and Values: A Study by Deloitte and the Billie Jean King Leadership Initiative,* Deloitte Development LLC, 2016.

133   Ekaterina Walter, "Want to Find Brand Ambassadors? Start with Your Employees," *Forbes,* October 15, 2013, https://www.forbes.com/sites/ekaterinawalter/2013/10/15/ want-to-find-brand-ambassadors-start-with-your-employees-2/?sh=78b83ffc5ef6.

134   J.K. Harter, F.L. Schmidt and T.L. Hayes, "Business-Unit-Level Relationship Between Employee Satisfaction, Employee Engagement, and Business Outcomes: A Meta-Analysis," *Journal of Applied Psychology* 87, no. 2 (2022): 268–79, https://doi. org/10.1037/0021-9010.87.2.268.

135   Amy C. Edmondson, *The Fearless Organization: Creating Psychological Safety in the Workplace for Learning, Innovation, and Growth* (John Wiley & Sons, 2018).

136 Claire Cain Miller, "Larry Page on Regulation, Maps and Google's Social Mission," *New York Times*, October 17, 2012, https://archive.nytimes.com/bits.blogs.nytimes.com/2012/10/17/larry-page-on-regulation-maps-and-googles-social-mission/.

137 Jacob Morgan, *The Employee Experience Advantage: How to Win the War for Talent by Giving Employees the Workspaces They Want, the Tools They Need, and a Culture They Can Celebrate* (Wiley, 2017).

138 Howard Schultz and Joanne Gordon, *Onward: How Starbucks Fought for Its Life Without Losing Its Soul* (Rodale Books, 2011).

139 Stever Robbins, *Get-It-Done Guy's 9 Steps to Work Less and Do More* (St. Martin's Griffin, 2015).

140 *Diversity, Equity and Inclusion in a Global Pandemic,* Society for Human Resource Management, 2021.

141 Christine S. Mueller, Sustainability Blogs: New Integrated Report, SAP, March 24, 2015, https://community.sap.com/t5/sustainability-blogs/new-integrated-report-out-sap-quantifies-its-social-and-environmental/ba-p/13166787.

142 "Herb Kelleher Completes His Service on Earth," Modern Servant Leader, January 3, 2019, https://modernservantleader.com/servant-leadership/herb-kelleher-completes-his-service-on-earth/.

143 Carmine Gallo, "Southwest Airlines Motivates Its Employees with a Purpose Bigger Than a Paycheck," *Forbes*, January 21, 2014, https://www.forbes.com/sites/carminegallo/2014/01/21/southwest-airlines-motivates-its-employees-with-a-purpose-bigger-than-a-paycheck/?sh=217fa4845376.

144 "The Whys and Hows of Generations Research," Pew Research Center, September 3, 2015, https://www.pewresearch.org/politics/2015/09/03/the-whys-and-hows-of-generations-research/.

145 Talmon J. Smith, "The Greatest Wealth Transfer in History Is Here, with Familiar (Rich) Winners," *New York Times*, May 23, 2023, https://www.nytimes.com/2023/05/14/business/economy/wealth-generations.html.

146 *World Happiness Report 2024,* Wellbeing Research Centre at the University of Oxford, UK, March 2024, https://worldhappiness.report/.

147 *World Happiness Report 2024*, Wellbeing Research Centre.

148 Ian McGugan, "Why a Report on Global Happiness Should Worry Canadian Investors," *Globe and Mail*, March 23, 2024, https://www.theglobeandmail.com/investing/markets/inside-the-market/article-why-a-report-on-global-happiness-should-worry-canadian-investors/.

149 Melissa De Witte, "Gen Z Are Not 'Coddled.' They Are Highly Collaborative, Self-Reliant and Pragmatic, According to New Stanford-Affiliated Research," *Stanford News*, January 3, 2022, https://news.stanford.edu/2022/01/03/know-gen-z/.

150 Becky Boyle, "US Gen Z Shopping Habits & Retail Trends for 2024," GWI, February 22, 2024, https://blog.gwi.com/trends/3-us-gen-z-retail-trends/.

151 William H. Frey, *The Millennial Generation: A Demographic Bridge to Americas Diverse Future,* Metropolitan Policy Program at Bookings, Brookings Institution, March 2018, https://www.brookings.edu/

wp-content/uploads/2018/01/2018-jan_brookings-metro_millennials-a-demographic-bridge-to-americas-diverse-future.pdf.

152   Alec Tyson, Brian Kennedy and Cary Funk, "Gen Z, Millennials Stand Out for Climate Change Activism, Social Media Engagement With Issue," Pew Research Center, May 26, 2021, https://www.pewresearch.org/science/2021/05/26/gen-z-millennials-stand-out-for-climate-change-activism-social-media-engagement-with-issue/.

153   *State of Gen Z 2018,* Center for Generational Kinetics, 2018, https://genhq.com/generation-z-research-2018/.

154   *The Truth About Youth 2018,* McCann Worldgroup, 2018, https://www.mccann-nworldgroup.com/truth-about-youth.

155   Kelvin Claveria, "YouTube, Netflix and Amazon are Gen Z's Top Brands in 2023, New Research From Rival Group Finds [press release]," Market Dive, May 17, 2023, https://www.marketingdive.com/press-release/20230517-youtube-netflix-and-amazon-are-gen-zs-top-brands-in-2023-new-research-fr/.

156   Melanie Hanson, "Student Loan Debt by Generation," Education Data Initiative, September 24, 2023, https://educationdata.org/student-loan-debt-by-generation.

157   "U.S. Annual Household Expenditures 2022, By Generation," Statista, November 3, 2023, https://www.statista.com/statistics/825887/us-annual-household-expenditures-by-generation/.

158   Josh Zumbrun, "How to Tell If a 'Fact' About Millennials Isn't Actually a Fact," *Wall Street Journal,* November 27, 2014, https://www.wsj.com/articles/BL-REB-29210.

159   Christine Barton et al., *Traveling with Millennials,* Boston Consulting Group, March 18, 2013, https://www.bcg.com/publications/2013/transportation-tourism-marketing-sales-traveling-millennials.

160   "How Many Gen Z and Millennials Are Really Living at Home with Their Parents," YPulse, April 20, 2023, https://www.ypulse.com/article/2023/04/20/how-many-gen-z-and-millennials-are-really-living-at-home-with-their-parents/.

161   Joeri van den Bergh and Mattias Behrer, *How Cool Brands Stay Hot: Branding to Generations Y and Z,* 3rd ed. (Kogan Page, 2016).

162   Melissa Hoffmann, "Attention Brands: This Is How You Get Millennials to Like You," *Adweek,* October 6, 2014, https://www.adweek.com/brand-marketing/attention-brands-how-you-get-millennials-you-160575/.

163   Steve Conway, *Millennials and GenZ: How Different Are They,* ConvergeHub, n.d., https://www.convergehub.com/blog/millennials-and-genz.

164   Andrew Smith, "Millennial Shoppers & Reviews: A Deep Dive," Power Reviews, June 23, 2021, https://www.powerreviews.com/generate-more-reviews-millennials.

165   Nick Shore, "Millennials Are Playing With You," *Harvard Business Review,* December 12, 2011, https://hbr.org/2011/12/millennials-are-playing-with-y.

166   Oriana Schwindt, "Comedy Central's David Bernath Out as General Manager, Tanya Giles to Replace," *Variety,* February 28, 2017, https://variety.com/2017/tv/news/comedy-central-gm-david-bernath-tanya-giles-1201998942/.

167   Michael Bush, "Study Finds Millennial Generation's Power to Influence Is Increasing [press release]," Edelman, December 4, 2012, https://www.prnewswire.com/news-releases/study-finds-millennial-generations-power-to-influence-is-increasing-182017681.html.

168   Paul Taylor and George Gao, "Generation X: America's Neglected 'Middle Child,'" Pew Research Center, June 5, 2014, https://www.pewresearch.org/short-reads/2014/06/05/generation-x-americas-neglected-middle-child/.

169   Heidi Shierholz and Elise Gould, "A Lost Decade: Poverty and Income Trends Continue to Paint a Bleak Picture for Working Families," Economic Policy Institue, September 14, 2011, https://www.epi.org/publication/lost-decade-poverty-income-trends-continue/.

170   Diane J. Macunovich, *Birth Quake: The Baby Boom and Its Aftershocks* (University of Chicago Press, 2002).

171   William Strauss and Neil Howe, *Generations: The History of America's Future, 1584 to 2069* (William Morrow & Co., 1991).

172   Smith, "The Greatest Wealth Transfer in History."

173   Valerio De Stefano, "The Rise of the 'Just-in-Time Workforce': On-Demand Work, Crowdwork, and Labor Protection in the 'Gig Economy'," *Comparative Labor Law and Policy Journal* 37, no. 3 (2016): 471–504.

174   *Freelance Forward 2023*, Upwork, December 12, 2023, https://www.upwork.com/research/freelance-forward-2023-research-report.

175   *OECD Employment Outlook 2023: Artificial Intelligence and the Labour Market*, OECD, July 11, 2023, https://doi.org/10.1787/08785bba-en.

176   Bettina Kubicek et al., "Working Conditions and Workers' Health," Eurofound Publications Office, 2019, https://doi.org/10.2806/909840.

177   "COVID-19 and the Future of Business," IBM, August 2020, https://www.ibm.com/thought-leadership/institute-business-value/en-us/report/covid-19-future-business.

178   Bank of America, *2021 Homebuyers Insights Report*, Sparks Research, 2021.

179   Shaun Callaghan et al., *Still Feeling Good: The US Wellness Market Continues to Boom*, McKinsey & Company, September 19, 2022, https://www.mckinsey.com/industries/consumer-packaged-goods/our-insights/still-feeling-good-the-us-wellness-market-continues-to-boom.

180   *How Sustainability Is Fundamentally Changing Consumer Preferences*, Capgemini Research Institute, 2020 , https://www.capgemini.com/wp-content/uploads/2021/02/20-06_9880_Sustainability-in-CPR_Final_Web-1-2.pdf.

181   *D2C and the New Brand Loyalty Opportunity Report*, PYMNT.com and sticky.io, 2020, available at https://www.pymnts.com/study/d2c-and-the-new-brand-loyalty-opportunity/.

182   Carla Morla, "New Nextdoor Insights Show Neighbors Strongly Support Local Businesses," Nextdoor for Business, February 10, 2023, https://business.nextdoor.com/en-us/small-business/resources/blog/new-nextdoor-insights-show-neighbors-strongly-support-local-businesses.

183   *Future Workplace Index 2.0,* Ernst & Young Global Limited, November 2022, https://assets.ey.com/content/dam/ey-sites/ey-com/en_us/topics/real-estate-hospitality-and-construction/ey-future-workplace-index-2.pdf.

184   Johnny Wood, "These 3 Charts Show the Global Growth In Online Learning," World Economic Forum, January 27, 2022, https://www.weforum.org/agenda/2022/01/online-learning-courses-reskill-skills-gap/.

185   Jay Baer and Daniel Lemin, *Talk Triggers: The Complete Guide to Creating Customers with Word of Mouth* (Portfolio, 2018).

186   "When It Comes to Advertising Effectiveness, What Is Key?" Nielsen, October 2017, https://www.nielsen.com/insights/2017/when-it-comes-to-advertising-effectiveness-what-is-key/.

187   *Five Keys to Advertising Effectiveness: Unlocking the Assets That Can Make or Break Your Advertising Strategy,* NCSolutions, 2023, https://info.ncsolutions.com/hubfs/2023%20Five%20Keys%20to%20Advertising%20Effectiveness/NCS_Five_Keys_to_Advertising_Effectiveness_E-Book_08-23.pdf.

188   "From Retail to 'Me-tail,'" ERT, May 19, 2017, https://ertonline.co.uk/opinion/from-retail-to-me-tail/.

189   Kirk Hallahan, "Content Class as a Contextual Cue in the Cognitive Processing of Publicity Versus Advertising," *Journal of Public Relations Research* 11, no. 4 (1999): 723–42, https://doi.org/10.1207/s1532754xjprr1104_02.

190   Natasha Bach, "Propel: Journalists Responded to Fewer than 3% of Pitches in Q2," PR Week, July 19, 2023, https://www.prweek.com/article/1830639/propel-journalists-responded-fewer-3-pitches-q2.

191   "7 Companies Hurt by Bad Publicity," MarketWatch, August 18, 2014, https://www.marketwatch.com/story/7-companies-hurt-by-bad-publicity-2014-08-18?page=7.

192   Stanford GSB Staff, "When Is Bad Publicity Good?" Stanford Business, February 1, 2011, https://www.gsb.stanford.edu/insights/when-bad-publicity-good.

193   Travis M. Andrews and Fred Barbash, "'I'd Like to Buy the World a Coke': The Story Behind the World's Most Famous Ad, in Memoriam Its Creator," *Wahington Post,* May 17, 2016, https://www.washingtonpost.com/news/morning-mix/wp/2016/05/17/id-like-to-buy-the-world-a-coke-the-story-behind-the-worlds-most-famous-ad-whose-creator-has-died-at-89/.

194   Paul Stringer, "Why Media Quality Will Take Centre Stage in 2024," WARC, January 22, 2024, https://www.warc.com/newsandopinion/opinion/why-media-quality-will-take-centre-stage-in-2024/en-gb/6531.

195   James McDonald, *Global Ad Spend Outlook 2023/24: Withstanding Turbulence,* WARC, n.d., https://www.warc.com/content/paywall/article/warc-data/global-ad-spend-outlook-2023-24-withstanding-turbulence/en-gb/152362?.

196   Stephanie Chevalier, "Retail E-commerce Sales Worldwide from 2014 to 2027," Statista, February 6, 2024, https://www.statista.com/statistics/379046/worldwide-retail-e-commerce-sales/#:~:text=In%202023%2C%20global%20retail%20e,estimated%205.8%20trillion%20U.S.%20dollars.

197   Matthew Woodward, "Ecommerce Statistics 2023—Everything You Need to Know," Search Logistics, July 18, 2023, https://www.searchlogistics.com/learn/statistics/ecommerce-statistics/.

198   Eric Gregoire, "E-Commerce Poised to Capture 41% of Global Retail Sales by 2027—Up from Just 18% in 2017 [press release]," Boston Consulting Group, October 31, 2023, https://www.bcg.com/press/31october2023-ecommerce-global-retail-sales.

199   Chevalier, "Biggest Online Retailers in the U.S, 2023."

200   Alphabet Inc., Form 10-K, United States Securities and Exchange Commission, December 31, 2022, https://www.sec.gov/ix?doc=/Archives/edgar/data/1652044/000165204423000016/goog-20221231.htm#.

201   "L'Oréal Paris Discovers the Beauty of Search for Building Brand Love," Google, June 2014, https://www.thinkwithgoogle.com/marketing-strategies/search/loreal-paris-builds-brand-love-with-search/.

202   Andrew Hutchinson, "TikTok Shares New Insights into How Users Respond to Promotions in the App," Social Media Today, June 15, 2022, https://www.socialmediatoday.com/news/tiktok-shares-new-insights-into-how-users-respond-to-promotions-in-the-app/625586/.

203   Stacy Jo Dixon, "Number of Global Social Network Users 2017–2027," Statista, August 29, 2023, https://www.statista.com/statistics/278414/number-of-worldwide-social-network-users/; World Population Projections, Worldometer, 2022, https://www.worldometers.info/world-population/world-population-projections/.

204   McLachlan, "23 YouTube Stats That Matter to Marketers in 2023."

205   Michael Stelzner, *2023 Social Media Marketing Industry Report,* SocialMedia Examiner, 2023, https://www.socialmediaexaminer.com/report2023/.

206   Simon Kemp, *Global Social Media Statistics,* DataReportal by Kepios, October 2023, https://datareportal.com/social-media-users.

207   Jeffrey M. Jones, "Social Media Users More Inclined to Browse Than Post Content," Gallup, January 9, 2023, https://news.gallup.com/poll/467792/social-media-users-inclined-browse-post-content.aspx.

208   Rohit Shewale, "Social Media Users and Statistics for 2024 (Latest Data)" Demandsage, January 1, 2024, https://www.demandsage.com/social-media-users/.

209   Esteban Ortiz-Ospina, "The Rise of Social Media," Our World in Data, September 18, 2019, https://ourworldindata.org/rise-of-social-media.

210   Ana Durrani, "Top Streaming Statistics in 2024," *Forbes*, February 2, 2024, https://www.forbes.com/home-improvement/internet/streaming-stats/.

211   "Synergy or Interference? How Product Placement in TV Shows Affects the Commercial-Break Audience," *Forbes*, September 8, 2014, https://www.forbes.com/sites/onmarketing/2014/09/08/synergy-or-interference-how-product-placement-in-tv-shows-affects-the-commercial-break-audience/?sh=3c2ec2c353da.

212   Jeanine Poggi and E.J. Schultz, "How Coca-Cola's 'American Idol' Deal Transformed TV Advertising," *AdAge*, December 18, 2014, https://adage.com/article/media/coke-s-american-idol-deal-transformed-tv-advertising/296309.

213   Poggi and Schultz, "How Coca-Cola's 'American Idol' Deal Transformed TV Advertising."

214   "13 Podcast Statistics You Need to Know," Backlinko, January 29, 2024, https://backlinko.com/podcast-stats.

215   Todd Bishop, "Amazon Unveils Echo Pop, New Echo Buds; Reports >500M Alexa Device Sales as AI Upends Market," Geek Wire, May 17, 2023, https://www.geekwire.com/2023/amazon-unveils-echo-pop-new-echo-buds-reports-500m-alexa-device-sales-as-ai-upends-market/.

216   "Chatbot Market Size, Share & Trends, Analysis Report by Application, by Type, by Vertical, by Region, and Segment Forecasts, 2023–2030," Grand View Research, https://www.grandviewresearch.com/industry-analysis/chatbot-market.

217   "They Love Lucy, $8,000,000 Worth," *New York Times*, February 19, 1953, 32.

218   Michele Majidi, "Average Cost 30-Second Advertisement Super Bowl U.S. Broadcast 2002–2023," Statista, September 27, 2023, https://www.statista.com/statistics/217134/total-advertisement-revenue-of-super-bowls/.

219   "Why Do Big Companies Still Advertise on TV Instead of Social Media?" *Forbes*, March 1, 2019, https://www.forbes.com/sites/quora/2019/03/01/why-do-big-companies-still-advertise-on-tv-instead-of-social-media/?sh=fbd7b03dd41a.

220   Stacy Jo Dixon, "Facebook Users in the United States 2018–2027," Statista, November 6, 2023, https://www.statista.com/statistics/408971/number-of-us-facebook-users/.

221   McDonald, *Global Ad Spend Outlook 2023/24*.

222   "US CTV Ad Spend (2023–2027)," Oberlo, https://www.oberlo.com/statistics/ctv-ad-spend.

223   "Canadians and Their Television Watching Habits," Ipsos, August 28, 2001, https://www.ipsos.com/en-ca/canadians-and-their-television-watching-habits.

224   Danielle Commisso, "Here's What Watching TV Looks Like for Americans Today," Civic Science, September 21, 2022, https://civicscience.com/heres-what-watching-tv-looks-like-for-americans-today/.

225   Daniel Frankel, "Nearly 60% of Americans Now Stream Video Daily on Smartphones, Tablets and Computers," Next TV, August 25, 2022, https://www.nexttv.com/news/nearly-60-of-americans-now-stream-video-daily-on-smart-phones-tablets-and-computers.

226   "TV vs Smartphone: How Netflix Viewing Changes by Device," Digital i, May 23, 2022, https://digital-i.com/research/tv-vs-smartphone-how-netflix-viewing-changes-by-device/.

227   Ashley Stewart, "Salesforce Is Trotting Out Matthew McConaughey Amid Cost Cuts and Employees Aren't Happy, Leaked Messages Show," *Business Insider*, August 8, 2023, https://www.businessinsider.com/salesforce-matthew-mcconaughey-deal-sparks-employee-criticism-messages-show-2023-8.

228   "Nielsen Releases Audio Today 2023 Report," Radio Insight, June 19, 2023, https://radioinsight.com/headlines/253927/nielsen-releases-audio-today-2023-report/.

229   "History of Radio Advertising," Study.com, September 10, 2017, https://study.com/academy/lesson/history-of-radio-advertising.html.

230   *Current Population Report: Illiteracy in the United States: October 1947,* US Department of Commerce—Bureau of the Census, 1948, https://www.census.gov/content/dam/Census/library/publications/1948/demo/p20-020.pdf.

231   Brad Adgate, "Nielsen: AM/FM Radio Reaches 91% of U.S. Adults Each Month," *Forbes,* July 26, 2023, https://www.forbes.com/sites/bradadgate/2023/07/26/nielsen-amfm-radio-reaches-91-of-us-adults-each-month/?sh=474002f9a155.

232   Marie Charlotte Götting, "Number of Radio Stations Worldwide 2016, by Country," Statista, January 8, 2021, https://www.statista.com/statistics/793283/number-of-radio-stations-country/.

233   "Share of Adults Listen to Radio in the Car," Radio Advertising Bureau, 2023, https://www.rab.com/whyradio.cfm.

234   Audrey Rawnie Rico, "Radio Advertising Costs: A Simple Guide to Ad Spend," Fit Small Business, July 7, 2023, https://fitsmallbusiness.com/radio-advertising-costs/.

235   "48 Direct Mail Statistics," Postalytics, 2024, https://www.postalytics.com/direct-mail-statistics/.

236   Melanie Wells, "Cult Brands," *Forbes,* April 16, 2001, https://www.forbes.com/global/2001/0416/072.html?sh=1174373471fa.

237   "The K Car: Variations on a Theme Helped to Save Chrysler," *New York Times,* January 29, 1984, https://www.nytimes.com/1984/01/29/automobiles/the-k-car-variations-on-a-theme-helped-to-save-chrysler.html.

238   Sam Dean, "Goodbye, Staples Center, Hello, Crypto.com Arena," *Los Angeles Times,* November 16, 2021, https://www.latimes.com/business/story/2021-11-16/crypto-staples.

239   Dean, "Goodbye, Staples Center."

240   Valentina Dencheva, "Global Influencer Marketing Value 2016–2023," Statista, September 27, 2023, https://www.statista.com/statistics/1092819/global-influencer-market-size/.

241   Walter Loeb, "Influencer Impact on Consumers Increasing—Facebook Has Less Power," *Forbes,* February 3, 2022, https://www.forbes.com/sites/walterloeb/2022/02/03/influencer-impact-on-consumers-increasing--facebook-has-less-power/.

242   *Nielsen 2021 Trust in Advertising Study,* Nielsen, 2021, https://www.nielsen.com/wp-content/uploads/sites/2/2021/11/2021-Nielsen-Trust-In-Advertising-Sell-Sheet.pdf.

243   Anita Elberse and Jeroen Verleum, "The Economic Value of Celebrity Endorsements," *Journal of Advertising Research* 52, no. 2 (2012): 149–65, https://www.hbs.edu/faculty/Pages/item.aspx?num=40853.

244   Celinne Da Costa, "Creating the Oprah Effect—How Brands on the Edge Can Change Their Future," *Forbes,* March 21, 2021, https://www.forbes.com/sites/celinnedacosta/2021/03/21/creating-the-oprah-effect---how-brands-on-the-edge-can-change-their-future/.

245   Jami LaRue, "Handsome Dan: A 130-Year-Old Legacy," *YaleNews,* July 3, 2019, https://news.yale.edu/2019/07/03/handsome-dan-130-year-old-legacy.

246   Mike Ives, "A Rogue Mascot Causes Headaches for a Japanese City," *New York Times*, January 22, 2019, https://www.nytimes.com/2019/01/22/world/asia/japan-mascot-chii-tan-otter.html.

247   "LBB and MPC Release Exciting New Research on the Advertising Value of Mascots & Characters," Little Black Book, September 22, 2021, https://www.lbbonline.com/news/lbb-and-mpc-release-exciting-new-research-on-the-advertising-value-of-mascots-characters.

248   "LBB and MPC Release Exciting New Research," Little Black Book.

249   S. Shyam, "Mascot Marketing—A Declining Trend," LinkedIn, June 28, 2021, https://www.linkedin.com/pulse/mascot-marketing-declining-trend-s-shyam-1e/.

250   "LBB and MPC Release Exciting New Research," Little Black Book.

251   *Quaker History,* Quaker Oats, accessed May 6, 2023, https://www.quakeroats.com/about-quaker-oats/quaker-history.

252   "Leo Burnett," *AdAge,* June 1971.

253   Stephen Fox, *The Mirror Makers: A History of American Advertising and Its Creators* (William Morrow and Co., 1984).

254   Edd Applegate, *The Ad Men and Women—A Biographical Dictionary of Advertising* (Greenwood Press, 1994).

255   Charlotte Olsen, "Disney Movies: Anthropomorphism," Be Creative (blog), March 25, 2016, https://cjo589.wordpress.com/2016/03/25/disney-movies-anthropomorphism/.

256   Report Linker, "Global Breakfast Cereals Market to Reach $107.9 Billion by 2030 [press release]," Globe Newswire, February 16, 2013, https://www.globenewswire.com/news-release/2023/02/16/2609907/0/en/Global-Breakfast-Cereals-Market-to-Reach-107-9-Billion-by-2030.html; Brooks Johnson, "How Kellogg's Cereal Spinoff Heightens the Competition with General Mills," *Star Tribune*, September 24, 2022, https://www.startribune.com/how-kelloggs-cereal-spinoff-heightens-the-competition-with-general-mills/600209806.

257   Karen M. Lancendorfer, JoAnn L. Atkin, and Bonnie B. Reece, "Animals in Advertising: Love Dogs? Love the Ad!" *Journal of Busines Research* 61, no. 5 (2008): 384–91, https://doi.org/10.1016/j.jbusres.2006.08.011; Sherril M. Stone, "The Psychology of Using Animals in Advertising," (Northwestern Oklahoma State University, 2014).

258   Richard Foster, "Bringing in the Dough, Boy," *Roanoke Times*, November 24, 1995, https://scholar.lib.vt.edu/VA-news/ROA-Times/issues/1995/rt9511/951124/11240025.htm.

259   Samantha Cole, "Clippy's Designer Wants to Know Who Got Clippy Pregnant," *Vice*, April 26, 2017, https://www.vice.com/en/article/xyj55a/microsoft-clippy-creator-interview-kevin-atteberry.

260   Jel Sert, *Mascots Matter: Gender and Race Representation in Consumer Packaged Goods Mascots,* Geena Davis Institute on Gender in Media, n.d., https://geenadavisinstitute.org/research/mascots-matter/.

261   Masahiro Mori, "The Uncanny Valley," *Energy* 7, no. 4 (1970): 33–35; Christine Looser and Thalia Wheatley, "The Tipping Point of Animacy: How, When, and Where We

Perceive Life in a Face," *Psychological Science* 21, no. 12 (2010): 1854–62, https://doi.org/10.1177/0956797610388044.

262   "Thermos Company—Company Profile, Information, Business Description, History, Background Information on Thermos Company," Reference for Business, n.a., accessed January 21, 2024, https://www.referenceforbusiness.com/history2/70/Thermos-Company.html.

263   "Starbucks Raises the Bar with Industry-Leading Employee Benefits, Outperforming Competitors [press release]," Starbucks, November 6, 2023, https://stories.starbucks.com/press/2023/starbucks-raises-the-bar-with-industry-leading-employee-benefits-out-perform-competitors/.

264   Thomas Friedman, "Thomas L, Friedman's Commencement Address," The Source, Washington University in St. Louis, May 21, 2004, https://source.wustl.edu/2004/05/thomas-l-friedman-commencement-address/.

265   Sean Peek, "Creativity Is Not Innovation (But You Need Both)," *Business News Daily*, January 30, 2024, https://www.businessnewsdaily.com/6848-creativity-vs-innovation.html.

266   Keman Huang et al., "The Devastating Business Impacts of a Cyber Breach," *Harvard Business Review*, May 4, 2023, https://hbr.org/2023/05/the-devastating-business-impacts-of-a-cyber-breach.

267   David A. Aaker and Erich Jochimsthaler, "The Brand Relationship Spectrum: The Key to the Brand Architecture Challenge," *California Management Review* 42, no. 4 (2000), https://doi.org/10.1177/000812560004200401.

268   Judy Kirpich, "House of Brands," Grafik Agency, n.d., accessed February 19, 2024, https://grafik.agency/insight/houseofbrands/.

269   Michael Schrage, "Lafley's P&G Brand Cull and the 80/20 Rule," *Harvard Business Review*, August 4, 2014, https://hbr.org/2014/08/lafleys-pg-brand-cull-and-the-8020-rule.

270   Avi Dan, "It's Time to Rebuild Brand Loyalty," *Forbes*, February 22, 2010, https://www.forbes.com/2010/02/22/brand-loyalty-google-apple-starbucks-zappos-cmo-network-avi-dan.html?sh=6a5eac835b9a.

271   Shep Hyken, "Businesses Lose $75 Billion Due to Poor Customer Service," *Forbes*, May 17, 2018, https://www.forbes.com/sites/shephyken/2018/05/17/businesses-lose-75-billion-due-to-poor-customer-service/?sh=2d38003e16f9.

272   Anthony Shorrocks, James Davies, and Rodrigo Lluberas, *Global Wealth Report 2022*, Credit Suisse, 2022, https://www.credit-suisse.com/media/assets/corporate/docs/about-us/research/publications/global-wealth-report-2022-en.pdf.

ABOUT THE AUTHOR

Kim Derrick Rozdeba is a strategic branding expert and a force behind some of the most iconic Fortune 500 brands. With over three decades of experience, Kim has honed his skills in strategic planning, branding, and executing multimillion-dollar advertising and marketing campaigns, PR, and corporate communications. His expertise spans various industries, including agriculture, pharmaceuticals, petroleum, airlines, fast food, telecommunications, and automotive.

From his year in his teens exploring Europe on a shoestring budget of ten dollars a day, to becoming a Fortune 500 corporate leader, Kim's life has been filled with exciting adventures and discoveries. He has carried the Olympic torch, he dabbles as an amateur chef and oenophile, and he's a Mousquetaire, snowboarder, blogger, and mentor to young professionals.

His first book, *Branding Queens: Discover Branding Secrets from Twenty Incredible Women Who Built Global Brand Dynasties*, was met with great acclaim. It introduced the concept of the five C's of branding and explored the nuances of brand building throughout history.

Today, Kim lives with his wife in Calgary, Canada, with three adult children. He serves as the VP of Communications at one of the top 100 global brands, while sharing his insights and experiences more broadly through his writing. His latest offering, *LOYALNOMICS: The Power of Branding*, is a testament to his deep understanding of branding and its power to drive customer loyalty.

DEAR READER,

Thank you for taking the time to journey through *LOYALNOMICS: The Power of Branding*. Your support means a great deal to me. If you found value in this book, I kindly request that you share your thoughts by leaving a review on the online bookstore site where you purchased it or on Goodreads.

Your reviews help me improve my work, and they guide other readers in their book selection process. Please feel free to share your opinions, praise, or critiques. I read every single review and sincerely appreciate your insights and suggestions. You can also follow my blog at **www.rozdeba.com** and connect on LinkedIn @derrickrozdeba.

Thank you once again for your time and consideration. Your support fuels my passion for sharing knowledge and wisdom through my writing.

Best regards,

www.ingramcontent.com/pod-product-compliance
Lightning Source LLC
Chambersburg PA
CBHW080759300326
41914CB00055B/948